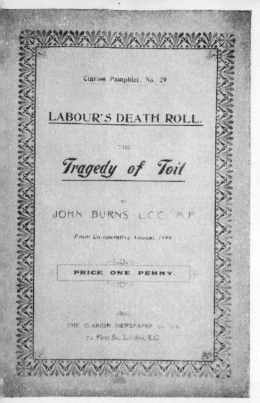

Clarion Pamphlet. No. 29

LABOUR'S DEATH ROLL.

THE

Tragedy of Toil

By

JOHN BURNS, L.C.C., M.P.

From Co-operative Annual, 1899.

PRICE ONE PENNY.

1899.

THE CLARION NEWSPAPER Co. Ltd.
72, Fleet St., London, E.C.

JOHN BULL
and his
Unemployed.

A Plain Statement on the Law
of England as it affects
the Unemployed.

By J. KEIR HARDIE, M.P.

ONE PENNY.

LONDON,
INDEPENDENT LABOUR PARTY

SOCIALISM &
SERVICE
By T. D. BENSON

Price
One
Penny.

PUBLISHED BY THE INDEPENDENT LABOUR PARTY, 10,
RED LION COURT, FLEET STREET, LONDON, E.C.

UNEMPLOYMENT:
ITS CAUSES AND CONSEQUENCES.

BY THE COUNTESS OF WARWICK.

Price One Penny.

The Labour Story

WITHDRAWN

Books by the same author

THE BRITAIN I WANT

WHEN THE MEN COME HOME

CONFLICT WITHOUT MALICE

THE
LABOUR
STORY

EMANUEL SHINWELL
P.C., M.P.

MACDONALD : LONDON

First published in 1963 by
Macdonald & Co. (Publishers) Ltd.
2 Portman Street, London, W.1
Made and Printed in Great Britain by
Purnell and Sons, Ltd.
Paulton (Somerset) and London

Have the elder races halted?
Do they droop and end their lesson, wearied over there beyond the seas?
We take up the task eternal, and the burden and the lesson,
Pioneers! O pioneers!

WALT WHITMAN

Preface

When in 1955 my autobiography, *Conflict without Malice,* was published several friends commented on the absence of important episodes in Labour history. They suggested that my long association with the Party should enable a more ample picture of its birth and growth to be presented. This volume, still admittedly incomplete, is the result.

Although the events described in the following pages relate chiefly to the present century, and coincide with almost sixty years of my Party membership, adequate presentation entailed some reference to political and industrial conflict in the latter part of the eighteenth century and the whole of the nineteenth, leading to the formation of the Labour Representation Committee in 1900.

It was my privilege to know most of the pioneers when the Labour Party was still in the embryonic stage. I have argued with Keir Hardie, taken the chair for Robert Blatchford, the editor of *The Clarion,* and the author of *Merrie England* and *Britain for the British*; shared the public platform with that romantic figure, Robert Cunninghame Graham, the descendant of Scottish kings; with Robert Smillie, perhaps the greatest of miners' leaders; Tom Mann and Ben Tillett, notorious for their trade union and Socialist activities; Ramsay MacDonald, Philip Snowden, George N. Barnes, Arthur Henderson, J. R. Clynes, George Lansbury, Fred Jowett and a host of others.

The later chapters of this book refer to events more familiar to the general reader. In contributions I made to the *Sunday Times* in 1960 and the *Sunday Telegraph* in 1961, some incidents were mentioned, though in a somewhat different form. I make due acknowledgements to the editors of both newspapers.

The research involved could not have been undertaken without facilities afforded by Labour Party headquarters and by officials of the Parliamentary Labour Party. Miss Rose Davy of the secretarial staff of Transport House, Frank Barlow, the secretary of the Parliamentary Party, and his assistant, Harry Mitchell, were most helpful in directing my attention to essential documents relating to

Party activities since the formation of the Labour Representation Committee in 1900. Nor can I fail to acknowledge the valuable help I have obtained from the large number of biographies and autobiographies of Labour pioneers and others who have served the cause of Labour; especially G. D. H. Cole's *The History of the British Working Classes;* Max Beer's *History of British Socialism;* Herbert Tracey's *British Labour Party* (Vols. 1, 2 and 3); William Stewart's *Keir Hardie;* L. McNeil Weir's *The Tragedy of Ramsay MacDonald;* "Iconoclast's" *Ramsay MacDonald, the Man of Tomorrow;* Philip Snowden's *Labour and the New World;* Ramsay MacDonald's *Socialism, Critical and Constructive;* James Cockburn's *Biography of Keir Hardie; Labour Party Conference Reports* (1900–1962); Parliamentary Labour Party Records, and pamphlets issued by the I.L.P., S.D.F., and the Fabian Society.

EMANUEL SHINWELL

PARTY CHAIRMEN

The Labour Representation Committee

W. C. Steadman	1900–1905
David Shackleton	1905–1906

The Parliamentary Labour Party

Keir Hardie	1906–1908
Arthur Henderson	1908–1910
George Barnes	1910–1911
Ramsay MacDonald	1911–1914
Arthur Henderson	1914–1917
William Adamson	1917–1921
J. R. Clynes	1921–1922
Ramsay MacDonald	1922–1931
Arthur Henderson	1931–1932
George Lansbury	1932–1934
C. R. Attlee	1934–1955
Hugh Gaitskell	1955–1963
Harold Wilson	1963

Contents

List of Illustrations

The author and publishers wish to thank the Labour Party for supplying photographs of H. M. Hyndman and John Burns.

Introduction

The Age of Revolution in which we live, and in which our descendants are likely to go on living, developed slowly, the social conscience and the emotional disquiet limping behind the conditions which made these reactions inevitable. Expanding industry created capitalism and the proletariat, though the significance of the ideological change was not a matter of conscious concern.

By the middle of the eighteenth century Europe was beginning to organise industry and to exploit every possible source of profit, both in merchandise and the human beings who produced it. The United Kingdom was the leading nation in this race towards modern civilisation, followed at a considerable distance by France.

In terms of greatness based on what are now outmoded ideas Great Britain's golden age was the eighteenth century. Between the years 1700 and 1800 English navies and English armies had subjected India, opened up the whole of North America, and gained a foothold in Africa. English explorers had pushed into the Antipodes and across Canada. English trade followed closely behind them all.

The enormous industrial developments which were thus made possible confirmed the results of the Agrarian Revolution. Peasant proprietors became farm labourers. Craftsmen became factory employees. Competition destroyed small merchants and created the merchant houses and merchant bankers.

Labour, displaced economically from its varied and fairly independent way of life, was also displaced physically as it moved into the industrial towns, at first built near water to provide power and then near the coal which would drive the machines. Competition meant more discipline, less leisure, and lower rates of pay.

The benefits of rationalised industry and mass production in lowering production costs were paid for largely by an appalling reduction in a labourer's earning capacity. Textiles, long England's great manufacture and based on cottage weaving, dropped in price from 39s. 9d., for a standard length, in 1795 to 5s. by 1830. In the lifetime of many weavers, earnings from hand looms declined by eight times, and becoming a machine minder in a mill did little to improve a weaver's financial situation. *Hansard* records that in

15

1819 weavers in Carlisle were working 14–17 hours a day, six days a week, for 5s. to 7s.

The conditions in the textile industry and in the mines—probably the two worst of all major industries—did not unduly worry workers in the craft industries still unaffected by the machine. The skilled artisans—carpenters, metal workers, and some kinds of farm workers—were in whole-hearted agreement with the guilds of tailors, goldsmiths, shipwrights and other crafts that the labourers in the machine-powered factories were of a distinctly lower class —as indeed they were, when employers came to rely more and more on children, women, and men reduced to near-bestiality by poverty.

The class consciousness of the early nineteenth-century craftsman was as great then as now. He was strongly conservative in outlook, hanging on grimly to the *status quo* and contemptuous of the straits in which the hapless servants of the new-fangled industries found themselves. He had little to conserve, but that little he jealously guarded.

Thus it was that Radicalism was the province of the idealist, and not of those most likely to benefit from it. The battle for human rights had to be conducted despite, and not with the help of, the mass of the impecunious, landless and voteless classes.

The majority of the men who exploited the unskilled workers were themselves of working-class origin, or had among their forebears a humble worker a generation or so back. The financiers, merchants and factory owners were self-made men, contemptuous of the State and arrogant in their self-assurance that they could run their business well. They had in fact created a new form of feudalism infinitely worse than the original which, with all its faults, had been shaped and re-shaped by men who had ruled according to tenets of religion and law.

The old nobility which had held the reins of power for centuries still filled most of the seats in the Commons and, of course, in the Lords. Apart from those peers who found fortuitously that their estates lay over coal or iron ore, few of these men who were responsible for running an ostensible democracy took an active part in the industrial revolution or, indeed, understood its implications.

Most of Britain's legislators considered the earth to be the inheritance of Masters, and labour to be the destiny of Men. The industrialists were also the Masters and could be left to use their Men as they wished.

Only civil unrest, serious crime, and very occasionally blatantly outrageous cases of human misery stirred Parliament to sporadic action. Revolution in France, and then a prolonged world war, both alleviated the worst facets of unemployment during long trade depressions and focussed attention on national dangers greater than internal trouble from the masses.

But the signs of potential upheaval were there long before the Napoleonic Wars were over. Minor riots over the price of food occurred periodically in the industrial towns from 1800 onwards. The anti-machine riots, which were triggered off by the hosiery factories at Nottingham, created the Luddite movement, which spread in the second decade of the nineteenth century to the textile towns of Lancashire and Yorkshire, the shipyards of Sunderland, the iron foundries of Wolverhampton, and among the farm workers of East Anglia.

Although the Luddites eventually attracted extremists and trouble-makers who liked to boast of political motives, but preferred to practise looting and poaching, these riots were really economic in origin. The rioters were starving, and the only changes they experienced were either dismissal from their jobs through redundancy or lower rates of pay to meet competition.

Their lack of literacy, the absence of direct political representation, and the slow and inefficient dissemination of news, made the small nucleus of rioters—they probably did not total more than 100,000 in outbreaks extending over ten years—quite unaware of political movements working on their behalf. The huge mass of despairing and resigned workers who remained quiet certainly had no conception whatever that Radicalism had emerged and was sending them on the long, slow journey to their emancipation.

Radical pioneers had been at work since the latter part of the eighteenth century. The House of Commons occasionally listened to pleas for reform, though it of course ignored them. Earl Stanhope produced a treatise on Parliamentary reform as far back as the seventies. In 1780 the Society for Constitutional Reform gained a few members and managed to get a question or two asked in the Commons. But, characteristic of the caution of the English publicist, the evidence of this reform taken to its logical conclusion, as portrayed by the excesses in Paris, caused most of the enthusiasm to die away and indeed encouraged its adherents to decamp hastily to the side of reaction.

The outbreak of war conveniently provided the authorities with an excuse to curb free speech and suppress inimical political activities. Consequently organisations like the Society of the Friends of the People, bravely formed in 1792 at the height of the horror stories from France, and the London Corresponding Society,

B

whose object was to join with political groups in other towns, were hamstrung by the Seditious Meetings Act of 1795, and finally destroyed when, in 1798, the Government arrested the principal members of the London Corresponding Society.

But after the peace of 1815 the repression of movements which were often solely humanitarian in character was no longer possible on grounds of treason against a nation fighting for its life. By then, too, riots, prayers, and protests had been proved to be unavailing as a way to improve the lot of the industrial classes.

From 1816 agitation was political, in that it was directed towards Parliament. The distressed areas, notably around Manchester, were the focal points of plans to march to London and protest to Crown and Parliament in person. Few if any of the provincial unemployed got that far. Those who did not fall out from exhaustion were dealt with by the military, the magistrates and the clergy who, in this dire crisis, saw as one. A Secret Committee of the House of Lords convinced both Houses that the country was on the brink of revolution and various repressive measures, including the suspension of *habeas corpus*, were put into force. In fact the majority of the reported insurrections existed only in the pages of official reports. Agents provocateurs of the government tempted men driven to extremes of anger to equip themselves with a knife or a bludgeon. This was sufficient to get them branded as traitorous conspirators and imprisoned.

Political societies were easily classified as seditious and suppressed. A few courageous people in the north, noting that the Seditious Meetings and Assemblies Act excepted societies run for charitable purposes, formed groups with such euphemistic names as The Society for the Promotion of Human Happiness, which even the most resourceful of Home Office agents could not contrive to prove traitorous. These groups managed to obtain, distribute and discuss pamphlets by such men as Tom Paine and William Cobbett.

A further idea to circumvent the dangers of illicit assembly occurred spontaneously in the midland and northern industrial towns. Thousands of men and women had from childhood been accustomed to the class meetings of John Wesley, which their parents had been encouraged to organise. These were basically family prayer meetings, which expanded to include neighbours and friends. Hundreds of these class meetings provided a quiet and individually private occasion yet were units of a tightly knit organisation going through local and area levels to the national direction of the Methodist movement.

The religious class system itself expanded in many instances into political classes, and was closely copied by scores of Radical movements. When through sheer size, and as the result of the relaxation of repressive tendencies, these associations came into the open, the objectives were reform of Parliament as the immediate goal; and universal suffrage, annual parliaments, and vote by secret ballot as the rather vague aims for action in the somewhat distant future.

This comparative moderation attracted the craft workers and those in trades not so seriously affected by recurrent depressions and the competition of machines, as well as humanitarians and some of the professional classes who were in favour of better conditions for the deprived so long as they were obtained with the minimum of civil disturbance.

Consequently demonstrations in favour of reform were large and popular. Petitions were frequent. When the Reform Bill was passed in 1832 it was indeed through popular clamour, but the noise was quite genteel, and it was this moderate section of the population which found the greatest satisfaction in the Bill. The working classes were not long left in any doubt that they had been betrayed by a façade of reform disguising a *status quo* so far as most of them were concerned. There was proof enough of this in the fact that most of the political unions declined or were formally wound up, their task completed.

An exception was the National Union of Working Classes, an organisation which by name and policy had little truck with the predominantly middle-class political unions. It had originated as a group pledged to study and spread the gospel of Robert Owen's co-partnership theories.

Owen, with that far-sightedness, resourcefulness and political consciousness which has marked so many Welshmen, had proved in his own cotton mill at Chorlton that there was an optimum working day beyond which toil benefited neither employer nor employee. Owen was a hero to the cotton workers for his success in getting at least a distorted form of his factory legislation on the Statute Book in the shape of the Factory Act of 1819.

There were, however, plenty of people, even among the depressed classes, who regarded him as a crackpot, principally on account of his theory that environment was all and if workers lived in pleasant homes alongside a pleasant factory all would be well. They also felt animosity towards Owen because of his avowed scepticism that the mysterious ways of the Deity were in some secret way for the best. People who had little else to accept as a reason for their

miseries in this life somewhat naturally suspected a man who took
even that comfort from them.

The National Union was therefore a suspect organisation, and
thereby attracted to itself extremists who liked nothing better than
to be different from their fellow men. Notable in the movement
was Henry Hetherington who edited the union's newspaper, the
Poor Man's Guardian. It was possibly illegal in content and certainly in price, for it sold at one penny and bore no Government
stamp. The National Union probably never had a big membership.
At one stage it boasted that it had reached 40,000, which was infinitely fewer than the claims of some of the more moderate
Radical associations in their heyday. But its influence was
tremendous. Primarily a London organisation, it was copied in
many provincial centres by groups which affiliated or were content
merely to adopt some form of its name.

The National Union without doubt developed into an extremist
organisation. When it plastered London with handbills calling for
a national convention to influence Parliament the authorities had
to act. The result was the so-called Battle of Cold Bath Fields in
the neighbourhood of Gray's Inn Road when a lot of people got
cracked heads and a policeman was killed. It was a futile clash
with authority and sounded the death knell of what was the first
workers' organisation of any national importance.

A more level-headed and constructive association replaced the
National Union. This was the Radical Association, founded by
Fergus O'Connor. Its objects were wholly political and would
today be described as the aims of typical intellectuals. Universal
suffrage, annual Parliaments, no property qualifications—the
familiar political tenets were bruited. There was nothing about
higher wages, shorter hours, or better working conditions. Those
evils, it was inferred, would automatically disappear when Radicals
were elected to the Commons in sufficient numbers.

Despite this suspicious middle-road policy, the survivors of the
National Union agreed to amalgamate with the Radical Association
in 1835. The latter organisation was the progenitor of the Chartist
movement which existed, though it only sporadically flourished,
from 1836 until 1848. The Charter, supposedly drawn up with a
lively realisation of the miseries of the industrial workers, followed
the old Radical recipe of changing Parliament first and putting the
people's welfare right when the visionaries got into Westminster.
Among the eight persons who led the Chartist movement only two,
William Lovett and Henry Vincent, could possibly be described as
"working men" in the conventional political sense of the term, and

none of the others had much direct experience of workers' living and working conditions in the midlands and the north.

Police agents who infiltrated Chartist meetings were able to report that the audience was middle-class, middle-aged, and "clad in discreet black". The more restless members of the movement, who advocated force if other methods failed, were dubbed "the physical force men" and virtually ostracised. They did not gain any real influence until 1840, when the moderates backed out—the middle classes becoming more intrigued by the aims of the Anti-Corn Law League as an agitation of more direct benefit to their own pockets—and the extremists took over.

Chartism then became the front for political malcontents. The decade of revolutions in Europe, culminating in the abdication of Louis Philippe of France in 1848, titillated every political renegade in Britain, and the Chartist movement was a convenient medium for fomenting revolution without too tender a regard for the worries of the working classes.

The famous Chartist petition was largely an excuse for a show of force. The organisers announced that the petition, carrying five million signatures, would be carried at the head of a procession of a hundred thousand. Actually the petition contained about one and a half million signatures, many of them forgeries, and the crowd never consisted of more than 25,000 even before the police and Wellington's troops broke it up.

Soon afterwards, agents tipped off the police that the Chartist leaders were meeting at the Angel tavern, Blackfriars, allegedly for the purpose of planning a second fire of London. They were arrested and the Chartist movement was finished.

1

KARL MARX'S WORLD

1850–1880

Britain halfway through the nineteenth century, lapsed into one of those phases of smug self-satisfaction which have bedevilled her social progress. The repeal of the Corn Laws in 1846 had eased the worst of the miseries of the urban working population.

Benjamin Disraeli, leader of the so-called Young England Party, had been the virtual leader of the Conservatives for years, though its nominal head remained Lord George Bentinck. Disraeli brought a reinvigorated spirit to politics, and in his brief tenure of office as Chancellor of the Exchequer, in 1852, he hinted at the sort of policy he would pursue when he took his famous "leap in the dark" and subsequently introduced more sweeping reforms than the country had ever known. Disraeli had, like so many men who have foreign antecedents, richly endowed himself with all the traditional vagaries of his adopted country's way of life. He venerated the Throne, and admired the nobility and aristocracy which carried out its commands. He also had a deep regard for the civic rights of every subject, but he loathed the irresponsibility of the new moneyed industrialists and the disinterest of the landowners and aristocracy who preferred to ignore the new economic situation rather than to try to grapple with it.

It was Disraeli who pandered to the lethargic satisfaction of the masses so that they could forget the horrors of the famine in Ireland of 1845–6 and shudder instead at the excesses born of revolution in Europe. Not for the first time did the Channel become very wide, isolating the "slavery" of Europe and safeguarding the "liberty" of the Island. That it was a liberty permitting starvation, slums, and exploitation of human beings did not seem to matter. It was the order of things in which it had pleased God and the Queen to place the working class.

The economic situation helped to maintain this national quiescence. Trade was improving. Industrialists did not have to cut wages even if they had no intention of raising them. There was

23

more work available. The working classes were no longer typified by the gaunt fanatic brandishing an incendiary torch or axe handle. He was an obsequious and serious citizen dangling one or two of his numerous progeny on his knee.

Such social progress as there was came, not from the agitation of the sufferers, but from aristocrats inspired by sentiment and idealism—men like Lord Shaftesbury who championed the expansion of the Ragged Schools for the workers' children and the Ten Hours Bill for their parents.

Beer remained cheap. Saturday became a half holiday. Trains and coastal steamers offered inexpensive outings. The new literacy produced thousands of serious young artisans who studied improving books and dabbled in political theories, often attending lectures at which refugees from revolutionary Europe were the guests of honour.

The artisan of the eighteen-fifties was not, as yet, reading Socialist theory. That was being slowly and venomously written by Heinrich Karl Marx, who had been converted to Socialism after reading Proudhon. After living in Paris, Brussels, and Cologne, usually moving on when the authorities reacted to his subversive newspaper articles, Marx settled in Highgate and spent his days in the serenity of the British Museum, morosely studying economics and envisaging the suicide of capitalism while devising theories on how that end could be accelerated. His *Communist Manifesto*, published in 1848, caused no more stir than a spate of other political treatises, now forgotten, which appeared in that year and every year before and after it.

Marx was then thirty, and in the onward pace of the social and economic revolution that was taking place around him he was regarded as a little old-fashioned. He was, like all philosophers of his generation, fascinated by the most momentous event of the world into which he was born—the French Revolution. He summarised this, reasonably enough, as the replacement by force of an outdated feudal régime by the bourgeoisie, which created a new capitalist class to control and exploit the capital freed from the tyranny of a few hereditary owners.

The use of capital by this new class itself then produced yet another class—one which Marx saw all around him as he walked from Highgate to Bloomsbury: the industrial proletariat all too obviously exploited and victimised by the bourgeoisie.

These were the facts; from that point Marx saw visions. Revolution was inevitable. Just as the feudal classes had yielded to the bourgeoisie so the bourgeoisie would give way to the proletariat.

The new factory-employed class was as potentially revolutionary as the bourgeoisie of eighteenth-century France.

That this was visionary without being logical is now obvious. When Marx was brooding on the future of man it was not unreasonable to believe that violence of a severity unknown even in the earlier stages of his revolutionary theories was inevitable. All his life Marx had lived in a Europe alternately torn to pieces by the victorious revolutionaries of France or subjected to civil upheaval as revolution followed in the wake of war. When he came to England the Chartist movement was at its zenith, and as a foreigner he could not have recognised its basic superficiality. He was inevitably misled by the spectacular rioting in London and the reports of revolutions throughout Europe. In the nineteen years he took to write his famous *Das Kapital* Marx ignored the placidity of an England enjoying the wonders of the Great Exhibition, the growing prosperity as British trade spread to every corner of the earth, the pride in the possession of the colonies, and the generally implicit belief that, with England in control, the world had entered an era of everlasting peace.

If he did note these things, his poverty, his aggravating ill-health, and his belief in violence encouraged him to adapt his theory of inevitable evolution to one of planned revolution.

Marx, in co-operation with his lifelong friend Engels, brought a new, and more embittered, conception into the problem of class. Before him most of the thinkers on social problems had produced systems which were highly romantic in concept, rightly earning for the authors the title of Utopian theorists.

One of the most venerated in Europe and in America, for example, was François Fourier, who advocated planned communities of adults, each working at a task for which he had liking and talent, and all benefiting according to their contributions. It was just workable in an isolated agricultural community, as a few groups who adopted Fourierism in America proved.

Although he was older than Fourier, the Comte de Sainte-Simon had a better appreciation of the importance of industrial activities as compared with agriculture, but his system also respected the old order of the classes. A benign autocracy of the clergy and savants, the one to look after the spiritual and aesthetic sides of life, and the other to provide culture and scientific training, co-operating with the "industrials", who would perform the menial tasks of society. In return for their labour the industrials would be cared for and would share in the communal wealth on a basis which was admittedly pure Socialism.

Systems like these were doomed to failure when factories grew bigger and bigger and events proved that the clergy and savants were classified by the workers as allies, or lackeys, of the aristocracy.

Marx's exciting call, "Let the ruling classes tremble at a Communist revolution. The proletarians have nothing to lose but their chains. They have a world to win. Working men of all countries, unite!" fell, not only on deaf ears, but into a vacuum. The international organisation which had asked Marx and Engels to draft the proclamation of the Manifesto was disbanded in the same year that their Manifesto appeared.

The harsh realism of Marx demanded a more disillusioned and angry proletariat than existed in Britain and Western Europe at least until the closing years of the nineteenth century. More varied techniques in industry and a growing complexity of trades and business had helped to produce numerous classes within the working class. The skilled artisan, the foreman, the shopkeeper, and the fast-growing army of office workers had all found some semblance of status and advantage to safeguard, and a good many of the unskilled workers of the eighteen-fifties saw at least a chance of advancement within their class—if not for themselves then for their sons.

The worker of today may have a car, a washing machine and a TV set to lose as well as his chains; the mid-Victorian labourer also considered that chains were by no means his sole possession.

Trade expanded steadily throughout the world in the nineteenth century, and Britain easily held the lead. However bad things were, there were millions of workers who could tell themselves that conditions were a little better than the year before and indisputably improved as compared with their childhood or the stories their fathers told them of their own beginnings as wage-earners.

In this atmosphere of the workers' acquiescence to the degradation of spirit and the inequalities of privilege the romanticists inevitably had another field day. Men would have to be taught that they should not live by bread alone.

It produced the William Morris concept of progress by going backwards. Morris boasted that he was a dreamer. Petulantly he asked, "why should I strive to set the crooked straight?" The son of a rich financier, Morris believed that Socialism could be made to work once he had convinced everybody that there was joy in labour provided it produced beauty. He depicted craftsmen returning to a rosy-tinted theory of life in the Middle Ages where each man painstakingly made goods which were both useful and beautiful, at the same time singing verses of his own composition while he toiled. The machine was evil because it made such artistic labour impossible. By the time Morris had accepted the fact that the machine could not be destroyed he was nearing the end of his life.

Morris left his mark on machine-produced goods; his influence on Socialist practice has been negligible. In that he was no different from scores of less well-known Socialist theorists of his generation. Neither they nor their innumerable successors have ever learned that the proletariat dislikes being categorised as a unique human species which, for some reason, should be told what is good for it while other classes can work out their destiny for themselves.

It was inevitable that such progress as the working classes falteringly made in the nineteenth century was through the unimaginative but highly practical activities towards trade unionism.

As the Webbs have indicated, the modern association of men in a particular industry or trade has nothing in common with the mediaeval craft guilds. Those were groups of almost wholly self-employed craftsmen and very often merchants; both types could be fairly said to fall into the category of the bourgeoisie. Even when the industrial revolution brought the competition of machine production, the skilled artisan in the ancient crafts clung jealously to his status despite the fact that he was often earning no more than the semi-skilled factory employee. At first he held aloof from the worker-union.

Early in the emergence of the powered workshop and factory its workmen naturally gathered at some near-by inn for a friendly drink and inevitably to discuss their woes. Technically any such group which came to an agreement to try to improve conditions were acting illegally; not (at first) because the employers had contrived legislation to make combinations of workmen illegal, but because they were in combination against the Crown, which had from time immemorial regulated trade customs, prices and wages, though the Crown had long since abandoned this duty.

But with the example of what could happen in the French Revolution, the Crown and Parliament were ready enough to collaborate with the new industrialists and pass potentially savage and repressive legislation, such as the Combination Acts of 1799 and 1800.

This legislation had driven the harmless social groups of workmen underground. They took on all the trappings of a secret society, with oaths and inflammatory speeches. They became fertile sources of supply of men for machine rioting, but otherwise had

little effect on the industrial scene, and certainly not as regards
bettering workers' conditions.

The Government was clearly unaware of the potential influence
dormant in these workmen's groups, and Francis Place, in co-
operation with a Radical M.P., Joseph Hume, was able to get the
Combination Acts repealed without the majority of M.P.s realising
the implications.

Place, a London tailor, was a master craftsman and really as
cautious in his outlook as any of his class. He was genuinely moved
by the suffering of the workers in the industrial areas, and as
genuinely inspired by reformers like John Stuart Mill and Robert
Owen. But he had the conservative attitude of so many of his kind
and regarded violent change with alarm. He can be credited with
fervent attempts to better the lot of the worst-exploited factory
operatives, but he can also be credited with devising the baton
charge to defeat those workers if they dared to resort to violence.

"I advised Mr. Thomas," (a police superintendent in the Westminster division), he wrote, "when he saw a mob prepared to make
an attack, to lead his men on and thrash those who composed the
mob with their staves as long as any of them remained together,
but to take none into custody, and if this were done there would
be no more mobs."

This was hardly a laudable attitude for a champion of the
workers to adopt, and is an indication that Place was a politician
and social worker prepared to do the workers' thinking for them,
but determined to deprecate any spontaneous thinking on their
own part.

In any event, the privilege he engineered so that workmen could
assemble, whether as a mob or as a more innocuous group, quickly
disappeared. Parliament passed a new Combination Act which
theoretically permitted workers to form unions, but in practice
meant that if they pursued any aims to further their own welfare
they were automatically breaking the law.

Despite this danger, many unions sprang up after the passing
of this new Act in 1825. Miners were an exception in the general
pattern of the membership of these new unions, which otherwise
comprised the better paid and more independent workers, including
carpenters, joiners, and engineers.

The first organisation of potentially nation-wide influence was
founded under the aegis of Robert Owen in 1834 with the title of
the Grand National Consolidated Trade Union. With Owen at
the head of it, its aim was not unexpectedly to effect a gentle and
painless change in the industrial society of the nation by a

policy of co-operation and co-partnership between employer and employee. The union proffered an olive branch to the master rather than threatening him with a bludgeon. This policy did admittedly evade the risk of prosecution under the Combination Act, but it did not do much for the union's members, despite a roll of more than half a million.

Many employers were unimpressed with Owen's lofty ideas of what they should do to improve working conditions, and they certainly did not believe in his prognostications of higher output and still larger profits if they did. A good many employers kept a piece of paper, soon known as The Document, which an applicant for work had to sign if he wanted the job. This paper demanded that the worker would leave any union he was in and confirmed his spoken pledge that he would join none while in the master's employ.

With half a million members, the Grand National inevitably had many adherents who lacked the patience and idealism of Owen. While the sentence of transportation to the six Tolpuddle farm workers for trying to build up a union frightened a large proportion of the union membership, it infuriated the more radically-minded minority who managed to organise a large number of small and usually ineffectual strikes. Between them, the timid and the impetuous brought the Grand National to its knees, and its effective life was soon over.

By this time the era of steady industrial growth had begun, and it fostered the formation of trade unions moving slowly and cautiously to some remote goal. Significantly, the still badly exploited unskilled men and the women were ignored by these new unions, which followed the modern pattern of restricting membership to a particular trade instead of organising workers in one area, as had been the earlier concept of workers' associations.

The most powerful union to emerge from these meek and moderate organisations was the Amalgamated Society of Engineers in 1851. It had full-time personnel, large subscriptions to maintain its highly efficient organisation, and benefits in the way of sick pay and so forth. Its practical advantages made an immediate appeal to those men in engineering jobs whose wages were high enough to enable them to pay the subscription.

The success of the society was such that it became known as the New Model, and many other groups were formed precisely on its pattern. The identity of operation, the restriction of membership to the "aristocrats of labour", and the personal contacts among the leaders made inter-union co-operation easy. The paradox occurred that, while general associations of working men irrespective of trade had not produced unity of action at times of crisis, the strictly craft unions could attain general agreement. Local branches of the unions in Glasgow, Manchester and other towns in the provinces linked together in loose and more or less unofficial federations. The London Trades Council, formally organised after the unions had shown that they could work in unity during the building operatives' strike of 1859, was an important step forward towards a national council, and in 1868 the Manchester and Salford Trades Council demanded a Trades Union Congress. The Congress could speak for only 150,000 workers, but they were in many trades and worked in every town in the country.

Men with little political knowledge and not much more political interest, who had banded together for a quite narrow purpose of improving their own conditions and without too many tears over their neighbours' troubles, had achieved a national movement which all the efforts, continuing for almost a century, on the part of the philosophers and idealists had failed to do. The march of the pro-letariat was not going the way Marx was prophesying and it was certainly not going the way the Radical reformers would have liked. Trade union leaders have never ceased to bear in mind that the Labour movement was born of trade unionism—a virgin birth with the politico-philosopher not participating in the parental activities.

The result may well have been so. The intention certainly was not. When the unions began to flourish virtually no member or potential member had the vote. A few obtained it after the Reform Act of 1867, but general male suffrage was not in force until after the Acts of 1884–5.

If the unions did not realise the dormant political power they were harnessing, outsiders did. The upper classes were seriously alarmed and the Government appointed a Royal Commission to investigate the movement. The hard-headed union chiefs were in no mood to give cap-in-hand evidence. They had the cash to employ talented lawyers and they could both pay and attract skilful publicists. The Commission's recommendations were in effect a verdict in favour of encouraging trade unionism.

The result was a series of Acts abolishing the risk of prosecution or arrest whenever the situation tempted the Government to make use of the earlier legal measures of repression.

The new prestige and privileges of trade unionism soon had their testing time. A period of trade depression and unemployment arrived, with the consequent excuses for the employers to drive hard bargains and the failure of workers' discipline in refusing to yield.

None of the unions emerged without a severely depleted membership, but none of the major ones was in financial trouble or false to its aims. These facts lent justification to the determination of the unions to pursue their policies just as they had been doing, and without interference from would-be friends and allies. The union leaders felt that, with all its faults, the social structure of their country was the inevitable one, and that it fortunately left room for movement as regards their own people's welfare. The aim was to improve members' conditions, but without changing the overall design of a bourgeoisie democracy.

This was all very well for men with a trade who could gain promotion to foremen, possibly open their own businesses, and expect that at least one of their sons would become a white-collar worker. But such aims made no appeal to the mass of unskilled and semi-skilled workers who did, however, note and learn the powerful advantages of forming a trade union. They were too badly paid to obtain the practical benefits which the high subscriptions to the skilled workers' unions offered. The craft unions were attracting members because they were mutual insurance societies, providing a cheap and excellent method of dealing with the ever-haunting terrors of the impecunious: sickness, accident, old age, and burial. No doubt the majority of members joined and rigidly maintained their subscriptions because of these practical benefits quite as much as for action to shorten working hours and increase working wages—attainments which a slump had indicated could be nebulous.

When the unskilled workers formed unions their mutal insurance benefits were either non-existent or extremely small. Neither was there much improvement in working conditions or wages; and many members were dismissed without much in the way of union retaliation.

The unskilled workers' unions had two hopes of betterment for their members: strike action and political change. Strike action might, and sometimes did, work, but it was painful. Its victories were costly in terms of hunger and misery for the member's family and himself.

Political change offered immensely greater hopes. The concept of a proletariat, organised, represented in Parliament, and acting as a social class, grew fast. It was not at first an attitude of the supremacy of the proletariat; Marx was still largely unread. But this was a Socialist, not merely a Radical, dream.

The situation was ripe for the emergence of new political groups. There were many men unimpressed with the smug satisfaction of the middle classes of Victorian England, and alarmed by the era's vaunting Imperialism. They came to encourage, instruct, and unfortunately too often talk down to, the mass of workers feeling their new power but mystified about how to use it. Those workers, members of the New Unionism, as the emerging organisations were called, prepared the way for the birth of the Labour movement as a political force in Britain.

2

THE FABIANS; THE S.D.F.; THE I.L.P.; THE LIB.-LABS.

1880–1900

For those who live in the second half of the twentieth century it is difficult to realise how "modern" their predecessors of eighty years ago felt themselves to be. Comparatively speaking, the decade in which I was born—the eighteen-eighties—represented to the average person something approaching the apex of technological and economic development; while many thinking men accepted, as those of today do, that moral and political developments were lagging behind the tangible and practical progress of mankind.

In sixty years of the nineteenth century western technology had changed more markedly than in the previous two thousand years. People were awed by the triumphs of science and engineering, and an increasing number were being educated sufficiently to believe they could participate in their benefits. One third of the fathers, and one half of the mothers, of the children going into the factories and offices in the eighties were illiterate, but their children were the New Generation, products of the compulsory education which affected every child on its fifth birthday after 1870.

Never before or since has there been such a hunger for something to read. The angry young men of nineteenth-century literature caught the mood of the masses and fed the hunger of disquiet. Social problems, science, and morality preoccupied them all. The quizzical social propaganda of Dickens was replaced by more thoughtful, and more alarming, works, such as Butler's *Erewhon,* the earlier of Shaw's plays and the writings of John Ruskin. The wonders of science were dramatised by Jules Verne and they developed steadily as part of propaganda media culminating in H. G. Wells's fiction-prophecies of the 1900's. Outright propaganda poured out in a flood of penny and halfpenny pamphlets, paving the way for more serious and responsible works.

Propagandist material for the literate masses had effects of incalculable dimensions. Capitalism of that era failed to recognise the existence of an enormous market for sales, and the potent means of moulding men's minds, by catering for this new readership. The future Northcliffe, with his information disguised as entertainment, was a laggard compared with the social and political propagandists of the day.

Phenomenal if uneven economic expansion, generally good international relations, improved humanitarianism, and a profound sense of optimism about the future, made the closing years of the nineteenth century a time of hope for the common man.

In late Victorian Britain, and perhaps in most of Western Europe and the U.S.A., the common man lived in conditions of some injustice, entrenched opposition, and great exploitation, but he could look ahead hopefully and there were innumerable advisers to tell him how he could speedily reach a Golden Age. The absence of cynicism, the loftiness of plans, and the spirit of brotherhood were there. In its way it was already a Golden Age, and the tenuous clues to a coming century of violence were ignored.

Nietzsche's superman, acting without mercy because he was beyond good and evil, was a figure not of fear, but of amusement. Such a philosophy, like that of Marx, was all very well for foreigners, but this was Britain, the Unique Land. Just as it preferred to work out its own social revolution so it would retain its own economic domination. True, the monopoly in many industries had gone, but it hardly mattered; Britain would by divine right and the prowess of her people simply substitute supremacy for monopoly.

The genuinely Socialist movements of the time were, then as now, furthered by middle-class intellectuals whose knowledge of working-class conditions and working-class thought was either theoretical or based on subjective examination.

Middle-class groups will always yield a rich supply of thoughtful people anxious to extricate themselves from a basically sedate and boring way of life. Some will consider self only and rise to the upper class as self-made men; a few will profit from their chances to study without undue economic restrictions and become intellectuals; still fewer will cast aside self and throw themselves into good works on behalf of the stomachs, minds, or souls of the class below them. And all will retain something of the smugness which is characteristic of their class and persist in believing their own ideas to be uniquely right.

Apart from spontaneous restlessness, economic and political factors will periodically bring home to the middle classes the inherent insecurity of their position. This occurred in the eighties when there was a short but sharp trade recession, bringing a pause in income increases and a rise in the cost of living—both particularly galling to a class which depends on steadiness and security for its way of life.

Thus the Fabian Society, formed in 1884, found a ready reception among both the lofty-minded and the rather timorous. Its origin was in the Fellowship of the New Life, an organisation designed to reform society "in accordance with the highest moral principles" by a woolly-minded American named Thomas Davidson, a prophet who found little honour in his own country. The vagaries of observance of morality eased any qualms that there might be anything revolutionary or treacherous in the Fellowship, and it found some sources of momentum among the meek but disturbed middle-class tradesmen and clerks. They gained some vicarious comfort in discussing ways and means of bettering the world and finally deciding to proceed very cautiously.

The Fabian Society, the brain-child of Sidney Webb, Bernard Shaw, Sydney Oliver, and Graham Wallas, intentionally indicated that it conformed to this middle-class attitude in the adoption of its name, derived from the Roman general Fabius, who had, principally through the weakness of his adversaries, proved that victory can sometimes be gained by avoiding battles.

Although the Fabians were later to boast that they directly inspired the formation of the Labour Party, nothing was farther from the thoughts of the majority of the society's founders. The enthusiasts who formed the Fabian Parliamentary League in 1886 quickly discovered that their colleagues were not merely uninterested but slightly shocked. Edward Pease had to abandon his ideas of a distinct party with representation in Parliament before he could become the Fabians' secretary.

The whole campaign, culminating in the publication of Shaw's essays in 1889, and sustained by the tracts to which Webb and Shaw contributed, was designed to infiltrate members, and to influence non-members, within the Conservative and Liberal Parties. The former naturally proved sterile ground, but the Liberals included Radicals and a new generation amenable to social propaganda. Not only was the Fabians' campaign directed to influence these, but proletarian activities in the provinces, an area always strange and suspect to the Fabians, which appeared to envisage an independent Labour movement, were discouraged by lofty pronouncements of their inherent foolishness.

Webb did not consider the trade unions of much political importance. He had the characteristic suspicion of the London

intellectual as regards provincial thought and hope, particularly
when the hard-headed and ill-educated spokesmen talked first
about practical benefits and added phrases about "highest moral
principles" just as an afterthought.

Nor did the other great movement of the eighties, the Social
Democratic Federation, offer much to the trade unionists. Like the
Fabians, the S.D.F. was a London organisation and tended to regard
London as the centre of the universe, an attitude certain to arouse
the suspicion and hostility of nine-tenths of the nation.

Henry Mayers Hyndman was nearly forty years old when his
reading of *Das Kapital* and his talks with Marx influenced him to
write *England for All,* an intelligent work on Marxist thought,
produced with the slickness that his journalistic background made
possible and with the sound reasoning of a highly educated man.

Based as it was on Marx's teachings, Hyndman's book was fiery
stuff, and his ensuing speeches and pamphlets were more fiery still.
With the true aristocrat's withering contempt for the middle classes,
he cared nothing for the large numbers of people who put their
faith in gradual change. He consolidated the working men's clubs
in the London area and channelled their discontent into a frankly
revolutionary movement.

With his hero Marx dead in 1883, Hyndman probably dreamed
of succeeding him as the prophet of the coming proletariat's
paradise. He followed Marxist teachings slavishly and spent a
lot of his time reciting them. I recall hearing them in an impassioned
speech of his in the City Hall in Glasgow in 1908. His pamphlets
and his oratory left most of his prospective adherents more
mystified about their rôle in the coming social revolution than
before. Hyndman's preoccupation with land nationalisation might
have inspired an audience of peasants, but it did little to excite
the working men of London or in the provinces.

Hyndman did, however, attract the intellectuals of the day like a
magnet. Middle-class renegades found in this formidable bearded
figure, always immaculately dressed in top hat and frock coat, a
sort of father figure they felt they could trust. In front of his blood-
red banner emblazoned with the call of "workers of all nations,
unite", Hyndman enthralled minor writers, retired army officers,
clergymen and lesser officials whose advanced thinking had set
them at odds with the Establishment.

These were the leader and his disciples who, by sheer enthusiasm,
created a forceful organisation pledged to hasten the victory of
the proletariat—if possible by a revolution which Hyndman himself implicitly expected to break out within ten years.

Thanks to the virility of Hyndman, but with only half-hearted aid from Eleanor Marx, who had joined the S.D.F. despite her knowledge that her father had thoroughly disliked the one Englishman making a serious attempt to translate Marxism into coherent English, the S.D.F.'s campaign did touch the heart of a few forward-looking working men. Notable among them were Tom Mann, John Burns, and Will Thorne, who were out of step with the old-style trade union and Lib.-Lab. leaders in that they envisaged something more than a workers' organisation which restricted its activities to bettering conditions for its own members, while ignoring problems of a wider social significance.

Hyndman had the self-opinionated intolerance of the self-appointed man of destiny. He stormed about London speaking and haranguing street-corner audiences and lecturing in working men's clubs. His measure of success was that he left a branch behind him, often consisting only of three branch officers and perhaps three bewildered members. Such tiny units were ideal for Hyndman's autocratic browbeating. The Federation rank-and-file followed the headlong course of the leader with little objection. However, the more thoughtful nucleus of foundation members became uneasy. The ageing William Morris broke away from the S.D.F. and founded the Socialist League, as impractical as the S.D.F. was materialistic. Apart from sponsoring some poems by Morris the League had no influence, and it gently passed away six years later.

Meantime, the S.D.F. gained a superficial appearance of strength by its rigid policy of no compromise and its crusading zeal at a period when a trade recession was producing that condition of empty stomachs so conducive to active brains.

Hyndman, with his mental fixation that some mysterious historical cycle would surely make the centenary year of the French Revolution, 1889, the inevitable time for the British Revolution, encouraged the drilling of workers on military lines. In the London riots of 1886, when the gentlemen in Pall Mall clubs were alarmed as brickbats came hurtling through their windows, and in the Trafalgar Square meeting so redolent of imminent civil upheaval that the Commissioner of Police was forced to resign, Hyndman and his friends, notably John Burns, became the darlings of the mob, if the bogeys of the bourgeoisie.

In retrospect the early years of the S.D.F. appear to be those of an extremist organisation bent on fomenting strife. But it contributed much useful material to the Socialist movement of the morrow. It was, in theory, a nation-wide movement. It trans-

formed Socialist doctrine into practical politics. It had the
enthusiasm needed to attract attention. Its tenets were imposing
enough to gain the attention of a wide range of intellects. Among
the malcontents and the renegades there was also room for idealists
like Morris, workers' champions like Tom Mann, John Burns, and
Ben Tillett, thoughtful youngsters like Ramsay MacDonald, and
professional men like Bruce Glasier. If the S.D.F. had all the
attributes which would today make it a proscribed organisation it
was in the eighties the only movement which gave men the opportunity to organise, argue, and plan.

The efforts of Hyndman achieved great notoriety; they did not
provide him with the sort of army he envisaged to man the London
barricades. As the decade ended the S.D.F. had fewer than 5,000
members with paid-up subscriptions.

Its membership roll was small because the most potent source of
recruits, the trade unions, remained obstinately anti-socialistic. The
official organ of the S.D.F., *Justice,* edited by Harry Quelch,
maintained a steady campaign of bitter attacks on the reactionary
tendencies of some union officials. In a pamphlet Quelch issued in
1892 he wrote:

"We still talk of 'fair' wages, and 'fair' profits, of 'good' and
'bad' employers. We still recognise the right of the capitalist to
exploit, so long as he does his exploiting gently and conforms to
trade union rules. We still set up a standard of wages as one might
set up a standard for the guidance of robbers. . . . The new unionism
is only trade unionism, not Social Democracy."

The new unionism the S.D.F. found so exasperating was, through
sheer size, the most significant trend of the period. Between the
years 1872 and 1889, 666 unions were registered in England, 65 in
Scotland, and 88 in Ireland. Many of them had just a brief existence; still more amalgamated. By 1889 the number of unions had
declined to 265 in England, 28 in Scotland, and 33 in Ireland, but
membership was far greater. Although it was true that the overwhelming majority of workers remained unorganised, the 886,000
members represented at the Trades Union Congress held at Dundee
in 1889 comprised a body of men far in excess of any comparable
social group, even if it had little unity and no agreed goal to attain.

The trade unions, from the outset of their respectability as organisations legally exercising their influence on the nation's
industrial life, were wary of identifying themselves with any political
movement which might swamp them.

The extension of the franchise in the eighteen-sixties made it
perfectly feasible, if costly, for working-class voters to elect one of

themselves to Parliament. The rank and file refused to support such candidates. Quite a number of candidates in the election of 1868 were of the working class. They were all unsuccessful.

In the election of 1874, which was to restore Disraeli as Prime Minister, there were thirteen working-class candidates, all identified with trade unions. The two who were elected, Alexander Mac-Donald and Thomas Burt, were mining officials in the Staffordshire and Morpeth areas. Both found it possible to stand for election by means of a cap-in-hand respect for Liberalism, which satisfied the party organisation and produced the correct image for the electorate.

Burt was a typical miners' union official of the time. He was a devout Primitive Methodist, and his father and uncle, both preachers, had been prominent organisers of strikes in the forties. From 1863 he had devoted all his energies to the organisation of the Northumberland Miners' Mutual Confident Association, making it one of the most prosperous and powerful miners' unions in the country.

The political ambitions of men like Burt and MacDonald were not to use the strength of the unions in the shaping of national policy, but merely to hold a watching brief over trade union legislation. The unions were almost to a man content to identify themselves with Gladstonian Liberalism, which was willing to leave negotiations on wages and working hours to employer and employee.

However, the unions had sensed some duplicity in the party of their choice. In 1871 Parliament had conferred its blessing on unions by enacting that the funds of unions registered as friendly societies would be under State protection, thus raising unions to a status of utmost Victorian financial respectability. But at the same time a Criminal Law Amendment Act virtually destroyed the right to strike by making picketing and intimidation criminal offences.

Union leaders in close contact with their Liberal M.P.s might acquiesce to this double-edged example of Liberal tolerance; the rank and file were not so satisfied, and from it came men who were to make their reputation in politics. They were, of course, working men. Their minds were stimulated by trade union politics, but they were not politico-unionists when they began their agitation. At the time it was all too clear that politics and trade unionism did not mix. The older unions had worries of a more immediate kind. The mild benefits they had obtained, consolidating their members' position as aristocrats of labour, were seemingly in jeopardy as the "submerged tenth" began to organise and demand a bigger share of such privileges as were going.

The organisation of the semi-skilled and unskilled trade unionist was going from strength to strength. The men who ran these unions, and the men who joined them, were simple realists. They pinned their immediate hopes on Liberalism and they were anxious to endow themselves with that Victorian respectability which would gain public favour and possibly prove that persuasion of employers was as effective a policy as intimidation.

If they failed to discover the employers' better nature their moderate policies certainly proved profitable in public sympathy. The first major evidence of a new orientation of thought towards the underprivileged worker came in an unexpected place and through the activities of an unlikely personality.

Mrs. Annie Besant was the perfect example of an un-Victorian woman. Married at twenty to a Lincolnshire clergyman, she revolted against the foundations of family life by becoming a free-thinker and getting a legal separation within six years. Wiseacres could point out that a clergyman's wife who was co-editor with Charles Bradlaugh of the *National Reformer* would almost inevitably disgrace her sex and her class by becoming a Socialist as well.

Greatness, however, will out—and Annie Besant was a great woman. When she started *The Link* it was not so much to propagate her Socialist ideas as to preach the social decencies. When she heard of the conditions endured by the women working in a match factory in East London she wrote a series of exposures where indignation was carefully balanced by objective recording of facts and figures, all carefully checked by long interviews with an informant, an employee in the factory who was dismissed when her activities became known.

The woman's fellow employees, who had perhaps only realised how disgraceful were their working conditions after they had read Mrs. Besant's description of them, came out on strike. Mrs. Besant hurled herself into the battle on their behalf, aided, incidentally, by members of the S.D.F.

Seldom has one woman, championing a relatively small and unimportant group of workers, achieved such success. Mrs. Besant rejected a direct challenge to the employers as a trial of strength she knew she and the girls could not win. She instinctively made a wholly emotional appeal to the public conscience. She won within a fortnight. The women were re-engaged under better conditions.

This was the triumph of workers outside any trade union. The next strike, though inspired by two trade unionists, John Burns and Tom Mann, was also a victory for many non-union workers. Their campaign was organised by Will Thorne, a gasworks labourer, who managed to get the majority of the workers at London's three largest gasworks to strike for a decrease from a twelve-to a ten-hour working day and a slight increase in wages. Once again, public sympathy, despite the considerable inconvenience hundreds of thousands of people experienced, helped the gas-workers to gain their victory.

Throughout the country thousands of unskilled and semi-skilled workers, who had joined trade unions ten or fifteen years before and had let their membership lapse when short hours and un-employment in some trade recession added the final sense of despair about unions which lacked militancy or policy, now re-joined or formed new organisations and branches.

The trade union leaders had responsibility thrust upon them by events. John Burns and Tom Mann were regarded as trouble-makers by many of their colleagues in the Engineers' Amalgamated Society because they constantly talked of the political implications of the trade union movement. Ben Tillett, the dockers' leader, was also politically alert, and an attempt to organise his fellow dockers had not destroyed his faith in the virtues of direct action.

The result was the historic dockers' strike for sixpence an hour and the protest against the system of casual labour during the closing weeks of 1889. Once again public opinion was the big ally. Thousands of a middle and upper-class people subscribed to the strike fund, not because they had heard much of what Tillett, Burns and Mann, supported by the romantic figure of Cunninghame Graham, descendant from the old Scottish kings, had to say, but because Charles Booth's horrific exposure of poverty and misery in *London Life and Labour* had shown the docker to be one of the most ill-used victims of the commercial juggernaut.

The success of the dock strike was not only an inspiration to unorganised unskilled workers but also suggested a sense of pur-pose to the existing unions. Despite the diehards of the older craft unions, there were more chances for men whose energies had hitherto been devoted to political work obtaining a hearing at union meetings and gaining a foothold as branch officials. The old idea that collective bargaining was the sole aim of union action moved aside to allow room for agitation for industrial legislation and thereby, almost automatically, for the eventual setting up of an independent working-class political party.

"The regeneration of the trade union movement dates from this great social event," Ben Tillett recalled when writing about the dock strike in his memoirs. "Trade unionism among general workers, let me repeat, was an absolute weakling regarded as an illegitimate offspring, and treated like one, by the well established and respectable unions of the skilled crafts and trades."

Soon after the dock strike the total trade union membership passed the one and a quarter million mark for the first time, and the bulk of the membership consisted of the lower ranks of labour. They knew little about any kind of politics, let alone new philosophies like those of Marx. They still cared nothing for Hyndman's revolutionary plans, but they had a healthy suspicion of the established trade union leaders who seemed to have achieved little over years of activity. The new trade unionism was a truly democratic movement, where the rank-and-file saw that they held the real power.

Their hopes were clear-cut and simple: better working conditions. That these had not happened spontaneously slowly influenced the bulk to suspect their leaders' faith in enlightened capitalism and their trust in the eventual working of the employers' consciences. They distrusted trade union leaders calling for patience, but at the same time they had not adopted doctrinaire Socialism. In short, the trade union leaders had responsibilities for action thrust upon them, for trade union members in the unskilled sections were adopting Marxism without knowing it. The narrow-minded and reactionary attitude to the political contribution the workers' organisations could make which was tenaciously held by the craft unions and the Old Guard had to yield in the face of facts.

Trade unionism was spreading to every branch of industry—even, thanks to the work of Joseph Arch, to the biggest unskilled labour force of all, that in agriculture. Both the diversity and number of the newly organised groups made political action inevitable. Consciousness of the potential force of a working-class political party was enormously strengthened by the propaganda of Robert Blatchford, the son of an actor, who worked on a Sunday newspaper during the riots and strikes of the London of the eighties. He was modern, gay, and cynically critical about his betters. He started the *Clarion* on a capital of £400, he and his friend A. M. Thompson mortgaging their insurance policies to find most of the money. The paper did fairly well, selling 40,000 copies an issue.

Blatchford, highly skilled at writing human-interest material, but with no pretensions as an orator, had filled in the time while on the Sunday newspaper by writing a semi-satirical work, *Merrie*

England, selling at a shilling. He gambled on mass sales and brought it out as a multi-paged pamphlet for a penny. It sold three-quarters of a million copies within a year and gained an additional 20,000 readers for the *Clarion*. It has rightly been said that for every convert to Socialism made by *Das Kapital* there were a hundred made by *Merrie England* in the twenty years that it was essential reading for every thoughtful young man in the working classes.

Blatchford preached outright Socialism. He could wring the heart with descriptions of evils and uplift it with practical plans for the future. He had little time for Marxist economics, a fact which appealed to the masses, and hardly any more for religion, which gained him enemies. He wanted all land, mills, mines, factories, works, shops, ships, and railways to be the property of the people. In short—"Britain for the British". It was a typically sweeping statement; the methods and details he left to others.

Blatchford's strong personality aroused the jealousy of Keir Hardie, who had hitherto enjoyed solitary glory as the leading prophet of the Socialist world of the morrow. Hardie was dour, morosely preoccupied with the evils of the present, and an abstainer. Blatchford, in contrast, was by character gay and optimistic. He revelled in good company and the drinks that usually went with it. The rivalry, inevitable through clashes of temperament, was increased by the difference in opinions. On the desirable policy for defence the controversy these two men let loose was even more acute than among persons and groups of the Labour movement of today.

If Blatchford wrote brightly and entertainingly he did so because he knew his public. He recognised, as he once said, "the people could not cotton on to the idea of a third party. They had been bred and born in a two-party tradition. The Tories they knew and Liberals they knew, but an independent party which took orders from neither of the old parties, but opposed them both, they could not believe in. These Socialist and I.L.P. men must be dupes or jackals of the Tories, bribed to break the Liberal ranks."

And unfortunately there was some proof that the belief might be true. The S.D.F. were not above agreeing with their political enemies to put up a couple of candidates for the election which put the Salisbury Government in power. It was a costly intrigue, for the few votes the S.D.F. candidates won worked out at £8 each on the Tory election bill.

The attitude that the known demi-god of Liberalism was better than the unknown devil of Socialism made any campaign of political enlightenment, calling for vigour and action, even violence, virtually futile from the outset. Victorian veneration for moderation exerted a cloying effect on people of all classes. They found the Fabian policy of gradualness greatly to their liking. Even those who had little to show for the century of sporadic social progress, free as it had been from the upsets of revolution, obstinately voted for moderation and resisted calls for violent change. Liberalism retained a reputation for humanitarianism, a social conscience, and sense of duty.

When in 1896 Keir Hardie said, "Which of the parties is it that is bound to get crushed in the struggle between Commercialism and Socialism? My reply is the Liberal Party," he was laughed at. Whatever might happen to the imperialists and the bosses, Liberalism was as much part of the fabric of the nation as Queen Victoria; both seemed to most people to be immortal, in spirit if not also in fact.

James Keir Hardie was born in the fifties—a decade which saw the birth of so many of the founders of the Labour movement, among them Blatchford, Lansbury, and Webb.

Given no schooling, Hardie was working at the age of eight and knew the bitterness of unemployment and starvation at ten. While still a child he was seeing at first hand the contrast between wealth and poverty between mine-owner and mine-worker in the Lanarkshire and Ayrshire pits. His illegitimate birth and his childhood experiences coloured his actions and outlook for the rest of his life, although he was usually at pains to insist that he did not preach class warfare.

"Socialism declares war upon a system, not upon a class," he proclaimed, and later on he was insisting that the movement had no desire for class-conscious Socialists. "We want conscious Socialists," he said.

While his colourful and sometimes harrowing cameos of working-class life as he had known it might have been merely a condemnation of a system which made them possible, his audiences listened to his vivid stories of harsh employers, and most of them must have gone away with the idea that there was a class of people who were as guilty as the system which they upheld. But it served Hardie to create the image of a man who loved all men and thus justified the missionary zeal of his actions. He insisted that the philosophy underlying and inspiring him was a New Holy Crusade.

Like all zealots Hardie brooked little rivalry. He blamed trade unionism for the existence of class warfare in the movement. For good measure he added the S.D.F. as a culprit. "For twenty-one years," he said in 1901, "the S.D.F. has based its propaganda on the class war theory and the result is dismal failure. How could it be otherwise?"

Beneath the cloth cap which he deliberately wore when he first entered Palace Yard as a Socialist M.P. in 1892 was an astute brain, seeing the future of the movement with far more clarity than most of his contemporaries. He had complete confidence in the eventual victory of Socialism. In addressing the electors of South West Ham after his election victory he ignored their immediate problems and painted a picture set in a rosy future.

"The Government or local councils might with advantage own and manage all mines, banks, railways, docks, waterways and tramways," he told his audience. "These and similar measures to lighten and sweeten the cheerless lot of the workers would find in me a willing advocate."

The politics of Hardie were not the sort which could possibly find acceptance even by the most Radical of Liberals of that decade. Here was a man with all the uncompromising obstinacy of his Scottish origins, all the jealous contempt of conventional attitudes that his unconventional birth and upbringing made part of the fibres of his being. Though the belief was a long time a-dying, Hardie's election to Parliament sounded the death knell for any lasting Lib.-Lab. marriage. With justification and an innate sense of the appropriate, Independent was the first word of the party which he helped to organise.

The need for the Independent Labour Party, and the opportunity for it to emerge, had come with yet another of the recessions which alternated with short booms in the latter part of the nineteenth century. Some unions were losing members through unemployment; others were returning to the non-militant friendly society policy of the past. The Liberals were again in power, though for the new generation their appeal was as anachronistic as Gladstone, their octogenarian leader. The significant political event of the time had been the arrival at Westminster of John Burns, of the Engineers, James Havelock Wilson, the seaman's leader, and James Keir Hardie, the miner, in 1892—all elected as Independent Labour M.P.s.

Few knew that they were temperamentally as ill-assorted a trio as one could find. Burns was jealous of his one-time disciple Hardie, and generally tiring of his Socialist colleagues as well as of Socialism. Havelock Wilson had found it convenient to evince acute political awareness on the hustings but once in Parliament reverted to narrow trade unionist attitudes. Only Hardie was a true politician, and so convinced of the fact that his presence could become unbearable to colleague and adversary alike.

However, the façade hid the defects of personalities, and all was set for the formation of a Labour Party independent, not of other Socialist movements, but of the enveloping Liberal skirts to which so many working-class politicians, amateur and professional, still preferred to cling.

Some 120 delegates arrived at Bradford on January 13, 1893, for the first national conference of the Independent Labour Party. The overwhelming majority represented the newly formed and flourishing I.L.P. branches in the industrial towns of the North. There were also delegates from the Scottish Labour Party, formed by Hardie when the Liberals refused to support Hardie's candidature in a by-election in Mid-Lanark in 1888 and thereby defeated him; from S.D.F. branches and the Fabians, and from minor societies such as the Eight Hours League. Four small trade unions and four trades councils represented the trade union interest in the event.

With the workers' organisations suspicious of the new Party, particularly as it staunchly refused to restrict the choice of Parliamentary candidates to trade union members, the I.L.P. fell into the usual pattern of relying more and more on intellectuals and middle-class radicals. This meant that a journalist like Ramsay MacDonald, a local government expert like F. W. Jowett, and a civil servant like Philip Snowden, all found through membership of the I.L.P. the means of standing for Parliament.

The I.L.P. managed to amalgamate the interests of its diverse delegations by proposing federation rather than amalgamation, though even this tolerant link was too strong for the S.D.F. and the Fabians. Without the membership of these two bodies and without any overtures from major trade unions (which would incidentally have delighted Hardie) the I.L.P. quickly became an organisation consisting solely of local I.L.P. branches.

Even with all its members ostensibly converted to Socialism the party found it impossible to persuade them to agree to any change of name embodying the word Socialist. The best that Hardie, running the organisation for himself and trusted friends in a manner which was hardly democratic, could arrange was that the object of the I.L.P. was formally stated to be to work for "an industrial commonwealth founded upon the Socialisation of land and capital".

The I.L.P. lacked in size all that it possessed in zeal. In the nineties it lived a hand-to-mouth existence depending literally on the 3d. affiliation fee of each member, of which the paid-up total ranged from 35,000 in the early enthusiasm down to a little over 5,000 in 1899. But in that year fresh hope came for the cause for which the I.L.P. had laid the soundest foundations of all the nineteenth-century Socialistic organisations. More than a million voters were about to have their political eyes opened.

The T.U.C. passed its historic resolution:

"That this congress, having regard to its decisions in former years and with a view to securing a better representation of the interests of Labour in the House of Commons, hereby instructs the Parliamentary committee to invite the co-operation of all co-operative, socialistic, trade union and other working-class organisations to jointly co-operate on lines mutually agreed upon, in convening a special congress of such representatives from such of the above-named organisations as may be willing to take part to devise ways and means for securing the return of an increased number of Labour members in the next Parliament."

Trade unionists justifiably regard this 1899 resolution as the origin of the modern Labour Party. It is worthy of note, however, that the vote of 546,000 in favour and 434,000 against indicates that the enthusiasm was half-hearted.

3

THE LABOUR REPRESENTATION
COMMITTEE

1900–1906

The conference on Labour Representation held on February 27 and 28, 1900, in the Memorial Hall, London, could hardly be described as an enthusiastic overture for Marx's conception of the proletariat welding itself into a united and formidable front against the other two sections of society. Historic the meeting was to become, but at the time the significance of the occasion was not recognised by the nation as a whole and certainly not by many of the half million or so whose interests it represented.

The conference was convened on the instructions of the T.U.C., and the agenda was designed to ensure that any person who succeeded in getting into the House of Commons would be sympathetic to the aims and demands of the trade unions. To this end the executive committee was to consist of twelve representatives from the trade unions, ten from Co-operative Societies, and two each from the I.L.P., the Fabians, and the S.D.F. As the Co-operative Union refused to instruct its organisations to send delegates the unions had a two-to-one majority.

Standing orders provided that each delegate represented 2,000 members or a fraction thereof. Voting was to be on one card for every 1,000 members. Again, this meant an overwhelming superiority for the unions. The I.L.P., with 13,000 members, had seven delegates; the Fabians, with 861, were represented by one delegate. The S.D.F. optimistically claimed 9,000 members and were authorised to send four delegates. From the trade unions came 121 delegates representing more than 545,000 members. They could rely on 126 votes out of the 129 the delegates could deploy.

W. C. Steadman, an M.P. who represented a mere 400 members of the Barge Builders' Union, was elected chairman. His attitude was hardly one of pugnacity and enthusiasm for a new political movement. He confessed that he had until recently followed the conventional trade unionist's attitude of keeping negotiations

48

Keir Hardie as Socialist agitator and Party Leader.

H. M. Hyndman, exponent of
Marxian Philosophy.

John Burns, the hero of Trafalgar
Square.

Keir Hardie presenting Ramsay MacDonald with oil paintings of him and his wife, at the Labour Party Conference, Birmingham, 1912.

Labour Party Executive, 1910. Left to right sitting: R. J. Wilson, Keir Hardie, Ramsay MacDonald, Ben Turner, W. C. Robinson, Tom Fox, George Roberts. Left to right standing: J. Middleton, A. Peters, J. Hodge, A. Henderson, E. R. Pease, J. J. Stephenson, J. R. Clynes.

between employer and employees out of politics. He admitted that events had made him change his mind, but stressed that he still had an open mind on forming a Labour Party or on the question of working-class M.P.s allying themselves with other political parties in the Commons.

Nor was there any enthusiasm for the job of secretary. Brocklehurst of the I.L.P. suggested that there should be two, one for the unions and one for the Socialist societies. Hodge of the Steel Smelters suggested Brocklehurst, who declined and proposed Ramsay MacDonald in his stead. The careful plans of the I.L.P. thus worked out precisely as Keir Hardie had hoped. They also worked out as MacDonald intended that they should.

Ramsay MacDonald was then a journalist of thirty-four. Like the majority of Scottish boys of his generation, his life had been hard. MacDonald felt it to be harder because he constantly sensed the stigma of his birth even when among people who were unaware of his illegitimacy. The sense of martyrdom which he carefully nurtured was an effective goad to better himself as well as a means of keeping constantly in his mind the inequalities of his class among people who had everything they wanted.

It can also be said that heredity played its part; many rumours, both absurd or feasible, have been spread about MacDonald's paternal lineage. He probably believed the more impressive of them so that throughout his life he regarded himself as a born leader. The vision of greatness was also displayed before him by his grandmother, a woman as proud as only a clanswoman who could trace pure descent from the romantic warriors of Skye could be. The obstacles which MacDonald's birth and childhood poverty created were the very reasons why he was spurred to an ambition which took him to the peak of a Highland boy's wildest hopes. That he tottered after he had reached it was partly the penalty of ailing health in advancing age but as much a glimpse of the truth his ambition and inspiration had helped him to conceal for so long. MacDonald was a classic example of a man irresistibly attracted by success but without the divine spark that could make it wholly real.

When, like thousands of the sons of the croft before and after him, he came to London, the extreme poverty he suffered was all of a pattern of the rough Victorian road to success. His privations were insufficient to turn him into a revolutionary.

"At one end of the scale people were a little too poor; at the other a little too rich," he wrote.

It was the tolerant disquiet of the typical Liberal: things were wrong, but not so wrong but a little compromise could not put them

D

right. This attitude enabled him without undue twinges of conscience to join the Fabians who, while dubbing themselves Socialists, were all for gradualism.

The Fabian Society gave him a few entrancing glimpses of the comfortable life of the middle classes and an occasional one of the wealthy. He revelled in meetings at the charming houses of the Webbs, Graham Wallas and others, while carefully maintaining himself on a food bill of about 4s. 6d. a week. A chance meeting with a Mr. Thomas Lough, who had political ambitions, got MacDonald a pleasant job as private secretary. MacDonald wrote the candidate's speeches, dealt with his correspondence and assisted at electioneering. He thus got an insight into political campaigning, saw the sort of world in which a politician moved—and, more important, was convinced that it was through his efforts that his employer got elected.

The four years MacDonald spent as Lough's private secretary altered his previous ambitions, which were almost certainly to be a journalist or author. He tried to get the Liberals at Southampton to adopt him as one of their two-member candidates. They rejected him. Soon afterwards Liberals refused to support a trade union candidate at Attercliffe. Those two events decided MacDonald. He would throw in his lot with the Labour theorists, always provided that they were not too far left.

A few years earlier MacDonald had been in correspondence with Keir Hardie, pledging support to the latter on behalf of a minor organisation called the Scottish Home Rule Association, whose aims MacDonald furthered as honorary secretary in London. It was the sort of group with lofty aims, and virtually no chance of reaching them, which appealed to MacDonald's masochistic temperament. He had told Hardie of the "powers of darkness leagued against us". These satanic powers were, he admitted, merely English editors of Scottish newspapers and partisan wire-pullers, but they were the type of people who made martyrs of their opponents.

From that time MacDonald watched Hardie's career with some admiration, albeit qualified. He recognised the "poor boy making good" atmosphere around Hardie, ten years MacDonald's senior. He approved the patience with which Hardie had awaited gestures of friendship to workers on the part of the Liberals. And he undoubtedly considered Hardie's little-concealed contempt for nine out of ten of his colleagues as the correct attitude of one great man to the lesser individuals he had to put up with. But primarily MacDonald's change of heart was due to impatience with the Liberal

Party, as personified by the senile Gladstone, now concerned with nothing, so far as the man-in-the-street could see, but the pacification of Ireland.

MacDonald was joint author with Hardie of the resolution which cleared the way for a Labour group in Parliament. Hardie was unusually amenable to MacDonald's wording. He had undoubtedly fallen under the spell of a fellow Scot who somehow appeared to be at one and the same time his social superior and his social comrade. When MacDonald wanted to ingratiate himself he could do so with consummate skill, and few others had ever succeeded in such an activity with the suspicious and cautious Hardie.

MacDonald recognised that his record of political activity was not sufficiently spectacular to impress the rank and file of the I.L.P. and the S.D.F. As a non-unionist he could expect little support from the unions. But he also recognised that Hardie was the only man who really mattered.

It was a risk to stand for the secretaryship on such a basis. MacDonald was almost unknown to the delegates. In fact, many of them voted for him in the belief that he was James MacDonald of the S.D.F. who had on the first day moved a resolution with all the revolutionary fervour of his Federation. He was a tailor and a man committed to Marxism in its undiluted originality, and as unlike his namesake as any two men ostensibly members of the same movement could possibly be.

Ramsay MacDonald was, on name, elected unanimously, but the absence of opposition did not mean that the conference felt much enthusiasm about the appointment. Hyndman wrote that MacDonald was not a man he cared to waste much space about, and then proceeded to cover several pages with a vitriolic and disturbingly accurate assessment of his character.

"Personal ambition has been his one motive throughout," Hyndman said. "I do not blame him much for that. As was said of a far abler and more prominent man, 'We did not even object to his having cards up his sleeve but we felt a little hurt when he solemnly told us that they were placed there by Providence.' It has been pretty much the same thing with Ramsay MacDonald."

But there are worse persons than a man of strong personal ambition at the helm of a young and struggling organisation. MacDonald, with little money—and of that only 6 per cent contributed by the non-union organisations—had got fifteen L.R.C. candidates in time for the Khaki Election which came within eight months of the inaugural conference.

That only two candidates—Richard Bell at Derby and Keir
Hardie at Merthyr—were successful was hardly MacDonald's fault.
All he had to spend on the entire general election campaign was
£33. Moreover, the nation as a whole was in the throes of jingoistic
rejoicing as the Boer War took a turn for the better, with Kimberley,
Ladysmith and Mafeking relieved, the Orange Free State and the
Transvaal annexed, and Johannesburg occupied, coming as one
Empire-building triumph after another.

To their credit, many Socialists had refused to succumb to the
war fever of the time and a stream of anti-war pamphlets had been
appearing for months.

Hyndman, in a vitriolic essay entitled "The Transvaal War and
the Degradation of England", claimed that the conscience of the
whole civilised world was revolted by Britain's actions. John Burns
wrote that the war was "for territory, for gold, for capitalist
domination masquerading in the guise of freedom and franchise",
and for good measure added a list of names of shareholders in the
British South African Chartered Company. Harry Quelch demanded
the abolition of any standing army at all.

The Government of the day may have been wiser than it appeared
in tolerating this sort of thing during a war. The public reaction
was the opposite to that which the campaigners intended. Trade
unionists in particular revived their suspicions of purely Socialistic
advocates and turned to the moderate Lib.-Labs., of whom eight
were elected in 1900. Hardie, incidentally, was successful at
Merthyr only because the Welsh miners had been consistently anti-
war despite the sequence of victories in 1900.

MacDonald, who stood at Leicester, was vigorously anti-war, and
despite support from the local trades council, he lost.

Thus the infant party had been able to secure the election of only
two members, one of whom, Bell, was already a Lib.-Lab. in all
but name. It was therefore hardly in an atmosphere of triumph
that the second conference of the L.R.C. was held in Manchester
on February 1, 1901, just after the new reign of Edward VII had
begun. Yet the election results could bear analysis and produce
some encouragement. The fifteen candidates had polled 62,698
votes out of a total of 177,000 cast in the constituencies concerned,
and the only really disastrous result was at Rochdale, where in a
three-cornered fight the Labour candidate's vote decreased by 350
(as compared with the previous election)—901 out of a total vote of
11,290.

The conference got very little notice from the press because of
Queen Victoria's funeral, and the fact that the day following the

conference was to be treated much as a Sunday as regards news-papers, railway services and shop-opening. Possibly with a sense of decorum, but also because of the eagerness of the trade unions to observe the conventions of the social scene which they were ostensibly meeting to change, many delegates protested in horror at the suggestion that the conference should, if necessary, continue on the Saturday. An S.D.F. proposal for this was defeated.

Numerical progress had not occurred. Trades councils were now represented but some unions had dropped out. Delegates were down by 47; the members represented had decreased by some 110,000. The Co-operative Societies still hung back.

Trade union delegates, while ready enough to pay lip service to the proposals of the first conference regarding the organising of a political party exclusively representing Labour interests, showed little real enthusiasm for any vigorous campaign, and were still ready to extend the hand of friendly co-operation to both Tories and Liberals.

A gentleman representing 536 vellum account book binders, for example, stressed that it would be no bar to a candidate that he was receiving the support of either of the non-Labour political parties and yet voiced views acceptable to the local Labour organisa-tions, thus getting their support in an election.

This speaker, F. Rogers, believed the trade unions deserved on their record to enjoy the foremost place in the new political move-ment—a claim which brought a protest from Dan Irving of the S.D.F., who reasonably demanded that approved candidates should disclose their political opinions.

The S.D.F. delegates, notably Harry Quelch, were pledged to an uncompromising policy based on the Marxist class war. The two other political societies, the I.L.P. and the Fabians, were wary of the trade unions' doubts and preoccupations, typified in the com-plaint of one trade union delegate who disliked "any one side ram-ming their principles down the throats of the other side". Ostensibly the conference was a united body; in fact the allusion to one side and the other side was accepted as a self-evident fact of schism among the delegates. The conference was divided into two factions.

The underlying atmosphere of uncompromising controversy over policy that existed after that second conference, which brought reality after the initial enthusiasm of 1900, might well have resulted in the secession of the trade unions if it had not been for the Taff Vale judgment of the following summer.

The decision of the Lords in this case was that the Secretary of the 60,000-strong Amalgamated Railway Servants Union was liable for damages because some of his members had picketed stations in the Cardiff area during a railway strike. Not only was the secretary liable, but his union funds were not sacrosanct. The employers, the Taff Vale Railway Company, were awarded £23,000, which included their legal costs.

This decision did, of course, set back the privileges of the trade unions legally to organise strikes by almost half a century. It alarmed trade union officials everywhere, indicating that they could be attacked where it hurt most—in their unions' banking accounts.

The unions rushed to the Liberal Opposition for help in changing the Law. As the Opposition the Liberals were ready enough to promise criticism and complain in the Commons. It went little further than words, though admittedly the Tory majority of 134 made practical action difficult.

The result was some serious re-thinking by the unions who had failed to join the Labour Representation Committee, and by those contemplating resignation. MacDonald used his committee's pathetically small funds—his own income as secretary was an honorarium of £21 a year—to encourage the unions to come into the fold. A copy of *Labour and Politics,* a four-page leaflet, went to the secretary of every union in the country. As a result 30,000 were sold. This was followed up, after the Taff Vale judgment, by the distribution of 25,000 free circulars.

The opportunity to confirm that trade unionists had contrived a change of heart came with a by-election at Dewsbury. The friction over a suitable candidate was so intense that the L.R.C. decided to sit on the fence while the protagonists fought among themselves. The S.D.F., the I.L.P., the Clarion Fellowship, and the trades and labour councils all had their own ideas about candidates and the campaign. The S.D.F. insisted that there had been intrigue against their candidate, Quelch. The I.L.P. refused to withdraw their nominee, Hartley. The Clarion Fellowship suggested that the way out of the impasse would be to reject both candidates and substitute another, whose name they would in due course provide.

The S.D.F. refused to compromise. Quelch stood as a S.D.F. candidate without the support of the Trades Council or the I.L.P., and lost the election. And the L.R.C. lost the S.D.F. which, numerically unimportant, had at least created sufficient controversy to produce some enthusiasm at the earlier conferences.

This meant that when the third annual conference opened at Birmingham in 1902, whereas the trade union membership had increased to 455,000 the political groups, represented only by the Fabians and the I.L.P, had dropped to under 14,000. The Cooperators still hung back. The trade unions were in control and the result was a conference preoccupied with trade union interests, and Socialism was approved only when and only where it coincided with union policies.

Yet events, backed by the power that the union numbers created to engage in activity, meant that the political horizon of the trade unions was inevitably lifted. The huge Amalgamated Society of Engineers came into the L.R.C. during 1902, followed by the 103,000-strong Association of Lancashire Textile Workers early in 1903. The only important unions still holding back were the miners, content with the benefits their Lib.-Lab. nominees were bringing them.

The cotton workers had discovered their enthusiasm for Socialist politics as the result of a by-election in Clitheroe, when David Shackleton, a local textile trade union official, had a walk-over. This success could well have occurred at Cleveland two months later, but the bickering between the miners and the L.R.C. prevented the choice of a candidate, and the election was lost by default.

The L.R.C. had no powers to put forward a Parliamentary candidate. The best it could do was to suggest names of approved men and to attempt to bring the clashing factions round a table and persuade them to come to some agreement. MacDonald used this ostensible weakness of the L.R.C. to increase its indirect power. At the Newcastle conference in February, 1903, payment of L.R.C.-nominated M.P.s was approved. This solved an otherwise insuperable problem for candidates without union support, but it also gave the L.R.C. disciplinary powers over its authorised M.P.s, whether trade unionists or not. A side effect which MacDonald recognised and probably regretted was that inevitably the contributions of about £5 per thousand members per annum made the unions the real financiers of the Labour movement.

With close on a million members, plus an unknown number in the trades councils who were generally in favour of Labour candidates, the L.R.C. was by 1903 becoming a potentially formidable political power in the eyes of their political adversaries, if not in the opinion of the electorate.

The national situation was fluid. A. J. Balfour had taken over the premiership from Lord Salisbury, and soon there was a ministerial crisis with Joseph Chamberlain and other Government members resigning over Balfour's Protectionist proposals. Trade was bad, and the Tory press was blaming the growing intensity and victories of foreign competition on the laziness of the British worker. The aftermath of the Boer War and the Coronation celebrations had brought the usual sense of frustration and disillusion, plus a feeling that internal defects and injustices had been ignored overlong in favour of Regal Imperialism.

The country momentarily expected a general election. It did not come, but the L.R.C. had thirty-eight candidates ready, apart from the five existing M.P.s who could confidently expect to be re-elected.

A sequence of by-elections confirmed that political progress was being thrust upon the trade union-dominated L.R.C. whether it liked the responsibilities or not. At Woolwich, Will Crooks won a by-election in an established Tory seat, turning a Tory majority of 2,805 into a Labour one of 3,229. At Barnard Castle, in a three-cornered fight, Arthur Henderson gained a narrow but historic victory. At Preston, despite a deliberately contrived snap election with only five working days for a campaign, John Hodge, of the Steel Smelters and Chairman of the Conference, provided a happy augury for the future when he lost to the Tory by only 2,100 votes in a constituency where Keir Hardie had been defeated by more than 4,000 in 1900.

But the flirtations with the Lib.-Lab. conception tenaciously continued. At a Norwich by-election the L.R.C. candidate came bottom of the poll in a three-cornered fight, largely owing to the peculiar activities of Richard Bell, Labour M.P., who indicated his approval of the Liberal candidate during the campaign and afterwards sent him a telegram: "Great triumph for progress. Heartiest congratulations."

MacDonald, with the concurrence of Hardie, took matters into his own hands. With the Machiavellian delight in discreet intrigue which always surrounded him, MacDonald asked the chocolate industrialist George Cadbury to let his Liberal friends know that some mutual understanding might be acceptable to the L.R.C. for the sake of attack on the common enemy. This was news that the Liberal Chief Whip, Herbert Gladstone, had long hoped for and indeed confidently expected. The first feelers had been put out by MacDonald before the 1903 L.R.C. Conference, though nothing was said about them during the sessions. Indeed Keir Hardie, who was, of course, privy to the desired negotiations with the Liberals, had given a peroration warning the conference lest "you surrender yourselves to Liberalism, which would shackle you, gag you, and leave you a helpless, discredited and impotent mass. Let us have done with Liberalism and Toryism and every other 'ism that is not Labourism."

Undoubtedly Hardie and MacDonald had no wish for their plans to be misconstrued by the conference. A report by Hardie on overtures to the Liberals would have delighted most of the trade unions and infuriated most of the members of his own I.L.P. Moreover, the free hand MacDonald wanted would have been transformed into a formal gesture surrounded with provisos and controls.

In mid-February the first meeting between MacDonald and Jesse Herbert, the Liberal Chief Whip's personal assistant, took place. Both took good care that none of their junior colleagues or office staffs knew about it. The positive approach was MacDonald's, and Herbert was content to listen, knowing that however anxious the Liberal senior men were for an understanding it was anathema in most of the constituencies.

MacDonald was later reported to have said—and he never denied it—that most of the L.R.C. candidates due to stand at the next election were "earnest Liberals" who would support a Liberal administration. The offer of a tacit alliance was followed by something of an ultimatum: if there could not be agreement about opposition candidates then the L.R.C., with an election fund MacDonald expected would reach £120,000, would fight the Liberals up and down the country.

MacDonald regarded the taciturnity of his listener as indicative of his acquiescence. He told Hardie as much and the result was soon seen, when Hardie, speaking at a York political meeting, claimed that Labour and Liberalism were "as one in their anxiety to bring down the Government, and that there were cases of two-seat constituencies where the two parties could campaign in a way productive of good fellowship".

MacDonald continued to meet Herbert, who at length proposed a formal meeting with the Liberal Chief Whip so that some delegates of the L.R.C. could make the discussions official. MacDonald demanded that he alone should conduct the negotiations which would have to be in some hotel where neither party was known. Negotiations went on slowly but without acrimony for the best part of the summer. By August agreement was completed on some thirty-five seats in England and Wales where Liberals would be ready to stand down if L.R.C. candidates were available.

The Liberals had made a wise move in view of the enthusiasm of L.R.C. candidates, which was rapidly growing, for election battles against anyone and everyone not endorsed by the committee; there was no doubt that in a score of constituencies they could have split the vote and risked letting a Tory get in.

On MacDonald's side the move was not merely wise and

realistic; it was a triumph for his powers of persuasion and his obstinacy in not conceding one iota from the plans he and Hardie had made.

Probably this vigorous and efficient servant of the L.R.C., acting as its self-appointed leader, gained more pleasure from the personal realisation of what he had achieved than he could possibly have done from public plaudits. Long after the agreement was a fact, publicists and speakers were demanding that negotiations should begin. Even the suspicious and critical S.D.F., to whom the news would have been a godsend as proof of their contentions of the non-Marxist character of the I.L.P. and all its friends in the L.R.C., apparently failed to get wind of what had occurred.

It was as well that MacDonald's foresight had seen the necessity to arrange an understanding with the Liberals in good time before a general election. The Labour quintet already in the Commons was shaky and for the most part Liberal in politics if Labour in name. Bell's antics at the Norwich by-election and his behaviour in the Commons finally caused his omission from the L.R.C. list of approved members.

MacDonald fell ill during 1904 and was away for several months from the L.R.C. offices, now moved from Lincoln's Inn Fields to 28 Victoria Street, Westminster. Events indicated how dependent on his attention was the progress of the party. Membership dropped by 69,000 due to trade unions and trades councils dropping out; the Fabians were merely a figurehead group of 730 members; the I.L.P. had slightly increased by a thousand to 14,000; candidates for Parliament were lapsing because they declined to agree to the L.R.C. constitution.

Despite these difficulties and setbacks, when the L.R.C. Conference took place in Liverpool in January, 1905, delegates heard that forty-six approved candidates were ready for the election. Four would probably be unopposed, seven were in three-cornered contests, five faced Liberal opposition, and nineteen (thanks to the MacDonald-Gladstone arrangement) had only Tory opposition.

The 1905 conference marked the emergence of a purely political party attracting members for reasons apart from their trade union or political society interests, by authorising membership of constituency parties. In fact only two small local parties, from N.W. Durham and West Houghton (Lancs), joined in the ensuing twelve months, which mollified the early premonitions of the trade unions.

At the conference the proposal had been fought vigorously. Will Thorne claimed it was a dangerous precedent, and he wanted to know where it would all end if it was allowed. Ben Turner, of the General Weavers, said that if workers meant business they would form trades councils and obtain representation on the L.R.C. in that way. Freak, of the Boot and Shoe Operatives, forecast that the constituency parties would consist of blacklegs. But the trades councils and some smaller unions whose members were scattered through many constituencies helped to defeat the big unions whose powers were already causing jealousies. The constituency parties were to become part of the L.R.C.

The long-expected general election took place in January, 1906. The chief point of contention was tariff reform, on which the Liberal and Labour policies were almost identical. As a result the full impact of the arrangement MacDonald had achieved was seen. In Lancashire, where cotton workers and mill owners were in perfect harmony over the tariff issue, the Labour and Liberal parties co-operated enthusiastically to destroy a Tory stronghold. Thirty-two Labour candidates were freed from Liberal opposition, and in ten two-seat constituencies Labour and Liberal candidates fought in alliance against the Tory opponents. Twenty-nine of the fifty Liberal-Labour candidates won.

As the Liberal majority in the new Government was eighty-four over all other parties the victory was not quite so momentous as Labour enthusiasts tried to make out, and not quite so alarming as the disgruntled Tories insisted. Nevertheless, organised Labour as a political force had arrived. It was big enough to act as a pressure group, and it could with reasonable chances of success argue through the normal Parliamentary process of democratic government.

The big names of the next twenty or thirty years of British political history were coming into the limelight. It was the heyday for the pioneers of the movement; Keir Hardie was there as senior of the seven I.L.P. members. And there were Henderson, Snowden, Jowett, Barnes, Clynes, Crooks, and Thorne.

But most significant of all was the name of the member for Leicester who had polled more than 14,600 votes—Ramsay MacDonald. He had suffered defeat there in 1900, and the rebuff rankled. Moreover he knew that his 1906 victory was due more to Liberal support than to Labour enthusiasm. Skilfully MacDonald had conducted a campaign acceptable to virtually any Liberal elector. He had not been a Socialist candidate, but a L.R.C. nominee. There was no evidence that MacDonald believed in the genuine Socialist concept of political life, even if on other occasions he found it convenient to preach it.

4

FIRST PARLIAMENTARY LABOUR PARTY

1906–1911

The masses struggling to work and thrive fifty and sixty years ago had good cause to be restive. The Edwardian age was one of social turbulence, not serenity. On the one hand business was becoming more powerful and ruthless; it was the beginning of the era of the millionaire financier (often crooked as in the case of Whitaker Wright); of the monopolist in the Press, shipping, steel and a dozen other booming industries. It was an age of power without responsibility, and it was attacked by H. G. Wells and Bernard Shaw with growing effectiveness.

On the other hand there was the grinding poverty of nine-tenths of a nation which could rightly boast that it was the richest in humanity's history. Slums encroached on the town houses of Mayfair and were within a stone's throw of the London Stock Exchange. While Rotten Row offered a parade of men and women whose incomes were the concentrated wealth of the world's mightiest empire, around Marble Arch the processions of gaunt, shabby men and women, sometimes numbering 20,000, shuffled along with their banners demanding, "Bread for Our Children".

It was a time when a London child who died of starvation was duly docketed as "dead from natural causes" at the inquest, and a time when the Queen's gift of £2,000 for food to the East End unemployed brought, not deferential thanks, but another procession through the West End, whose banners bore the plea "Work, not Charity".

"It makes one sad and fills one with indignation," said Keir Hardie, "to see the need, year after year, for relief funds to keep the people from starving, to place our own people under an obligation to those who grow rich out of their misery."

The puny and ill-organised pressure to right these wrongs came from the small Labour group in the Commons. They had been goaded to action by the small electorate which believed in them.

It was the rank and file of the movement which recognised that the new era was dawning rather than any fervent anxiety by their representatives to rush ahead of events.

Not for the first time, and probably not for the last, the ordinary people of Britain had developed a political attitude in advance of expert political thought. Their image of their country was very different from that of the Palace, the Government, and the Press.

The atmosphere in the country in 1906 was not unlike that of 1945, although, of course, public sentiment which produced the Labour victory after the Second World War was not in the embryonic stage of 1906, when the famous Liberal administration took office.

But the parallels of the conditions and attitudes are worth noting. The Boer War had ended in victory and was therefore proof of the might of empire. Yet the British people had become more sick of conquest than they were proud of the power which produced it. The 1906 election repudiated the policy of vaunting nationalism and imperialism. Moreover, the rejection of Chamberlain's tariff reform programme indicated a trend towards internationalism despite the practical benefits which a wall round the mother-land and her dominions and colonies might have been thought to offer.

The Liberals have claimed credit for the advances in social legislation in the early years of this century. But the party's zeal for real reform had long been weakening because it was an old party, steeped in nineteenth-century political theories. That it discovered vigorous new blood, which gave it the chance to direct Liberal policy, was due very largely to the twenty-nine Labour M.P.s who were the Liberals' somewhat restive allies.

And behind these cloth-capped, rather unimaginative men who were without real political acumen, stood the masses, politically enlightened for the first time. More than a million trade unionists had at long last recognised that politics were inextricably bound up with employer-employee relations; the final kick which put the ordinary working man, skilled or unskilled, in the political arena, after the years of persuasion, lecturing and encouraging which had failed to lead him very quickly, was the Taff Vale judgment. That reactionary decision was the major and perhaps fatal action of the Lords; from that time the power of that assembly was steadily stripped away.

Class antagonism came into the open. A revolution, however bloodless and peaceful, had begun. The social reforms of the Liberal Government were, in some measure, Socialist reforms, unconsciously engendered by those twenty-nine Labour M.P.s and by thought of the masses they only symbolically represented.

As a body, the Labour M.P.s of 1906 had too little faith in themselves. They were usually content to tag along behind the Liberal Government, and opposition to Government proposals which had little to do with Socialism was virtually non-existent. There was too much evidence of cap-in-hand gratitude by those members who could never forget that they were in the Commons thanks to a Liberal standing down. By contrast, the Liberals were not so meticulous in observing the secret agreement MacDonald had arranged.

There were two by-elections during 1906. Both were three-cornered fights. At both the Labour candidate lost. At Cockermouth, where Bob Smillie, the Scottish miners' leader, was bottom of the poll, the Tory was elected on a minority vote. At Huddersfield the Liberals rushed the election after only seven days for campaigning, and the closeness of the votes for all three parties would have made a Labour victory certain if the Liberal had stood down, as he would have done a year earlier and should have done then.

The Labour M.P.s' first year's activities in Parliament were not distinguished. A couple of members were ill for a large part of the time; others found that their "heavy responsibilities" as trade union officials made it difficult to keep a good attendance record. Excellent work, however, was done on the Trade Disputes Bill, which was completely changed as the result of Labour action. There was also a commendable effort to organise school meals (a plan which was pushed by the Government into a Select Committee backwater), and significantly narrow-minded efforts to prohibit the admission of foreigners who might be used to replace strikers.

Keir Hardie, the chairman of the Party, dealt with the charge that the Labour Party's independence in the House was more assumed than real by saying it was useless to run amok at the Treasury Bench, and he denied the rumours of internal bickering by insisting that the trade unionist and Socialist members had worked together in perfect accord, thereby unfortunately confirming that the stories of dissension were widespread, and accepting as a fact that a trade unionist could not be automatically regarded as a Socialist.

This air of dissension had been inevitable from the moment Hardie obstinately insisted on standing for the chairmanship of the Parliamentary Party, despite his friend Bruce Glasier begging him to remain a free agent. Hardie trusted nobody and regarded himself, with some reason, as the only M.P. with sufficient experience and talent to manoeuvre the Party successfully. He had been automatically accepted as the father figure he considered himself to be, although at the outset there had been strong support for David Shackleton to be the first chairman. In fact, the members (MacDonald as secretary abstained) were equally divided, and it was only MacDonald's support which assured Hardie the necessary majority. Pointedly the Lib.-Labs. formed their own group under the hybrid title of Trade Union-Labour. It meant that there was a Bourgeois Party with a deep suspicion of Socialism and a Socialist Party with a jealous dislike of trade union self-interest within the Labour group.

Hardie would have preferred dictatorial powers, not because he was greedy for power, but because he rightly saw the need to be able to exercise his political experience, free from the niggling criticism and doubts of the Conference delegates. At the 1907 Party Conference Hardie was vigorously assailed for wanting freedom of manoeuvre for his Parliamentary Party. Ben Tillett said Hardie had not the respect for the delegates to which they were entitled; he protested against Hardie's language.

R. Morley, a respected and popular delegate, demanded that the Conference, and not the Parliamentary Party, should decide Parliamentary business. J. Baker said that members in the Commons were not only disregarding instructions but frequently voting against the wish of the Conference.

Thanks to Arthur Henderson, who made a conciliatory speech to offset Hardie's obvious impatience, the Parliamentary Party got a modicum of latitude: the time and method of giving effect to Conference instructions on activities in the Commons were to be left to the Parliamentary Party and the National Executive, which in effect meant that Hardie and MacDonald had a free rein.

It was thus opportune for Hardie to make a challenging gesture. In the last few minutes of the Conference, using a vote of thanks to the residents of Belfast and the local Press as his opportunity, he told the delegates he would resign from the Labour Party if he had to obey the Conference's opposition to women's franchise based on a property basis.

The gamble was, of course, a perfectly safe one. Hardie was given permission to vote contrary to Conference and Party policy on this issue—an early example of the escape route on grounds of conscience which has been a desirable, if upsetting, feature of Labour's history ever since.

The personality of profound influence asserting himself by the time of the 1907 Conference was Arthur Henderson, hero of the 1903 by-election at Barnard Castle. He was a typical product of the working class of his generation. He was born late enough to benefit more from the Education Acts than the other Labour pioneers, and the combination of intelligence and physical strength had enabled him to obtain skilled and comparatively well-paid work as a moulder. He had the serious intensity of the reformed character, for in his teens he had been converted to evangelical religion, with all the ardour which that entailed, so that his boyish amusements of betting, gambling and drinking took on all the evil of major vices in retrospect. It was probably his religion which eventually transformed Henderson from a trade unionist into a Socialist.

He studied politics as seriously as he studied the Bible, and there were few as knowledgeable as he, though his essential reticence invariably made him hold back in discussions except as a peacemaker. MacDonald found him invaluable as an assistant in preparing propaganda and sharing speaking schedules, especially as Henderson was clearly ready to obey and never to dispute the place in the limelight.

Henderson recognised the abilities of MacDonald but deprecated his lack of judgment when personal ambition clouded the issues. Henderson made mental reservations on the value of any close friendship with MacDonald, though, true to his Christian principles, he concealed what he doubtless thought to be a fault in his tolerance. He believed that much of what was fine in MacDonald's activities was the result of Mrs. MacDonald's advice and inspiration, and Henderson could enjoy conversation with her with an easier heart than with her husband. Between them they probably did much to save MacDonald from himself on more than one occasion in those early turbulent days.

Henderson acted as a strong link between the trade unions and the political organisations. His loyalty to both was an example which a few tried to follow and which influenced many more to restrain themselves from any real schism.

Diplomatically, Henderson, as Labour Party delegate to the 1906 T.U.C., noted that the Labour Party owed its existence to a T.U.C. resolution, and he begged the trade unionists to work for perfect unity in the Labour movement. His plea was not completely ignored.

For most of the vital year of 1906 it was Henderson who carried out the day-to-day secretarial duties of the Party. MacDonald had gone for a prolonged tour of the colonies, ostensibly for the benefit

Allied Reparations Conference, 1924. The group includes, from left to right, F. B. Kellog (U.S. Ambassador), Senator de Stefani (Italy) chatting to Ramsay MacDonald, J. H. Thomas, Baron Hayashi (Japan).

Ramsay MacDonald playing golf at Lossiemouth, watched by his daughter Ishbel and his son Malcolm.

George Lansbury
of Poplar.

The Seaham defeat of Ramsay MacDonald in 1935 by Emanuel Shinwell who is
seen in the centre of the group, hat in hand.

SHINWELL 38,380

MACDONALD 17,882

of his health, or, according to some trade union critics, for a holiday. Henderson worked without remuneration, and the Party Executive later tried to get him a token reward of £25. It was approved by the Conference after some captious criticism which was not directed against Henderson, but against MacDonald who, it was insinuated, ought to have paid Henderson out of his own honorarium which had been increased to £150. As Treasurer of the Party the controversy was extremely embarrassing for Henderson, particularly as he was a trade unionist in fact, and was entirely in sympathy with the typical trade unionist's timidity about the wild men of the political associations, of whom MacDonald could pretend to be one when the occasion demanded.

Henderson rode without mishap to greater power because of his deliberate refusal to commit hostile acts. He had many enemies, but open clashes were impossible when the potential adversary turned the other cheek.

Hardie undoubtedly regarded Henderson as a narrow-minded bigot and a Liberal masquerading as a Labour man just for the sake of the Party's support. Yet, like MacDonald, Hardie knew it was perfectly safe to thrust responsibilities and power on Henderson without risk to his own position. Henderson was the Party Whip— and got on extremely well with his Tory and Liberal colleagues— and was soon running the Parliamentary business of the Party without supervision, partly because Hardie fell ill. He collapsed in the House and went for a long convalescence, followed by a world tour. Labour's leading figures have always appeared to be particularly susceptible to the wandering sickness, and the hospitality and travel facilities offered were not always the selfless gestures of admirers that they seemed to be. The regular absences of MacDonald and Hardie were regrettable, though admittedly both had driven themselves to exhaustion. Nevertheless, as the most experienced men in the Party their wanderings took them away at a time when Labour needed all the publicity and propaganda it could get, especially to offset the circumstantial evidence that while Labour theorised Liberalism acted.

The Liberal Party was astutely stealing Labour's thunder after 1906, and even if the Executive could convince the Conference of the strong influences the Labour group had brought to bear their contributions had little impact in the country. To most people it was the Liberals, and the Liberals alone, who passed the Workmen's Compensation Act of 1906, the Trade Boards Act of 1908, which was designed to safeguard the interests of workers in the sweated trades, the Old Age Pensions Act of 1909, and the

Minimum Wage Law of 1909. In regard to the last piece of legislation it was notable that it excluded the miners, the group of workers who had so tenaciously clung to the Lib.-Lab. concept and the theory that welfare was best left to direct negotiations with the employers, and politics to the established Radical party.

The agitation over the conditions in which chainmaking, dressmaking and clothing operated forced the Government to introduce legislation in order to protect workers in those industries. Allegations about sweated conditions had been confirmed from various sources, so the Government brought in the Trade Boards Bill, which became the relevant Act.

It was remarkable that most of the trade unions objected to this kind of legislation because of their fears that it would lead to interference with collective bargaining and reduce the number of trade unionists. They thought that the workers in those trades being safeguarded by minimum wage rates, enforceable by law, would decline to join the unions. They now object to a wage policy enforceable by law for the same reason.

In fact the effect in 1908 was to boost trade union membership, because the organisers of the unions were able to argue that employers would fail to comply with the terms of the Act and the unions could best deal with them. I was a member of the Trade Board appointed in 1908, representing the Scottish Workers, and remained a member for three years. Among the members were Mary McArthur and J. J. Mallon. The meetings, which were held about once a month, gave me the opportunity of visiting London, making contact with trade union leaders and politicians, and also to visit the House of Commons to listen to the debates.

"The root trouble of our social system is the precariousness of living," Lloyd George told the nation, and in his Budget presented himself as the principal doctor capable of curing the national ills. Most of the electorate who benefited from the Liberal legislation were confirmed in their traditional Liberalism. It comforted them that a mild revolution could take place so placidly. There was no desire to lead the world in enlightened social progress; indeed, much of the smug Victorianism remained, and even the deprived section of the community was content to note that Britain was lagging behind many European countries in the adoption of new-fangled ideas, ignoring the fact that they were the inevitable developments of time and change, and the race was to the bold.

It is useful to examine the international conditions to which Britain mostly turned a blind eye in the first decade of this century.

They provide a remarkable contrast to today, when whatever sense of inferiority the people have about our economic and political influence, they are positive that in social affairs we lead the world.

In France the three most powerful forces of reaction, the Army, the Church, and the Royalists, had been weakened by a series of laws which automatically gave rein to progressive movements, notably, of course, Socialism. Some workmen's compensation benefits had been law since 1898, and within the first ten years of the century old-age pensions and restriction of working hours had become operative. As always, schisms split French political thought, but the Chamber of Deputies included fifty-four members who were Socialist in opinion by 1906, and there was a powerful United Socialist Party in operation throughout the country.

The progress of Socialism in France was due to the political consciousness of the trade unions. They had long taken the view that a union was a political movement as well as an economic organisation, and the Confédération Général du Travail was so unified and completely in control of its members that it was able to plan a general strike in 1906 in order to reduce the working day from ten hours to eight. The Government had to make mass arrests of the workers' leaders to prevent chaos.

German workers, kept in subjection by Bismarck until 1890, had quickly organised themselves, both politically and economically, after Wilhelm II came to the throne. The Social Democrats, representing mostly factory areas, grew in power as fast as Germany's industrial output. In a matter of ten years there were 110 Social Democrats in the Reichstag, and more than four million electors had a shrewd and united Party to represent them. They pursued an unrelenting class war against the militarist Junkers, the great landowners and the new industrial emperors. The weakness of the Social Democrats was that they hankered after the power available in the existing structure of German Government, and they made little attempt to change it.

Two other countries fascinated the British intellectual—Italy and Russia. The Italy of Garibaldi was inspiring and romantic, and the unification of the country suggested that it might become a great nation. It retained its tendency towards progressive politics, though in fact the left represented the impoverished south and the right the forces of reaction in the richer north. But from 1903 Italy was ruled by a Government of the left. There were old age pensions, compulsory insurance, flourishing trade unions, and a measure of nationalisation of service industries. The steady if unspectacular economic progress of the country increased the number of middle-class people, who quickly learned to fear the proletariat to which they had so recently belonged. It could be said, however, that before reaction, aided by political corruption, weakened the progressive spirit, Italy had outpaced Britain in many matters of workers' welfare and political emancipation.

Russia, then as now, was the great enigma. Feudal and without any large-scale industrial activity worth mentioning, as the new century opened new factories and mines began to turn part of a peasant population into an urbane one. The risk of revolution against the despotic régime then grew rapidly. Restlessness pervaded all classes. Intellectuals from the aristocracy wanted to change the primitive conditions which made life even for themselves uncomfortable. Minor officials and the bourgeoisie wanted to Europeanise their country and imitate the West's Parliamentary systems. The workers in the towns were subjected to a barrage of Socialist propaganda from the intellectuals, and intrigue, the second occupation of every Russian, flourished.

The harshness and incompetence of the Russian Crown and Government were proved after the disastrous Russo-Japanese war of 1905. The attempt at revolution which culminated in Bloody Sunday of January 22, 1905, was as much a patriotic protest against the shame brought on their country as the action of people driven to desperation by hunger and poverty.

The Duma which the Czar then promised satisfied the Liberals, but the Social Democrats and the workers' parties refused to participate. When the progressive forces thus split the Duma became a farce. A second, sitting in 1907, proved as obstinate as it was powerless; it too died. A third, elected by manipulation of the vote to favour the wealthy and aristocratic classes, did nothing so effectively that it made the revolution of 1917 inevitable, if surprisingly late.

Whatever its success or lack of it on the Continent, the philosophy of Socialism urged the masses to be on the move politically, socially and economically in the first ten years of the century. The triumphs and failures of Continental Socialists provided an inexhaustible source of argument in Britain. And only those blinded by their own self-satisfaction could deny that Britain's record of progress was none too bright. Unfortunately all too many were blind to the squalid facts, and those who had been voted into political responsibility spent too much time worrying about allegedly unethical and unconventional action which they regarded as mutinous and treacherous. Experience admittedly indicated that this belief was by no means without foundation from the activities of some of the wilder men who had studied Marx and found him wise.

Victor Grayson provided an early example of careerism, love of publicity, and lust for trouble-making which has since bedevilled the Labour Party much more than its adversaries, who are perhaps not so avid for bestowing democratic freedom on their adherents. Grayson's brief and brilliant career has since become almost the blueprint for succeeding extremists. Although there was little evidence in his life of much observance of religion he got his opportunity of a great career when his youthful loquacity impressed the Unitarian Church in Manchester. The result was that the Unitarians sent him to Manchester University to train for the ministry.

Grayson had been an apprentice engineer, and the physical troubles of the men he had known interested him far more than their spiritual health. He became the self-appointed champion of Manchester's unemployed and unorganised workers.

Keir Hardie and MacDonald liked neither the manner nor the matter of Grayson's rhetoric. Their animosity was increased by the near-idolatry for him of the rank and file in the local I.L.P. branches. Partly because the Party feared him and also because he upset the local trade union leaders, Grayson failed to get endorsement as Labour candidate when a by-election occurred at Colne. Characteristically he exulted in the opportunity to prove that he required no official help. He stood as a "clean Socialist", and took every opportunity to explain what he meant by that in relation to the activities of the existing Labour M.P.s. He won in a three-cornered fight and caused more consternation in Westminster than even Hardie's election in 1892. Lloyd George certainly pondered on it, not because he failed to see through Grayson's superficiality but because his extremist line found such enthusiastic audiences. Lloyd George did not fear the Hardie Parliamentarians—he had proof enough that they could be persuaded to co-operate in return for a few seats. But he did recognise that men who preached violent action and "clean Socialism" could wreck all his plans to make the Liberal Party the great social reform movement of the twentieth century.

"If at the end of an average term of office," Lloyd George told his colleagues, "it is found that Parliament has done nothing to cope seriously with the social conditions of the people . . . then a real cry will rise in the land for a new Party."

Clearly Lloyd George in 1907 did not consider the danger to be in the already existing Labour Party, but a new grouping of which Grayson could be the forerunner and even the organiser.

Fortunately, perhaps, for the Establishment in all three parties Grayson proved a poor Parliamentarian. His youth—he was only twenty-five when he entered the Commons—did not entirely excuse his execrable social and personal behaviour. He was naturally ostracised by the Tories and Liberals, and rejoiced in the fact. But he was as strongly ignored by the Labour members, which aroused his fury.

Hardie was particularly hostile. He hated the way his virtually unquestioned management of the Labour M.P.s was being undermined. He jealously recognised that the fiery restiveness of a mere boy was very similar to his own feelings before the years had banished it to a vague memory.

"What was pardonable in a Party of one is quite unpardonable with a Party of thirty-one," Hardie pointed out after Grayson had got himself suspended by a violent and ill-advised speech during a debate on unemployment.

The reproofs intimidated the Labour M.P.s, but that did not affect the rank and file in the country. Grayson went from strength to strength as a mob orator, lambasting the trade unions, the Labour Party, and the I.L.P. leaders indiscriminately.

Hyndman and Blatchford eagerly rallied beside Grayson, not because those astute and intelligent veterans of political propaganda were very impressed by the youthful member for Colne, but because he focussed the unorganised disappointment in the country about the Parliamentary Party's zeal which had produced an electoral vacuum.

They saw the chance of forming a new Socialist Party. Grayson tested his powers at a *Clarion* meeting at Holborn Hall, when he said that the organisers must choose either Hardie or himself as speaker. It was Hardie who was asked to stand down. Then at the 1909 I.L.P. conference Grayson managed to carry his proposal to delete the I.L.P. decision that it could no longer arrange meetings for him. Hardie, MacDonald, Snowden and Glasier thereupon resigned.

If Grayson had not been deteriorating rapidly in health, intellect and personal behaviour his victory might have been more than a futile gesture of defiance. As it was, his brief day was almost over, due to his own vices rather than the wishes of his tens of thousands of admirers. Before he disappeared from the political scene Grayson became the man behind the Green Manifesto, a pamphlet entitled *Let Us Reform the Labour Party,* which caused acrimonious and embittered quarrels within the I.L.P. but had little effect in the country. When, as the result of all this mutinous activity, the British

Socialist Party was founded in 1911 it was in fact merely a re-born S.D.F. and as such had no more and no less influence than that body had ever had.

A phenomenon of the time which was potentially as great a source of disruption of the Labour movement as the antics of Grayson and the intrigues of Hyndman and the S.D.F. was the Syndicalist movement.

Syndicalism was a European movement, attracting men who looked for something more constructive than anarchy and nihilism, but with the melodramatic spirit of those movements inherent in it. The Syndicalist felt uncompromising hostility to the State and he repudiated all the existing forms of Government. Essentially a *modus vivendi* for industrial nations, its principal aim was to organise all workers in a trade or industry into one union and then all such unions into a national organisation which would eventually become international.

Apart from the difference of attitude as regards political control of a nation, Syndicalism differed from Socialism in that its organisation of working people was intended to benefit only them, whereas Socialism aimed to organise them for the benefit of the community as a whole.

The basic self-interest of Syndicalism was somewhat in line with the narrow outlook of the trade unionists, and only its attributes of violence denied any appeal to the powerful and established unions. For the younger workers, and for those who were poorly organised or affected by the economic conditions of the time, Syndicalism made a big appeal.

The movement was largely an intellectual one abroad, its French exponents being Sorel, Lagardelle, and Berth. In the U.S.A. Daniel de Leon gained some notoriety, and it was of some moment in Italy. In Britain the be-all and end-all of Syndicalism was Tom Mann, one of the great Socialist orators among the pioneers. A Warwickshire boy, who was apprenticed as an engineer in Birmingham, he settled in London at the age of twenty and was, of course, one of the leaders of the 1889 dock strike.

Hardie at first cultivated Mann because he was a trade union rebel, and Hardie recognised that a trade unionist with great oratorical powers and a real enthusiasm for Socialism could be of inestimable value. Mann became the first secretary of the I.L.P. and stood for Parliament three times. He was always ready to contest impossible constituencies. At North Aberdeen he did so well that his narrow defeat influenced Hardie to run at the East Bradford by-election in 1896, where Hardie came bottom of the

poll. At Bradford Mann fought a Liberal, who was supported by
Lib.-Lab. M.P.s on the platform. Mann's inevitable defeat was
useful material for Hardie's case for trade unionists to have their
own members in the Commons.

After four years Mann gave up the secretaryship of the I.L.P.
and dabbled in more exciting extremist organisations such as the
London Reform Union and the National Democratic League. Then,
in 1902, he emigrated to Australia, where his political activities
landed him in prison. Hardie, on a world tour in 1907–8, met
Mann in Melbourne, and as a result Mann decided to return to
Britain. But this time it was not to work with his old friend, but to
preach the gospel of Syndicalism. His method was direct action
and the objective a general strike. In a matter of a few months
Mann, who could pack the largest halls in the country, was able to
hold a meeting in Manchester where he could call on 60,000 workers
to follow his banner, and outside the north, where he mostly
operated, there were double the number of young, restive trade
unionists ready to join Mann's revolt against the existing trade
union policies and to prove their distrust of the Labour Party
leaders.

Inevitably the forces of reaction within the trade union and
Labour movements closed their ranks and Mann found resistance
everywhere. The inevitable result was more extremism which set
him aside as a crank. To all intents and purposes his political life
ended when his excitable manifesto "Don't Shoot", circulated in
1912, landed him in gaol.

In any event, more immediate difficulties faced the workers'
movements, both political and industrial. The harsh facts of finance
had suddenly and unexpectedly become an acute problem as the
result of the notorious Osborne lawsuit.

The judgment in the Osborne case provided evidence, not for the
first or last time, of the political bias of some of His Majesty's
judges, which may not have tainted their legal decisions but influenced them to make comments on trade unionism and Socialism
which were sometimes clearly actuated by malice and suggested that
justice was not, in this case, blind to political interests.

Osborne, a railwayman, objected to paying a compulsory levy
for the remuneration of Labour M.P.s, which then stood at £200
per year each. The injunction he sought against his union started
a tiresome series of actions which went from the Appeal Court to
the Lords. There were three decisions under examination—first,
that political action came within the meaning of the Trade Union
Acts and was, therefore, not *ultra vires*; secondly, that the pledge

of Labour M.P.s to abide by the decision of the Parliamentary Party was contrary to public policy; and thirdly that the question as to a union's M.P. being a supporter of any particular Party was a matter for the union.

In the Lords the first question received three negatives, one affirmative, and one non-decision. The second yielded verbose comments which were in the main that the pledge of obedience could give reason for questions. The third brought no decision from any of the Law Lords.

Despite the lack of clarity the inference was all too clear. Unions could not engage in any action except that specifically mentioned in the Acts of 1871 and 1876. Although those Acts had been hailed as a progressive step to legalise political activities by the unions and that had been their intention, the fact that those activities were not mentioned rendered them illegal from December 21, 1909, when the judgment was delivered.

There was evidence that the Crown received some encouragement from the Government to take every advantage of the decision, and within a matter of weeks twenty-two unions were in trouble as injunctions against them succeeded.

Twenty-one trade unions hastily resigned from the Labour Party, and twenty Labour M.P.s faced the fact that they would be without maintenance as by a strict interpretation of the constitution they were no longer eligible for payments. The Labour Executive decided, however, to maintain their remuneration.

The Labour group raised the matter in the Commons, but the Liberals showed little sympathy for their Labour friends, and the Attorney-General suggested that a better solution than changing the law would be for the State to pay M.P.s. Months later, to quieten constant questioning and to mollify the widespread restiveness of the unions, Asquith hinted at future legislation to permit trade unions to maintain political funds provided there was no compulsion on any member to contribute to them. But it was not until 1913 that a new Trade Union Act permitted a separate political levy with the contracting-out proviso.

Through attempted breakaways within the Party, and with the trade unions intimidated and bereft of financial power over policy, the Labour movement was in a very weak position as the crucial election year of 1910 arrived.

The Liberals in the Commons doubtless felt they had little to fear whether they maintained their agreement over three-cornered battles or not. But in the Upper House the bogey of the ailing Socialist infant was far more ugly than the facts justified.

The Lords were ready to precipitate a political crisis because of their forebodings about the Labour Party. The Labour M.P.s did not realise that their demand, made in 1907, for the Second Chamber to be swept away had alarmed the peerage, even if the Commons seemed to have forgotten or ignored it.

Winston Churchill accurately put his finger on the cause of the Lords' mutinous behaviour over the Budget when he told the electors of Dundee that it was the growth of the Labour Party, and all that it implied, which had led the Lords to advance claims and pretensions which "we had all thought were disposed of generations ago".

Yet the first of the 1910 elections was fought on a policy which should have created a well-nigh perfect situation for another major Labour advance. The Lloyd George Budget of 1909 had been based on what was virtually a "soak the rich" programme in order to finance social and welfare legislation which alarmed the Tories and caused heart-fluttering among the elder Liberals.

Lord Rosebery, for instance, said that the people he described as his friends, because membership of the Liberal Party was their sole mutual interest, were "moving on the path that leads to Socialism". He pointed out what was all too obvious to the survivors of nineteenth-century Liberalism: "Socialism is the end of all."

When the Lords threatened to throw out the Budget with its increase in income-tax to 1s 2d. and the introduction of super-tax of 6d. in the £1 on income over £3,000, the issue was one of the Lords versus the People, which became the Liberal election slogan.

The Liberals, as so often occurred during the period of the secret agreement arranged by MacDonald and the Liberal hierarchy, had stolen the obvious and opportune Labour thunder, or rather they had produced it because of the silence on Labour's side. In competition with the astute mind of Lloyd George, born with a genius for electoral manipulation, none of the Labour members could hope to be recognised as the prodders of the Liberals, as indeed they were. Their latent power was in fact more realistically accepted by the Liberals than it was a conscious weapon of their own.

There were seventy-eight Labour candidates for the first of the 1910 elections, the increase being mainly due to the inclusion of miners' nominees. Forty were elected, and the reverses were due to losses where a Liberal opposed in a three-cornered contest. New seats were won at Derby, Wigan, and Manchester (East); existing seats lost were at Wolverhampton (West), Manchester (South West), Preston, Chatham, Sunderland, Gateshead, Jarrow and Woolwich.

Five years of propaganda and Parliamentary activity had increased the total Labour vote by only 183,506, the percentage being a little over a third of all votes cast. The fact that the membership of the Party stood at close on one and a half millions indicated that rank-and-file loyalty was not perfect, though of course many of the Party members, who included women, had no vote. But even allowing for this, the result was not good, and was an anti-climax compared with the high promise of 1906.

The election organisation had been chaotic. In Holmfirth the Labour candidate saw his Liberal opponent being fêted by the Labour Party in the adjoining division; almost to a man the local miners voted Liberal. In Swansea Ben Tillett, who had been dropped from the list of approved candidates because of criticism of the Party, fought an election in the face of posters all over the town which proclaimed, "Had I a vote in Swansea it would not be given to Tillett—J. Ramsay MacDonald"—the result of an ill-advised interview with a local Liberal newspaper. With Liberal leanings of this kind it was not surprising that no Labour candidate won a seat where the Liberals put up an official candidate, and there was little significance in the fact that Grayson lost his seat. His increasing alcoholism made him personally disliked by the electorate, and it was his personal defects that lost him the election rather than any warnings from the Labour Party organisation.

Nor was the brief interval before the Liberals again went to the country, in that year, sensibly or constructively utilised by the Labour Party to profit from the class antagonism which was the chief point of argument in the early 1910 election. The Liberal Party was fighting for its life, and it seemed that Labour was determined to assist it sooner than look after its own interests. So certain was the Liberal Party that it could rely on Labour support and ignore Labour hostility that it made no overtures to Hardie or MacDonald to share in the conferences with the Tories to see if some compromise on restricting the power of the Lords could be found, thereby avoiding the upheaval of an election. Nor did the Labour Party demand to be included in what was clearly an all-Party matter. In this second 1910 election Labour candidates decreased to fifty-six; forty-two were successful, including a newcomer, George Lansbury. The result was therefore better than in January, but the prospective candidates had decreased largely due to the lack of finance which the Osborne judgment had made inevitable. Five new seats were won—significantly and promisingly scattered around the country, at Bow, Bromley, Sunderland, Woolwich, Whitehaven, and West Fife. Three were lost—at Newton,

Wigan, and St. Helens. The decrease in candidates naturally lowered the total Labour vote by 134,000, but the percentage had crept up to 40.88. It was not an inspiring result in view of the controversies besetting the two major parties, but inspiration had been poor in the tragically barren record of the Parliamentary Labour Party during the short 1910 Government.

5

RAMSAY MACDONALD AND ARTHUR HENDERSON

1911–1916

In February, 1911, MacDonald told Hardie that he was worried about the question of a vigorous leadership of the Parliamentary Party. "Let it be led to the devil if you like," he said; "but do not let it be the nerveless thing of the past session."

MacDonald was, of course, in no doubt about who the leader should be, but he was stating the correct view that some positive personality was vital to banish the hapless drift which had rendered the Labour Party's contribution to the hectic Commons business of 1910 futile and puny. The Labour M.P.s had even lost the prestige of sitting on the Opposition benches, having to make do with a couple of benches below the gangway on the ministerial side.

George Barnes, the Parliamentary Party's chairman, had been ailing and was happy enough to hand over office to MacDonald. It was the attainment of a goal MacDonald had always borne in mind, and probably was the reason for his hanging on tenaciously to his career in a year when his personal world crumbled. Mac-Donald's virtues as a politician and as a friend might have been open to criticism; his affections as a son, husband and father were beyond questioning. In the year that he became a figurehead in the British Labour movement he lost a son, David; his mother, and finally his wife, Margaret, a woman of great beauty, intelligence, and wisdom, whose help in MacDonald's career only he could assess.

In status MacDonald had risen with his resignation as secretary, but his influence on the day-to-day activities of the movement had begun to decline. Over the years he knew better than anyone the power that the Party secretary could exert. That power was now in the hands of the diffident and almost self-effacing assistant who had gradually taken on more and more responsibilities while Hardie and MacDonald went on their tours and absented themselves through periodic illness.

When Arthur Henderson began quietly working to become the power behind the scenes of the Party—and his influence came from the fact that the trade union leaders trusted and liked him—he was not regarded as a Socialist in practice or in theory but as an old-fashioned Radical. But he was also a man of honour, and when MacDonald's resignation made Henderson the obvious choice for the secretaryship he had no wish to pay lip-service to Socialism without a genuine conversion. The Fabians, with their tenacious belief in gradualism of change, offered a reasonable solution. As a Fabian Henderson was, of course, perfectly acceptable to all but the extremists, and in addition to the office of Party secretary he was then enabled to take on the secretarial work of the British section of the Socialist International.

Henderson's level-headed and retiring character was of great value to the Party and especially to the political and union leaders in the years before the First World War. Hardie was a shadow of the man he had been. MacDonald was becoming didactic and intolerant. That there was no real revolt against MacDonald, so that the Parliamentary Party re-elected him year after year, or any real abandonment of veneration of Hardie as the all-wise grand old man of the movement, was due to the diplomatic activities of Henderson in maintaining a middle road between the Old Guard and the new prophets.

It was not an easy task. The divisions in the Party were deep, and little that the Parliamentary Party did made any contribution to healing them. Those who could speak most effectively in Parliament could hardly forbear to applaud the Liberal legislation such as the social insurance schemes; those whose unsullied Socialist outlook made them highly suspicious of the motives for these progressive moves by the Government usually gave a poor performance in the Commons.

Despite its lack of impact in the Commons, the Parliamentary Labour Party exerted far more indirect influence on the outcome of events in the years preceding the First World War than the public knew, the unions were ready openly to admit, or the Labour M.P.s themselves realised. An examination of the actions of both sides in the industrial disputes of the period suggests that a mood existed which must have resulted in national chaos as a preliminary to serious civil disturbance. Wherever workers struck, the Government's reply was to introduce hordes of police and to threaten military and naval action; troops and Navy men were actually used for strike breaking. Employers were in an angry mood. Strikes were answered by lock-outs. Negotiations with unions were refused.

Asquith, seemingly oblivious of the imminent danger of war and the necessity to conciliate the industrial classes at almost any cost, tainted his offers of Royal Commissions with a threat of the use of the hated troops if the suggestions were rejected; he appeared to be unaware that one duty of Government was to adjudicate between opponents within the State it governed.

Fortunately Lloyd George had a greater awareness of the disaster towards which the nation was drifting. And fortunately he was friendly with both MacDonald and Henderson. Without any doubt it was on the advice of MacDonald and Henderson, the one representing Labour political opinion and the other sound trade unionism, that Lloyd George demanded that the railway directors yield to their employees' demands for direct negotiation, and it was thanks to the same agreeable liaison that the miners' strike of 1912 ended in Government intervention with an offer of minimum wages legislation. Where union militancy was such that co-operation for the behind-the-scenes actions of the Labour leaders was difficult, the strikes degenerated into drawn-out battles of little advantage to either side. A case in point was the four months' strike in the London docks, broken by the use of more than 20,000 servicemen.

Thus the Labour Party unwittingly served its rank-and-file members well in pursuing a policy unspectacular in its methods but effective in its results. Understandably the trend towards peaceful negotiations did not find acceptance among the younger generation of trade unionists, who were equally suspicious of their leaders. Younger men, like Arthur Cook of the miners, were rising to power, and Syndicalist firebrands like Tom Mann exerted far more influence than the established leaders, either in the union offices or in the Commons.

The Triple Alliance, formed by the miners, railwaymen and transport workers in 1914, was founded for the purpose of direct action on Syndicalist lines, and its ambition was not restricted to an understanding among three unions but among all of sufficient size to exert political pressure. Had not war broken out this militancy would undoubtedly have spread, and in the inevitable show-down both the existing pattern of trade unionism and the Rightist character of the Parliamentary Labour Party would have been destroyed. If the change was merely the inevitable evolutionary movement of political growth among the masses, the war and its aftermath merely delayed it. The crisis which was imminent in the summer of 1914 did not arrive until 1926.

Nineteen-eleven was one of the most turbulent years in the industrial world even in this century. The Coronation of George V was overshadowed by strikes, rioting and arson. The basic causes were the steady rise in the cost of living and the violent bouts of unemployment in scores of industries. By the example of the Government's preoccupation with social legislation the deprived classes became more conscious that their miseries were a form of injustice and not a natural consequence of existence. They seethed with discontent, and more and more of them had little confidence that the gradualism of the majority of their M.P.s, both Labour and Liberal, would effect an improvement.

Strikes and lock-outs were too numerous to count. More than eight hundred had occurred before the summer ended. The Rhondda miners were starved into returning. Seamen or dockers—or both —paralysed Southampton, Liverpool, Cardiff, Glasgow and Hull, with arson and looting of the warehouses in some cases.

It was the Seamen's Union which triggered off this succession of strikes. Deck hands were sailing to the River Plate for £3 10s. a month; men in the stokehold (all ships were of course coal-fired then) were paid £4 a month. Many failed to get regular work and were many weeks without a ship.

The demand was made for £5 10s. a month and strikes broke out in every port. They began to end when the shipowners gave way and agreed to £5 a month, but many ports held out for £5 10s. and eventually got it. The result of the strikes gave Havelock Wilson, leader of the seamen, financial security which he had lacked for many years. His had been a hand-to-mouth existence; he had been made a bankrupt twice.

But, after fighting the shipowners, he made friends with them, promised to have no more strikes, and also made terms with them which included that no man could get a job without his union's card. This killed any freedom within the union, so inevitably there were breakaways.

A serious outbreak was the general strike in the Port of London. Carters, dockers, labourers, lightermen and tugboatmen threatened the life of the biggest port in the world. Ben Tillett, hero of the 1889 dock strike, was the hero of this one, and he set up something closely approaching a miniature revolutionary government on Tower Hill. Up north, in Liverpool, much the same sort of thing was happening under the leadership of Tom Mann, who believed that his dream of a nation-wide general strike was about to come true. The riots on Merseyside developed into pitched battles, and some of the troops brought to assist the police opened fire.

By mid-August maladroit handling of the genuine grievances of the workers had brought the country close to revolution, and while the strong hand of Churchill at the Home Office provided for the worst eventualities, the appearance of armed troops in the towns and Royal Navy vessels in the ports was not calculated to relieve the tension.

An important development during these years of strife and strikes was the emergence of two Socialist newspapers. A newspaper to reflect Labour opinion and to conduct Labour propaganda had long been an ambition of the Party intellectuals who recognised the growing influence of the new-style popular newspapers. The Party's lack of genuine enthusiasm to subscribe and get such a paper started was largely due to the trade unions involved, who saw nothing paradoxical in protesting that any success of such a newspaper would be at the cost of existing publications and could therefore prejudice the jobs of members of the printing and publishing unions. A similarly narrow attitude had been in evidence when Labour M.P.s and trade unionists representing members in areas of shipyard activity rejected resolutions condemning the naval arms race before 1914.

Of the two Labour dailies of the time the *Daily Herald* was first to be published, brought out by printers during a lock-out in January, 1911. It was largely a propaganda sheet and ceased publication after thirteen weeks. But its sale, which had hovered around the 10,000–15,000 mark without any national distribution, seemed to prove what the advocates of a Labour daily had been saying at the annual Conferences for a long time: a Socialist newspaper could be commercially successful.

The compositors and printers involved in the first version of the *Herald* were behind the new project, aided by Ben Tillett who badly wanted a propaganda sheet, and by the somewhat dubious approval in principle of the T.U.C.'s Parliamentary Committee. The first issue came out on April 15, 1912, and rapidly the sale climbed to 230,000, principally on curiosity value. Before the summer was over the £5,000 with which the paper had been started was gone. Fluctuating sales, sometimes down to 50,000, were bringing in nothing as a surplus. Lansbury, who was not editor in name until 1913 but had been responsible for most of the paper's contents from the first issue, persuaded well-known writers to contribute for nothing or just token payments, though Bernard Shaw contemptuously refused to help, gratuitously adding that "neither Lansbury nor anybody else could keep a daily Labour newspaper going". The result was a hodge-podge of violent Marxism, nostalgia for old-fashioned Radicalism, and furious outpourings by the Suffragists.

F

The Commons' debate reports were usually headed "The House of Pretence", and the wildest and most abortive strikes were hailed as hints of the coming Syndicalist dawn.

On the outbreak of war the *Daily Herald* raised its price from a halfpenny to a penny, and on September 6, 1914, became a weekly, surviving the war, when it again resumed daily publication.

Its rival was the *Daily Citizen,* launched in 1912 with a capital of £150,000 in £1 shares. MacDonald was chairman, and among the directors were W. C. Anderson and Bruce Glasier as journalists, and Henderson, John Hodge, and Edward Pease as Party watchdogs. The first issue appeared in October, 1912. Within a year the paper was in financial difficulties, and a deficit of £30,000 a year had to be met out of trade union funds. Sales slumped badly, but steadied with simultaneous printings in London and Manchester. The paper continued to lose money, and the T.U.C. was asked, first to endorse a compulsory levy to ensure publication, or alternatively a voluntary levy. Both proposals were rejected and the London edition was stopped. The last Manchester edition appeared on June 5, 1915, destroyed by the dead hand of unionist interference and unionist lethargy.

In the first months of their publication both the *Daily Herald* and the *Daily Citizen* had devoted a large amount of space to that burning topic of the day which served as a diversion for the more unwieldy issues of international relations and internal economics. This, of course, was the question of women's suffrage.

Of the women who were to the forefront of the suffragette movement a considerable number were of strongly Socialistic persuasion, a fact which did not always endear them to their colleagues. Mary McArthur, daughter of a prosperous draper in the town of Ayr, who became the wife of W. C. Anderson, the chairman of the I.L.P. executive in its golden years, was primarily an organiser of trade unionism for women in industry and thereby did a lot for the women's suffrage movement among a class of women which was hardly touched by the society ladies. Annie Besant, of course, embraced the movement with all the enthusiasm that she always had for emancipation and social justice of every kind. More influential were women Socialists in the provinces, including Edith Rigby, who was a member of the I.L.P. and on the council of the Women's Labour League; and Isabella Ford, a Quaker who pioneered trade unionism among women working in Leeds and Bradford textile plants. Ethel Snowden, who married Philip Snowden in 1905, was a Fabian, and although she was a prominent member of women's suffrage societies she never persuaded her husband to approve of the militant policy women pursued, a failure which also applied to Keir Hardie's private secretary, Mrs. Travers Symons, another enthusiastic worker for votes for women.

As the movement gathered momentum the shrewd minds behind the organisation saw that the mixture of bright young ladies of the aristocracy and serious-minded wives and daughters from middle-class homes was causing plenty of sensation but failing to move the mass of the population, feminine or masculine.

The way a few dedicated men, without money or influence, had built up a solid if still small political party appealing to the industrial class was noted and pondered over. In the industries where men predominated or made an exclusive contribution they saw that organisation was by the early nineteen-hundreds so good that they could elect men who were their own representatives to Parliament. In the industries, such as textiles, where women formed the bulk of the employees, trade union organisation was still weak but it was growing. These hundreds of thousands of women offered a potent source of political pressure if inspired and directed to seek the women's suffrage goal.

Trade unionism among women had been largely the product of lofty idealism. Mrs. Besant, with the match girls, had conducted what was almost a crusade. The Women's Trade Union League, formed in 1870, was prodded to action chiefly by clergymen of the Church of England and maintained in useful activity by its secretary, Mrs. Emma Paterson, at first only interested in women's votes but quickly more concerned with women's rights in their workaday world.

It is significant in appreciating the basically suspicious attitude of the trade union and Labour leaders towards women in politics that most of the older Socialists venerated the proverbial relegation of woman to the home and regarded the need for her to work as one of the numerous faults of the society in which they lived. They did not advocate sex equality because it suggested far too much independence for their own wives and daughters. In the trade unions many admitted women on sufferance, using the fact of their smaller wages as a reason to impose smaller dues and therefore to restrict the women members' influence on the management of union affairs.

The result was that a formidable part of the campaign for female emancipation concerned women's right to vote on equal terms with men in the unions, and the matter of a Parliamentary vote sometimes took second place. The most vigorous fighters on behalf of women trade unionists were Miss Eva Gore-Booth, the daughter of an Irish baronet (her elder sister, Countess Markievicz, was the first woman elected to the House of Commons), and Esther Roper. Neither was particularly Socialistic in outlook, but their rôle as ardent feminists influenced them to champion the women factory workers of Lancashire.

It was the campaigning of these two women which had helped to return David Shackleton as Labour M.P. for Clitheroe in 1902, the votes in the ballot of the local union which approved him being given by more women than men. Shackleton was pledged to press the claims for female emancipation, though his subsequent activities in this regard were not distinguished.

More significant was the women's success at the Wigan by-election in the general election of 1906. It was the women who selected Thorley Smith to stand as "Women's Candidate and Independent Labour", which automatically got him disapproved by the miners' union and the local trades council. To their credit the railwaymen's union protested at the decision but theirs was a minority view. Smith, surrounded by women wherever he spoke, and supported by an array of women speakers, including Mrs. Pankhurst, polled more votes than the Liberal although, as expected, he failed to gain a traditional Tory seat. He got some 2,200 votes, which were virtually the votes of the 96,000 women trade unionists in the Lancashire area who had shown almost frenetic enthusiasm for a campaign in which they had nothing but indirect influence on husbands and other male relatives.

The significance of this bizarre campaign was not lost on any of the political parties. The reaction of them all was much the same: to dig their toes in and resist women's emancipation.

In the Labour Party the reason was a matter of tactics. Keir Hardie, who was on most friendly terms with the Pankhursts, believed that complete enfranchisement for women was the correct goal, but at that time he rightly saw no chance of reaching it. All the trade unions and most of the 1906 M.P.s believed that the women's suffrage movement cut across all classes, and the tactical withdrawals which Parliament might be persuaded to make would merely result in partial emancipation favouring women who would vote Tory. Many women whose enthusiasm was for Socialism rather than sex equality held the same view. Margaret Bondfield, for example, who became the first woman cabinet minister in 1929, and who was at the time Assistant Secretary of the struggling Shop Assistants' Union, said, "Don't let the suffragists come and tell me that they are working for my class."

George Lansbury resigned his seat in 1912 and stood again in order to seek a fresh mandate from the electors of Bow and Bromley for his policy of votes for women. The Executive Committee refused to support his action, and he fought the by-election without any official support and lost it.

The Parliamentary Party excused itself for this action by saying that while discipline had never been enforced when a member had a very strong personal view, disregard of policy on Lansbury's scale could only result in chaos. This problem of conscience was looming in a far more acute form for many Labour M.P.s as the imminence of war drew nearer.

The pacifism of the Labour Party was not so much a policy as a deliberate disregard of facts. At the 1911 Conference the chairman Ben Turner, said, "German invasion! That is the cry. We do not believe in it. We know the friendly feeling of brotherhood which the German and French working men and women extend to us, and we reciprocate it."

By 1912 dedicated Socialists—and therefore invariably confirmed pacifists—were awaiting the chance to fight an election. They included the well-known pacifist Dr. Alfred Salter; Harry Snell, a leading personality of the Ethical Society; Ben Tillett, whose militant ardour was confined strictly to class warfare; Bruce Glasier, the accomplished writer and unconventional member of the I.L.P.; J. H. Hudson, another I.L.P. pacifist; Tom McKerrell, a noted and popular street-corner orator in the Scottish Lowlands; and Dick Wallhead, already famous for undiluted Socialist propaganda in Lancashire.

These men had all received the Executive's endorsement as approved candidates, though no doubt after some discussion and argument. Hardie, though a pacifist himself, could not understand the new spirit animating the movement, summarised in a comment of Alf Short, one of the younger trade union leaders, at the 1912 Conference that he wished to see the leaders of the movement in touch with the spirit of the rank and file.

The Labour Party was thus completely unprepared for the war of 1914. While not a year had passed without Conference speakers declaiming against armament manufacturers and gunboat diplomacy, and rather half-heartedly against imperialism, it was the general loathing of war that inspired these diatribes rather than awareness of its imminence. This attitude was, of course, general among the public, and particularly the working classes.

Socialism was a European movement crossing national barriers. That had also been true of Liberalism in the 1840's, but Liberalism had then inspired more practical action against existing political evils than Socialism in more than sixty years had managed to do. The international bodies of workers and Socialists of various beliefs were idealistic and emotional, congratulating themselves on their aims rather than making any serious attempt to see them carried out. The nationalism of these international bodies was never far below the surface, and the outbreak of war was instantly to result in every Party of any size ranging itself alongside the nationalistic Party of its country which it had purported to loathe. The optimists who clung to the belief that the Socialist International would effectively block any chance of a "class war" saw their hopes dispelled within a week of the bomb explosion at Sarajevo.

The Government's arrangements with France in the event of war with Germany were not known to the Labour M.P.s in that age of secret diplomacy and secret staff conversations. But if the actual agreements were unknown the policy was, of course, obvious. It was clear that Britain was committed to send an expeditionary force to the Continent and that zones of action had been allocated to the navies. While not even the Cabinet, let alone M.P.s of any Party, were acquainted with the precise details, these were communicated to the Russian General Staff and in some versions were passed on to Germany and thence to the Left political organisations of all the nations involved. It would have been a singularly obtuse politician who dismissed all these stories as mere rumour, and the Parliamentary Labour Party was not obtuse. MacDonald was preoccupied with the danger. Keir Hardie had attended a peace rally in Brussels attended by Socialists from all over Europe, and had returned confident that his talks with Jean Jaures of France and Haase of Germany would bear fruit. Jaures was assassinated a few days later.

As late as July 30 MacDonald sent a message to Asquith, on behalf of the Labour Party, hoping that on no account would Britain be dragged into a European war. All Labour organisations were called on to oppose in "the most effective way" any action which might involve the country in war.

As secretary of the British section of the Socialist International MacDonald was the organiser of a demonstration held in Trafalgar Square on August 2—yet he absented himself.

He was at the time indulging in that schizophrenic attitude which could separate the idealist from the careerist in his mind. Periodically his actions aroused criticism, on account of his friendly attitude to the Liberals. The truce could be obvious, but few, apart from Hardie, suspected that MacDonald had become personally friendly with Liberals and even with some of the progressive Conservatives.

Ostensibly these contacts were no more than courtesies in the Commons, but MacDonald's innate admiration of success influenced him to try to cultivate men like Lloyd George and Haldane. He sought to gain recognition on personal terms with Asquith, but the Prime Minister invariably rebuffed him. This failure was compensated by a considerable incidence of intimate friendship with Sir John Simon, John Morley, A. J. Balfour, and even Admiral Lord Fisher—the last representing everything Labour deprecated.

Keir Hardie, constantly in and out of the Party's offices, could not help but know something of MacDonald's social activities. But Hardie was ill and ageing rapidly, and that was undoubtedly the reason why open antagonism never developed. Hardie remained implacably pacifist; MacDonald, he suspected, might be persuaded to change his views by the company he kept.

That was the company MacDonald was in when the anti-war demonstration took place in Trafalgar Square. He was at lunch with Lloyd George, Sir John Simon, and some of their friends. Such men were fully aware, at long last, of the details of British commitments in the event of war, and MacDonald, alone of anyone in the Labour movement, knew the inevitability of a major conflict in which Britain must be involved.

As chairman of the Labour Party he was bound to observe the Party's resolution on neutrality. His own idealism and vivid imagination supported this policy. Against these sentiments was his eagerness for popularity, both with the masses and with the men who mattered. Both were, he suspected, in the throes of war fever.

The result of his dilemma was a speech in the Commons which was intended to placate both sides and in the event convinced neither.

In a House deeply moved by Sir Edward Grey's speech and not merely resigned to, but enthusiastic about, the inevitability of conflict, MacDonald began by claiming the Foreign Secretary's views were wrong. He denied the country was in danger and that therefore, in his opinion, the people represented by Labour could not be asked to offer their services in the common cause. But the whole speech was based on suppositions about the situation, and on admissions that if his suppositions were wrong then war might be justified.

This exhibition of meaningless rhetoric was in contrast to the many fine examples of oratory which MacDonald gave when the issues did not trouble his double sense of values. It did no good for the Labour Party, and nothing that Keir Hardie said subsequently on that day, with earnest dignity, compensated for it.

MacDonald's major faults were to denigrate Grey, then the idol of the country, and to base his whole criticism on the fact that Belgium remained intact. That country was invaded within twenty-four hours and the kernel of his argument was split asunder.

The National Executive of the Party met on the day following the declaration of war. A resolution, endorsed by the Parliamentary Party, was almost as vague as MacDonald's speech, but it did not condemn participation in the war, merely advocating the attainment of peace as soon as possible, which was the objective of the most diehard Tories as well. One reason why the majority of Labour M.P.s abandoned whatever pacifist views they may have had was through disillusion over the much-vaunted international solidarity of the working classes. French and Belgian workers' leaders were making fiery speeches about driving out the Germans, and the German M.P.s of the Left, betraying their previous anti-war declarations, had enthusiastically voted for money for the armed services.

On August 5 the Parliamentary Labour Party met to consider its policy over the service estimates to be introduced that afternoon by Asquith. The Party voted not to oppose them, whereupon their leader resigned—partly from pique but also to avoid a more serious personal crisis. By voluntarily resigning MacDonald was able to appear before the I.L.P. as a martyr in a lost cause. Henderson who had succeeded MacDonald as leader, characteristically had no wish for revenge or still more for acrimony, and there was no question of expulsion.

In Parliament the Labour group's identity virtually disappeared. It accepted the electoral truce Asquith proposed and actively co-operated in recruiting. In May, 1915, when the Coalition Government was formed, the political truce was stabilised when Henderson, both Labour leader and Chief Whip, was given the sinecure of President of the Board of Education so that he could act as Labour Adviser to the Cabinet and sit on Ministry of Munitions committees. William Brace became Under-Secretary in the Home Office, and George Roberts became Junior Lord of the Treasury. Although these were a trio of minor posts they were reasonable in view of the small number of Labour M.P.s in the House. In fact the Parliamentary Party had been opposed to participation in the Government, due to I.L.P. influence. The National Executive, however, approved the appointments and by a majority were able to overrule the Parliamentary Party at a joint meeting.

The absence of any Conference in 1915 meant that for the first eighteen months of war the Party had no direct estimate of rank-and-file opinion. When the annual Conferences were resumed in

1916 the wisdom of Henderson's control, which if it had been colourless had been consistent, was proven. W. C. Anderson, of the I.L.P., presided. In his opening address he was critical about the past and pessimistic about the future. This contrasted strongly with the trade unionists whose views were typified by Milligan of the dock labourers, who asked if any trade union secretary would dare go back to his men and say he was against the war. MacDonald, angry and contemptuous, made a rambling reply to the thinly veiled aspersions about his patriotism in a speech which David Gilmour, a Scottish miners' leader, described as a Scottish sword dance: the speaker had danced around the points without touching on any of them.

6

WARTIME CRISIS AND A NEW
CONSTITUTION

1916–1918

As 1916 drew to a close public disillusion about the war had increased. On the Eastern front both the Russian and Rumanian allies were being hurled back. Gallipoli was at last accepted as a disaster. On the Western front the armies were bogged down on the Somme. Kitchener was dead. The country was gradually taking sides—one, a resigned "make peace on the best terms you can" policy; the other, hoping for a not impossible "wage war more efficiently" design for ultimate victory.

The Tories had lost faith in Asquith's leadership. Most of them leaned more towards Lloyd George as his successor than towards their own leader Bonar Law (Balfour was old and ill). Labour's view was influenced principally by Henderson who, as a member of the Cabinet, had a close view of the intrigues which began to prevent Lloyd George taking supreme power. Henderson was at Buckingham Palace when Asquith refused to serve in a subordinate position in a new administration and Bonar Law finally advised the King to approve Lloyd George.

The new Prime Minister had been told that none of the former Tory Ministers, apart from Bonar Law, would enter the new Government. A handful of Liberals sided with Asquith. Lloyd George's first actions were to break through the Tory defences and to woo the Liberal rank and file; he managed both so effectively that the only problem remaining was that of getting Labour approval—a problem he did not consider as difficult as the other two.

When he invited a joint deputation of the Parliamentary Labour Party and the Party Executive to a meeting at the War Office on December 7, he quickly saw that he had the advantage because the delegates were so divided. It showed on their faces before a word was said.

Lloyd George's method was to show hearty ebullience in order to gloss over defects in his proposals which he knew were so fundamentally contrary to Labour's outlook that they might have rallied the divergent views of the deputation. He first told them frightening facts about the war situation, and disposed of the pacifist elements as represented by MacDonald and Snowden by making a joke about imprisonment for dangerous men. J. H. Thomas, rapidly becoming the most powerful personality in the trade unions, was enthusiastic about the whole business, contrasting with Ernest Bevin, glowering and suspicious of political slickness. The majority of the Labour M.P.s, listening to the Prime Minister's promises of Government posts for the faithful irrespective of Party, took up an attitude of silent veneration for the new miracle worker. His final bait was an announcement that in his War Cabinet of four Henderson would be a member—a Socialist sharing a quarter of virtually dictatorial powers. This promise, supported by an assertion that Labour M.P.s would head the new Ministries of Labour and Pensions, was enough to sway the doubters away from the pacifists and hostile trade unionists. Approval for allying the Labour Party with the new administration was given by seventeen votes to fourteen.

The promised rewards were soon announced. Henderson was in the War Cabinet (increased to five). John Hodge was in charge of the Ministry of Labour and George Barnes of the Ministry of Pensions. Three minor appointments were also made subsequently to strengthen Labour's acquiescence.

The 1917 Party Conference was held within six weeks of these momentous Government changes, and many delegates were worried about the inferences of the close liaison with the Liberals. The Conference president, George Wardle, sought to warn the delegates at the outset that criticism of the Parliamentary Party's co-operation would merely be sources of moral injury.

"After the election of 1910," he reminded the Conference, "an American critic prophesied that the Labour Party would eventually fail through absorption or through internal dissensions, and considered the latter more likely. Is this to be its fate?"

Many delegates thought it was. Philip Snowden summoned up all his venom to attack Henderson and Thomas, the apostles of Lloyd George, and he drew attention to the dangers of the block vote.

"The Conference is packed with huge block votes," he said, "the disposal of which has been decided upon before ever a single word has been said in debate, and we are going to have a unanimous vote of one union who in their own delegation had carried it only by a majority of one."

Inevitably, with the almost overwhelming support of the unions, the Executive had its way, after the ranting and roaring of the minorities, but there were some awkward moments, particularly when David Kirkwood spoke on behalf of the Clyde deportees.

This affair was the culmination of prolonged unrest in the Glasgow area, beginning as early as February, 1915, with a series of unofficial stoppages in the engineering plants. The sensitive place was the Parkhead Forge, then one of the biggest munition works in the country. Here David Kirkwood, who joined the staff in 1912, organised the workers on behalf of the Amalgamated Society of Engineers so effectively that by the outbreak of war it was virtually a closed shop. The relations between employers and workmen were then in fact quite harmonious.

Trouble began when the employers, obeying Government orders, planned to dilute the labour force with unskilled workers. The big unions appeared to be not merely powerless to prevent this but, through their representatives on the various Government war production committees, hostile to the Clydeside engineers' views. The result was the formation of the Clyde Workers' Committee, composed of shop stewards who at first exerted no political pressure but were solely concerned with the welfare of the men they represented.

Lloyd George went to Glasgow in December, 1915, to talk to the men. He was accompanied by Henderson. A meeting was arranged inside the Parkhead Forge, with Kirkwood in the chair. Kirkwood was honest but unwisely frank when he told the audience that he and his friends distrusted Lloyd George and that, by joining the Government, Henderson had lost their confidence as well.

This naturally made subsequent discussion difficult. Kirkwood's arguments, about free engineers being better than slave engineers and that workers with a sense of justice worked harmoniously and efficiently, were lost in the personal hatred Lloyd George had conceived for the man who had publicly branded him as an enemy of the workers and tainted with slavery. The man accustomed to adulation wherever he went was deeply angered when the "Red Flag" drowned out "See the Conquering Hero Comes" at Lloyd George's final meeting on Clydeside.

After Lloyd George's return to London the Socialist periodical *Forward,* edited by Tom Johnston, was suppressed; Kirkwood was forbidden to move around the works, with the result that his comrades went on strike. Stoppages in sympathy immediately occurred throughout Clydeside, and in the early hours of the following morning Kirkwood and eight other men were arrested. That evening they were deported from the area. There was no charge and no trial. They simply were forbidden to come within five miles of Clydeside unless they signed a document promising to carry out loyal work and obey their union chiefs.

The arrest of the leaders, including Kirkwood, Sam Shields, Arthur McManus and a few others, aroused the workers throughout the munition plants on Clydeside to furious resentment. A demonstration was organised on Glasgow Green to protest against the action of the authorities. A large crowd assembled. I was, as president of the Glasgow Trades Council, asked to take the chair. The two principal speakers were Jimmy Maxton and a young schoolteacher, James McDougall. Both made violent attacks on the Government and in particular on Lloyd George and the Labour members of the Coalition Government.

The result was that Maxton and McDougall were arrested and were each sentenced to twelve months' imprisonment. To my surprise no attempt was made to arrest me, probably because of my standing among the seamen and dockers on the Clyde. I had been asked by the Ministry of Shipping and the Admiralty to help in finding men to man the auxiliary naval vessels, a task by no means easy. Maxton and McDougall, on the other hand, appeared to represent nobody but themselves, though both enjoyed the high respect of the Clyde workers.

Meanwhile several prominent Socialists who had attacked the Government's policy were charged with sedition. In peacetime their speeches would have been considered harmless, but under war conditions the authorities became alarmed, and action was necessary against anybody who failed to toe the line. Willie Gallacher, not at that time a Communist but regarded as a rebel; John Muir, a quiet and thoughtful man, whose sincerity and activities on behalf of the Socialist movement had gained him much popularity; and Tom Bell all received terms of imprisonment. This in turn infuriated John McLean, perhaps the greatest of Scottish political propagandists, who, because of a series of speeches against the Government, was sent to prison for three years.

Subsequently Henderson had to face an outburst of angry calls when he stood up at the Conference a year later to explain his actions, or lack of them, in connection with the unrest on Clydeside and the official ruthlessness shown towards it. He was uneasy and nervous, hiding behind the unions concerned, claiming that the deportations had occurred before he, a Cabinet Minister, knew about them, and half-heartedly offering to resign so long as he could have a fair trial first.

It was a poor performance, where Henderson's transparent honesty was for once clouded by a weakly pose as a candidate for martyrdom. His innate sense of loyalty precluded him from criticising the Prime Minister, though Lloyd George's actions had created this personal crisis for the Labour Party leader.

It was not long before Henderson discovered the bitter fact that his own principles of loyalty were not reciprocated by the Prime Minister.

In June, 1917, the United Socialist Council, a body which had no official recognition but in fact reproduced the combined voices of the I.L.P. and the British Socialist Party, held an enthusiastic meeting in Leeds to welcome the Russian revolution and applaud the prospect of imminent peace. Although Lloyd George had reacted immediately after the March revolution with the opinion that Russia no longer counted as an ally of any value he subsequently clutched at any chance of help for continuing military action on the Eastern Front. He told Henderson to take Thorne and James O'Grady, both reliable trade unionists like Henderson himself, on a visit to Russia and to report on the situation there. Henderson returned from Petrograd considerably impressed with the infant Russian Democratic Republic, and not a little persuaded that now was the time to make peace on reasonable terms for both sides.

The rising clamour for an end to the war enabled Socialists in neutral Scandinavia and Holland to make formal arrangements for a "peace conference" in Stockholm.

The Executive, mindful of a Conference vote against any Socialist international conference at which German delegates were present but those of France, Serbia, Rumania and Belgium were not, rejected the invitation and retaliated with a proposal for a conference restricted to Allied Socialists in the summer.

Almost immediately the Russian workers' and soldiers' representatives telegraphed their idea for a conference to work out a peace policy, and the Executive had to appoint a deputation consisting of G. H. Roberts, M.P., and W. Carter, of the Miners' Federation, to go to Petrograd, and if they thought fit, to talk to Branting, leader of the Swedish Socialists and organiser of the Stockholm conference, on the way back.

Lloyd George's foreign affairs experts told him that the Russian invitation came from a section of the revolutionaries already challenging the Prince Lvoff administration, and facilities for the trip were not granted. This annoyed Henderson, who had not merely returned impressed by the Russian situation; he had been accompanied by four representatives of the Russian workmen's and soldiers' deputies. These visitors left the Labour Party Executive in no doubt that the Stockholm conference would proceed whether Britain was present or not. By five votes to two the Executive then agreed to accept the invitation on the basis that the British delegates would be fundamentally observers, without powers to participate.

The French Socialists were as wary of the Russian moves as were their British colleagues, and in order to clarify the position there were some pointless discussions in Paris followed by a special Party conference on August 10. At this meeting Henderson made a rambling but sincere statement of his views, dramatically opposed to many of his own earlier outlook and the current opinion of the unions, that enemy delegates should not attend. The resolution to accept the Stockholm invitation was adopted by 1,846,000 votes to 550,000.

The German Government, by this time eager enough to secure peace at any reasonable price, had readily granted passports to its Socialist delegates for Stockholm, and this fact, augmented by the increasingly frequent reports of excesses in Russia, meant that the British newspaper-reading public were instantly subjected to a flood of alarming reports on the treacherous pacifism in the Labour Party, much of it Government inspired.

Lloyd George, prodded by Bonar Law, decided to challenge Henderson. He was told to attend a Cabinet meeting at Downing Street late one afternoon. With presumed deliberate intent to insult him, Henderson was kept pacing up and down the passageway outside the Cabinet room for an hour before he was admitted. The wearing-down process continued for a few days, with hostile receptions in the Commons and continued exclusion from the War Cabinet deliberations. Henderson wrote his inevitable letter of resignation on August 11, enabling Lloyd George to destroy the demand for resignation written and ready on his desk.

The Labour Party was understandably deeply angry when the adjourned conference met ten days later. Although it was known that passports would not be issued for any visit to Stockholm a resolution to be represented at the conference was passed, but by only 3,000 votes. A suggestion by the British Socialist Party that Labour Ministers should all be withdrawn from the Government was by-passed on the pretext that there had been no time to consider such a vitally important move.

For the rest of the year there were innumerable conferences, conversations and commissions all of merely theoretical purpose in view of the facts of life at the time. Not only was the Government determined to prevent anyone leaving for Stockholm or Petrograd but the trade unions co-operated by working against their formal resolution for Britain to participate in the conference.

Ramsay MacDonald had consistently maintained his pacifism after his temporary doubts in August, 1914, and he had genuine hopes that Stockholm might find a way of stopping the carnage far more quickly than the generals' final battle plans. Perhaps foolishly, but in line with his views, he had spoken against demands for compensation for the families of British seamen killed by German U-boats, whereupon Havelock Wilson of the Seamen's and Fire-men's Union, a man with almost pathological hatred of the Germans, and a well-known dislike of the Labour Party, announced that no ship manned by his men would sail the North Sea with MacDonald on board. This was a more formidable barrier to MacDonald's participation in the Stockholm conference than any Foreign Office moves about withholding a passport, for even in wartime it would have been difficult to prevent a British subject going abroad; the trouble would only have arisen on his return.

My personal knowledge of the feelings of ordinary people, in-cluding bereaved families of victims of the U-boats, encouraged me to believe that if a ship could be found there would be no diffi-culty in finding a crew to man it for the sole purpose of getting MacDonald, and anyone else courageous enough to go, to Scandin-avia or Russia. A ship was available at Aberdeen and I collected a crew easily enough. A telegram was sent to MacDonald to tell him all was ready. There was no reply. Perhaps Post Office censorship was the reason; more probably MacDonald's flair for indecision until it was conveniently too late to decide was the cause.

The Stockholm affair was of little international importance, but it was the cause of a deep-seated crisis within the Labour Party. The astuteness and the ruthlessness of Lloyd George had effected a defeat of Labour views which, however, properly handled, could have seriously incommoded the victor, anxious as he was to main-tain his all-Party unity. The Prime Minister's cavalier treatment of a valuable and hard-working colleague, who had seriously prejudiced his own position on many an occasion in order to further the Government war policies, ought to have caused a closure of Labour's ranks and a realisation of the fundamental differences between Labour and Liberalism in peace or in war. But in virtually every move Lloyd George handled the difficulties as he wished and benefited from Labour's reaction. George Barnes meekly accepted Henderson's office when Lloyd George offered it, and the Party was

The Dockers' leaders on the eve of the 1924 strike. From left to right: James Sexton, Ben Tillett, Ernest Bevin.

A Labour house party at Easton Lodge, June 1923. Left to right sitting: Arthur Henderson, Countess of Warwick, Ramsay MacDonald. Left to right standing: Canon Adderley, Mr. & Mrs. Shinwell.

Two great trade
unionists: Arthur Cook,
the Miners' leader,
during the coal crisis
of May, 1926;
Ernie Bevin as
Minister of Labour,
1943.

easily mollified by George Wardle getting a minor job in the Board of Trade.

There were the seeds of Labour's dissolution in these events. That they grew instead into a strong Socialist plant was due as much to Henderson as the swiftly moving events in the last months of the war. It was the integrity of Henderson that shone through all the bewilderment and doubts. Upon his resignation from the Government he actively resumed the chairmanship of the Party and became the only man who could fashion a united movement out of the reactionaries, the avenging war fanatics, the pacifists, and the trade unionists. His experience in the war years had, in short, finally converted Henderson to Socialism—the only possible policy offering any hope of creating unity.

Moreover, he had imagination. He stirred the Trades Union Congress when he addressed it as fraternal delegate in 1917, with a vision of a League of Nations devoted more to international amity than unity of individual sections of nations for a class war. He lifted the eyes of men who had hitherto seen nothing beyond their own wages and working conditions to the influence they could exert on foreign affairs. Aided by J. H. Thomas, he taught the unions about the powers and responsibilities they now held as a political force. He bridged the gap between the unionists and the intellectuals so that he could confidently ask the Webbs to prepare a new constitution for the Party with a fair expectation of getting it through a Conference. Henderson, in brief, was in 1917 and 1918 moulding the Labour Party for government. Hitherto it had never really regarded itself as more than an opposition to whichever of the two parties was in power.

The stature which Henderson gained as a result of his experience in the Coalition Government was remarkable. He planned for his Party's future with a calculating regard for every eventuality. He saw women's suffrage as an immediate reward when the war was over and proposed four seats on the Executive for women. He expected that large numbers of the men in uniform who had come from the middle classes and the reactionary craft unions would be potential Labour voters in the new conditions of a changed Europe, and he allocated five Executive places for local Labour Parties, where membership for such newcomers would be offered to individuals irrespective of trade union, trades council, or political association affiliations.

In this way Henderson softened the impact of the 1917 Conference decision that members of the Executive should be elected by the vote of the whole Conference, and with the result that the unions

G

could always outvote the political societies by fifty to one. The block vote loomed over every move, but the framework on which those votes were given would henceforth be a sound Socialist one.

The constitution adopted on February 26, 1918, was a masterly success for all the hopes and schemes of Henderson and the Webbs. The now historic paragraph on Party Objects—"to secure for the producers by hand or by brain the full fruits of their industry, and the most equitable distribution thereof that may be possible, upon the basis of the common ownership of the means of production and the best obtainable system of popular administration and control of each industry or service"—was a Socialist aim which Hardie and the pioneers would have regarded as wildly unacceptable to any trade unionist. By 1918 the famous Clause Four was a reason for enthusiasm about the brave new world once peace had come.

Henderson was now so firmly in the saddle that the careerist policy practised by the Labour M.P.s participating in the Government when the war ended hardly caused a ripple of trouble. They all refused to resign despite the views of the National Executive; only Clynes, the Food Controller, eventually obeyed the Party's orders, though with obvious reluctance. The rest were expelled from the movement, and thereby Henderson cut out a considerable amount of dead wood, freeing himself for the tough battle presented by Lloyd George's snap election of December, 1918. He could at least go to the country with an honest brand of Socialism; not wholly Marxist in origin; not pandering to one workers' group more than another; but a decent British concept of social justice and honest government for the greatest good for a majority of the people.

The odds against a fair election were almost impossibly long, as Lloyd George had of course intended. Although the majority of the voters on the electoral rolls were voting for the first time, large numbers of eligible persons had been omitted because of the movements of the population under war conditions. The previous Liberal understanding with the Labour Party went overboard in view of the profitable results obtainable from Liberals joining with Unionists as Coalition candidates and electioneering with the coupon device of the outgoing Government. Virtually the whole of the resources of both Liberals and Tories were used to oust Labour, the only group Lloyd George feared.

Remarkable efforts, with the unions working in close harmony with the Labour Party and the I.L.P., resulted in 361 Labour candidates coming forward. Only fifty-seven seats were won, but the Labour candidates polled close on 2¼ million votes out of a total poll of 10.8 millions. Only 59 per cent of the electorate voted, and a good proportion of the missing votes belonged to people who received no ballot papers. Large numbers of men in the forces never received any, with the result that only a million of the four million eligible servicemen recorded their votes.

William Adamson became chairman of the Parliamentary Party, with Clynes vice-chairman. They believed that the Labour Party would become the official Opposition, their sixty-one members (which included unopposed members) far exceeding the group of "free" Liberals, usually calculated as numbering twenty-five. But within the 535 Coalition members there were numerous splinter groups which were soon opposing the Government. The Labour group did not receive the cachet of being regarded as His Majesty's Opposition, but in its activity as the session continued it earned the title. Henderson's months of work to influence public opinion were beginning to pay a dividend.

7

THE AMBITIONS OF THE T.U.C.

1918–1922

Peace quickly proved to be a travesty of everything the politicians had promised when demanding more effort and more sacrifice in the war, and of the peaceful existence the troops had envisaged once victory was won. The cost of living soared. Basic foods were in short supply and homes even at inflated rentals impossible to find. Instead of the foreshadowed trade boom there was soon a trade slump. Even peace itself was little more than a bitter description of half-war. Eastern Europe was in a ferment; Russia a dark continent of rumoured horror; India, Ireland and Egypt in the throes of rebellion.

After Europe's economic conditions improved, the tenuous advantages of industrial output Britain had briefly enjoyed in the first months of the so-called peace evaporated. Both wages and prices dropped, the former faster than the latter. And even at starvation wages jobs became fewer. By 1921 unemployment had risen to two and a half millions and the misery of the innumerable strikes and lock-outs, which in turn paralysed railways and deprived the nation of coal, police services, and all kinds of goods and facilities, paled before the unpleasant truth that the statesmen, whether Welsh wizards or die-hard Imperialists, had no solution for winning the peace.

It was the grand opportunity for the nation's third political force to show what it could do in place of the two established parties which were virtually confessing failure both at home and in foreign affairs.

In international affairs the Labour Party had also to wrestle with narrow views as difficult to weld into some practical plan of compromise as for the world statesmen at Versailles. The Secretariat of the International had been re-established in Brussels in the autumn of 1919, and a great congress was planned for Geneva in July, 1920. The T.U.C. and the Labour Executive agreed to send a British delegation of sixteen members to use the thirty votes allocated to Britain. Of these, twenty-four were for the trade unions and the remaining six for the political societies.

Immediately dissension began as to whether the political groups should recognise the Geneva conference or not. The British (Marxian) Socialist Party decided it preferred the rival Moscow International, and the I.L.P., at a Glasgow conference at Easter, 1920, decided to withdraw from the Second International but also rejected a proposal that it should join the Moscow competitor.

After the Armistice there was among Labour leaders a genuine conviction that international accord could be constructively fostered by the Socialist movements of Europe. Disillusion about the failure of the international workers' movement, symbolised by the Second International before 1914, had been minimised in the general optimism about a better new world. Yet the members of the Second International, who had talked freely about general strikes to make war impossible before the end of July, 1914, had in a matter of days become as belligerent as the governments they had determined to thwart.

While there was much talk among moderate Socialists both in the defeated and the victorious countries, the upshot of which was the formation of the International Labour Organisation as an autonomous body linked to the League of Nations, the Communists went quietly ahead with their plans. The Third International was presented by them as the rightful successor to the Second.

The Labour Party pinned its hopes on the negotiations at Geneva, but the I.L.P., in co-operation with a number of other European groups, decided to join a third international organisation launched by Fritz Adler in Austria. This, because it sought to formulate a policy midway between the reactionary and outdated remnants of the Second International (mostly agreeable to the Geneva proposals) and the Communist regimentation of the Third, was dubbed the Two-and-a-Half International.

I was one of the delegates sent by the I.L.P. to attend the Vienna International and subsequently became a member of its Executive. Among the Socialists I met there were Jean Longuet, a grandson of Karl Marx; Ledebour of Germany, Grimm of Switzerland, Otto Bauer of Austria, and of course Adler himself, who had gained notoriety for his part in a political assassination which preceded the collapse of Austria in 1918.

As is the custom of international organisations, pious resolutions were carried without much foresight, with every delegate aware that these were gestures of unity disguising their inherent impracticability. On any concrete matter necessitating definite action, discussions were fruitless. In fact, the arguments continued for years, fading into oblivion when the Second International was re-established and perpetrated the faults which had rendered it pointless in August, 1914.

For years afterwards, the negotiations to foster international Socialism lapsed into a turgid sequence of jealousies, controversies and self-aggrandisement. On one side were the survivors of the pre-war international workers' movements, by now reactionary with the serenity of advancing age and bestirring themselves only to re-fight the war over the conference table.

On the other side was the Communist-controlled and power-hungry dictatorship determined to absorb and destroy every Socialist movement which did not demonstrate its subservience to the Russian brand of Marxism.

To some extent the second movement could reasonably regard itself as the probable victor. It fed on the workers' disillusion, and there was plenty of that emotion at the time when the Russian experiment attracted malcontents and idealists alike.

The Communist Party in Britain was established in August, 1920. Arthur McManus, one of the Clyde deportees, its chairman, and Albert Inkpin, its secretary, promptly applied for affiliation to the Labour Party. The National Executive rejected the application, Henderson explaining that the Communist Party's objects "did not appear to be in accord with those of the Labour Party". A series of acrimonious letters ensued, but Henderson stood firm.

The Communists continued to press their claims, and as a diversionary objective began a process of infiltration into the Labour Party and more especially into the unions. While a Communist could not obtain membership of a local Labour Party or obtain approval as a Parliamentary candidate with local Labour support, he could and did infiltrate into the unions and then appear at the Party conferences as a delegate.

One of the most vigorous Communist propagandists was A. J. Cook, of the Miners' Federation. He came before the 1921 Labour Conference as a delegate of the miners, an executive member of their union, a miners' agent in one of the biggest of the Welsh coalfields, and, he added, "As a member of the Communist Party, for which I make no apology."

"God knows the Labour Party wants amending," he said, and he went on to warn the delegates, "Watch your leaders; they want watching, every one of them."

This was the type of speech which got wide publicity in the capitalist Press, and made a considerable impact on younger trade unionists. The public were duly informed by their morning news-papers that the Labour Party was falling into the hands of the British Bolsheviks. In the event, the Executive's refusal to permit the Communist Party to affiliate was overwhelmingly endorsed.

The readiness of the unions to allow Communists to control the branches and even reach the Executive was indicative of the dis-quiet and disappointment with the Labour Party and the Parlia-mentary group.

In the closing months of the war there was an agitation among the trade unions to form a political party of their own. J. B. Williams, of the Musicians' Union, was the moving spirit behind the proposals. He could point to several resolutions at the Trades Union Congress in 1916 and in 1917 which suggested that industrial politics could best be dealt with by a Trade Union Labour Party.

Some twenty trade union officials signed a circular proposing the founding of the new party, much to the alarm of the Labour Executive which thereupon appealed to the T.U.C.'s Parliamentary Committee to stifle the breakaway movement. The idea fell through, but was indicative of the ambitions of several trade unions to obtain more direct representation in Parliament. It was also a warning to the intellectuals, with their growing influence, not to forget that even if the trade unions could be cajoled they could never be ignored.

Immediately after the 1918 election the unions again showed their desire for independence when the Triple Industrial Alliance, the most militant of the trade union developments of the time, demanded that direct action to change the Government's policy towards Russia should be organised by the T.U.C. alone. "Direct action" was a euphemism for general strike action, not to settle any industrial dispute, but to change Government policy.

Their impatience was understandable because of the dilatory behaviour of the Parliamentary Party. Henderson wrote to Lloyd George on December 18, 1918, asking four specific questions about the policy towards Russia and the Government's reason for sending British troops to support the White Russians. More letters and enquiries were sent, but Henderson received nothing beyond a formal acknowledgment for the next five months. The trade unions naturally considered that the Labour M.P.s were either too weak to force the Prime Minister to answer the Party's secretary, or else their hearts were not in it.

The Parliamentary Labour Party was badly in need of new blood. The automatic admiration for a working-class representative manag-ing to get to Westminster had died before the war. There was nothing dynamic about it any longer. Further, the usual perorations of every Labour candidate since Keir Hardie, inferring that it was only necessary for the speaker to get to Parliament for a workers' paradise to appear round the corner, had become stale. The thoughtful, younger working men and ex-servicemen knew there was a long, slow battle ahead.

Most of the working class preferred that it should be a gradual, democratic process. The horror stories coming from Russia, albeit distorted in the sensational Press, had made their point. Men and women who had endured four years of war carnage did not want bloody revolution. But they did expect more tenacity on the part of the Labour M.P.s. They wanted some form of Socialism, at least in a form free from Liberalism. They wanted to see some tangible results now that the war-time political truce was over.

Unfortunately they did not find what they hoped. The refusal of men regarded as trustees of Labour's policy to leave the Coalition was regarded at the best as careerism; at the worst as perfidy. MacDonald and Snowden, differing violently in many opinions but accepted by huge groups as men who mattered, had failed to get re-elected because of their war-time pacifism. Henderson, the one man whose conduct could be respected by pacifist and non-pacifist alike, and perhaps the one man who could have discovered ways and means of strategy against the cunning of Lloyd George and the hostility of both the Parties which gave a masquerade of unity under his leadership, had also lost at the polls. There were only two names among Labour M.P.s which meant anything nationally—J. R. Clynes and William Adamson. Neither meant anything particularly impressive in the opinion of most of the rank and file. Conference speakers made pointed remarks about the poor record of attendance of Labour M.P.s. The Party's Parliamentary reports became an apology rather than a record of achievement.

The militancy of the trade unions and the growth of extremist groups, both affiliated and unaffiliated, which occurred in the first year or so after the Armistice were partly in the spirit of disillusion and unrest which is war's aftermath. But they were also symptoms of the disquiet and discontent of the rank and file as regards the Parliamentary Party.

The T.U.C., as a natural development of its traditional belief that trade unionists were the best people to look after the working classes, finally broke away to follow a completely independent line. For a generation it had tended to be ready to sell itself politically to the highest bidder, and whatever its formal liaison with, and support of, the Labour Party might be, a good many trade unionists, both inside Parliament and out, were never wholly converted from the Liberalism which had in practice, though under pressure, done far more to improve wages, hours of work and so on than the Labour movement.

Thus the T.U.C., while taking care not to sever any of its potentially useful political links, became a political force in its own right. The Parliamentary Committee of the T.U.C., which had been little more than a discussion group with Labour Party leaders who were largely out of sympathy with the trade union view on day-to-day affairs, was replaced by the General Council.

This body was a political hierarchy whatever its ostensible purpose. Under the revised constitution of the T.U.C., which came into force in 1921, the craft unions found their power and prestige reduced, and the strength of numbers predominated. The nation's unions were divided into seventeen groups, each with a representative on the General Council. Each representative was a member of a union within his group, and nominated by the unions, but the election to the Council was by card vote, which meant, of course, that power was with the big battalions.

Ernest Bevin, now beginning to emerge as a trade union leader, seldom failed to express cynicism about the politicians. Vigorous and energetic men within the unions saw in the General Council a target for their ambitions far more promising than election to Parliament, and a career in trade unionism thus made an appeal to men who disliked the formalism and ritualistic procedure of Parliament. Their preference was understandable, but it was one reason for the disaster of 1926, when the General Strike not only dealt a reeling blow to the T.U.C. but rendered ineffectual the position of the Labour Party.

But the sin of omission by the Labour Party in the 1919–1922 period was as much a cause of the 1926 debacle as the overweening ambitions of the T.U.C. to determine political policy for itself. Those who had direct responsibility for keeping the Party lively and in touch with the facts of politics failed to sense the obvious changes which were occurring in the new generation and the new electorate.

By 1921 the Party's rank and file were becoming more militant and more convinced of Socialism's purpose. Labour was not only celebrating its twenty-first birthday but was approaching the path towards maturity, with its earlier doubts and misgivings largely dispelled. That was the attitude of the rank and file—not of the men in Parliament who were supposed to give voice to Labour opinion.

They were badly out of touch with the progressive developments which had occurred so rapidly after the war ended.

The result was that at the Party's Conference at Brighton in June, 1921, the chairman, Alex Cameron, had a rousing reception for his sweeping statement, "The present capitalist system must go. Before the workers will be permitted to control industry effectively, or even the distribution of the products of their industry, they will first require to own the machinery and materials of industry. Such ownership will only be acquired when we capture political power."

Cameron was a prominent trade unionist, and all but 260,000 of the 4,158,000 votes at that Conference were in the hands of the unions. Their new sense of militancy and urgency, engendered by unemployment and economic hardships, was only part of the atmosphere of discontent with the Executive shown at the time.

Herbert Morrison, speaking for the London Labour Party, vainly tried to obtain better representation for constituency parties, appealing to the trade unions to refrain from suppressing local Labour groups. This was the muscle-flexing of a new and vigorous Socialist infant as restless as the unions, and extremely wary of the T.U.C.'s manoeuvres to obtain political power on its own or, failing that, to call the Labour tune. The reason for the challenge which had emerged was not hard to discover.

The only significant trend, auspicious for a future general election, was the remarkable growth of Labour representation in local government. War-time emergency laws had suspended local elections, but with their resumption in 1919 Labour gained some 6,000 seats on the local authorities.

Labour was now particularly strong in mining areas. Durham was a Labour-controlled county. A Labour majority existed on ten urban councils in South Wales. But the most striking development was in London, where in the elections in November, 1919, 572 seats were gained, giving Labour majorities in eleven boroughs and control, thanks to Labour mayors, in two more. It was a victory for Herbert Morrison, who had organised his campaign for the London Labour Party while doing farmwork in Hertfordshire as a conscientious objector. It was the opening chapter of the long story of Labour's rule over the greatest city in the world.

That co-operation between the T.U.C. and the Labour Party did not break down was due chiefly to the fact that the Miners' Federation gratefully accepted the simple lesson that political skill was vital for their interests—a lesson which brought the teacher Sidney Webb to the culmination of many years of wise if didactic contributions to the Labour movement. Webb and his wife, Beatrice, had, of course, exerted tremendous Party influence behind the scenes from the turn of the century. Whatever inspiration the Fabians bestowed on the movement—and it was indirectly very great indeed—the sinews were the construction of Webb. The growing awareness of Socialism's impact in the London area was the result of Webb's journalism and municipal work to a far greater extent than the tub-thumping oratory of the men who rode to success when London went Labour.

But Webb had simultaneously extravagant hopes and too much awareness of the long and difficult road to make much appeal to the pioneers of the movement who directed the Labour Party before 1914. He preached gradualism as the best way to consolidate electoral gains so as eventually to rank alongside the other two Parties. He was unmoved by ephemeral but dramatic problems of one group or another, and was consequently dismissed as an ivory-tower intellectual wanting too much while planning to attain it too slowly.

His emergence as the hero of the practically-minded men who had hitherto regarded him as an adversary occurred as the result of Webb's work on the Sankey Commission of 1919. The Miners' Federation could appoint three of their own members and nominate three experts from outside the industry. Webb was one of the trio they nominated.

In the event the miners learned that their moral victory was entirely due to Webb. Robert Smillie harangued the other side with characteristic melodrama about exploitation, starvation, and disease. It sounded well but made poor debating material in a Commission's report devoted to facts.

The facts came from Webb. Cool, calculated statistics devastated the owners' and Government's case. The Miners' Federation were not ungrateful. They saw that Webb topped the poll for the Party Executive and were the leading group which put him in the Chair in 1923. And they in due course took the remarkable step of inviting him to stand for Seaham, the preponderantly mining electorate returning him with a majority of more than 11,000, a wonderful testimonial for an intellectual of sixty-three whose Fabian Society was reluctant to accept working-class applicants for membership.

The reward of a Parliamentary seat was justified for the man who was the architect of the post-war Labour Party. His was the pen which drafted the new constitution and policy statement which became the blueprint of the inter-war period and indeed, despite attempts to modify it by some of the Party intellectuals, is still basically the Party policy. But it was neither to Webb's advantage

nor the benefit of the Party that he thus emerged from the back
room of propaganda and planning. He disliked and distrusted
MacDonald and was visibly contemptuous of most of the Party
leaders. Neither of his subsequent Government appointments was
distinguished. In fact, the performance Webb put up on behalf of
the miners was a *tour de force* and nothing more. It gained the
miners a moral victory but no practical benefits.

This disillusion with discussion, and the justifiable disgust with
a Government which rejected its own Commission's views, further
aggravated the anarchistic trend of the miners, but not before they
had tried very hard to obtain justice by political methods. The
"Mines for the Nation" campaign was one of the greatest propaganda activities the Labour Party and the T.U.C. had ever carried
out. It was run by Fred Bramley (T.U.C.), Frank Hodges (Miners'
Federation) and J. S. Middleton (Labour Party). A large number
of demonstrations were held up and down the country, and huge
quantities of leaflets distributed.

The only jarring note was the marked absence of the Labour
Party's best-known personalities at meetings, and when the Parliamentary Party failed to persuade the Government to introduce
legislation on the lines recommended by a majority of the Coal
Industry Commission the T.U.C. held an emergency meeting. This
voted against calling on all unions to participate in a general strike
and sank back on a vague plan for political action. Once again
the miners felt frustrated as their friends let them down. There was
another bitter lesson in the offing.

The acute militancy of the miners, which swept away their old-
style narrow-minded leaders, was inevitable after Black Friday,
April 16, 1922. It proved to the miners that they could not put
their trust in their fellow trade unionists.

On that notorious Friday—described by the *Daily Herald* leader
writer as "the heaviest defeat that has befallen the Labour movement within the memory of man"—the much-vaunted Triple
Alliance crumbled within hours. The railwaymen and the dockers
were uneasy about striking in sympathy with the miners should
the strength of the alliance be put to the test. A speech by Frank
Hodges, secretary of the miners, gave them the excuse they needed.
Bevin for the dockers and Cramp and Thomas for the railwaymen,
ungracefully retired from the battle, making the ultimate defeat of
the miners inevitable.

Hodges could subsequently complain of the falsity of his allies,
but his own behaviour had strained goodwill to the limit. He had
left a meeting in the House of Commons, at which the T.U.C. and

the subsidiary groups of the Labour Party seemed to be in complete agreement on solidarity in strike action, to talk to a group of Liberal and Tory M.P.s. Hodges was there on his own responsibility and his hint that the miners would accept a compromise was his personal opinion.

The union repudiated what Hodges had said, but the other members of the Triple Alliance clutched at Hodges' statement as the straw which could dispose of the strike pledge. Lloyd George seized on the cracks in what he had feared was a solid wall and drove his wedge into them. It was an easy victory which the Prime Minister badly needed. Not for the first time or the last Labour's political adversaries had been presented with a last-minute chance of victory through the divisions and schisms of the opponents.

The general election of November, 1922, was hailed as a vast triumph for the Tory Party—a needed victory and the first it had enjoyed for twenty-one years. The Tories obtained an overall majority of 77. Their success was not so dramatic as the Liberals' defeat; they had won only 55 seats for the Lloyd George National Liberals and 60 for the Asquith Liberals.

This disaster to the great Party of the previous twenty years served to disguise the more significant progress of Labour, which won 138 seats and became the Opposition, whether the two Liberal Parties combined or not. The Tories feared that Lloyd George would not accept defeat but would organise a middle-of-the-road radical Party, collecting a few of the Asquithian M.P.s, perhaps a handful of Coalition Tories, and all the Liberal-inclined Labour M.P.s. The last category was one that Bonar Law, the Prime Minister, feared as the most potent source of recruitment for Lloyd George. Like so many of Socialism's political opponents, Law could not envisage any M.P. preferring to remain outside the conventional political folds of one Party or the other.

Lloyd George's dreams and Bonar Law's fears about the venality of some Labour M.P.s might have been correct if it had not been for the gusty fresh breezes brought into the Party by the wild men of the Clyde, the newest and most dynamic members of the Parliamentary Labour Party.

The description of wildness was a Press commentary on a group of thirteen men from Glasgow and the surrounding area who were, for the most part, left of centre, and deserving of no description as revolutionaries or anarchists because of their progressive views. However, at the time, the mere mention of Glasgow and the Clyde was prone to arouse the direst forebodings in some quarters. Memories of war-time strikes had been sharpened by the unrest which occurred in the first weeks of January, 1919, when the industrial area along the Clyde experienced the full impact of the depression. In order to achieve a degree of fair shares for the thousands of unemployed from the war plants and the returning ex-servicemen, local shop stewards decided to demand a 40-hour week with no overtime and no reduction in wages. Most of the union leaders opposed strike action but the Glasgow Trades Council gave the movement its full support.

The enthusiasm of the meetings alarmed the Government, which had just dealt with mutinies at military camps along the south coast, and it persuaded a technically Labour member of the Government, G. H. Roberts, of the Ministry of Food, to brand the strike as revolutionary in character.

On January 31, when some 70,000 men were on strike in the Clydeside area, a mass meeting in George Square was broken up by the police with some bloodshed.

I was chairman of the Strike Committee. That night I was among those arrested for incitement to riot, and while I was in prison Glasgow was transformed into a military camp with tanks and steel-helmeted troops at strategic points. The repressive measures against the citizens and the punitive sentences my colleagues and I received did, of course, have the immediate effect of intimidating the workers of Clydeside. Ten of the strike leaders, including Kirkwood, were acquitted: William Gallacher and I were imprisoned. The movement had spread to other parts of the country, notably the Midlands. The eventual reaction was to consolidate all opinion in favour of Socialist policy. The I.L.P. contingent which the workers sent to Parliament in 1922 was the direct result of that 1919 reactionary act of suppression.

The majority of the men who received a send-off from Glasgow for Westminster did in due time attain some stature in the nation's political life, and none proved particularly dangerous to the peace and security of the realm.

One was John Wheatley, leader of the Labour group on the Glasgow Town Council. He liked to boast of his extremist views, but was in fact a rather cautious man, suspicious of extremist action in contrast to a liking for extremist oratory.

James Maxton, one of the finest orators of his day, was a schoolteacher. He had been chairman of the Scottish Council of the I.L.P., and during the war was a conscientious objector. He was deeply convinced that nothing short of revolution would put Britain's wrongs right, but his gentle nature and his indolence made it unlikely that he would ever lead the mob to the barricades.

He did, of course, become a great Parliamentarian and one of the best-loved men in the House of Commons during the twenty-four years he sat for Bridgeton.

George Buchanan was a pattern-maker and a trade unionist, though this was secondary to his political loyalties; he represented the Gorbals. The Rev. Campbell Stephen, Tom Johnston, David Kirkwood, and myself were others of a group who hardly ranked for the sobriquet of "wild", though compared with the old-style Liberal-leaning Labour M.P.s we were, I suppose, a new and alarming force. It was not long before we caused alarm and some despondency among the Old Guard who had for too long been deciding on the leadership for themselves. Unhappily, of all the Clyde Brigade who entered Parliament in the election of 1922, the only survivors are Tom Johnston, now in retirement, and myself.

The Clyde was not alone in sending reinforcements to the Parliamentary Labour Party in 1922. Some, like Charles Trevelyan, Arthur Ponsonby, Josiah Wedgwood and Lees Smith, had forsaken the Liberals and had become fully-fledged members of the Labour Party. It could hardly be said that they had accepted the Socialist faith; there were some who were disgusted with Lloyd George; others who felt that after the sacrifices of the war the people deserved a higher standard of living and security against another conflict. With them came men of high intellectual quality like E. D. Morel, the fighter for Colonial freedom, Sidney Webb, Clem Attlee, Arthur Greenwood, Patrick Hastings, a distinguished lawyer; and many others.

From Wales came Dick Wallhead, Vernon Hartshorn, and Ted Williams; from Yorkshire, Tom Williams, Will Paling and Tom Smith; from Durham, Jack Lawson, Joe Batey and Bob Richardson; from Lancashire, Joe Tinker and Alan Parkinson.

For the first time since the formation of the Parliamentary Party in 1906 the Opposition contained within its ranks men of experience in industry, the professions, in foreign affairs; a great array of talent to back up some of the old-timers: MacDonald, Snowden, Clynes, and Tom Shaw. Our expectations were high; the country would soon discover what a real Opposition could do.

During 1919 and 1920 Adamson had been absent from Parliament through illness, with the result that he could be conveniently and necessarily dropped from the chairmanship of the Parliamentary Party. Adamson was a dour and phlegmatic Scottish miners' leader very much out of his depth in the Commons. He took the complaints about the Labour M.P.s' poor record as a personal affront. His selection had been motivated by a desire to have a chairman who would create the minimum of trouble, so the movement got the results it deserved.

Adamson was followed by J. R. Clynes, a man whose militancy was certainly not in evidence in his demeanour nor in his record of unwilling retirement from the Coalition Government. But Clynes had considerable ability for organisation so long as imaginative action was unnecessary. He was, by the time he became chairman, fifty-one and already an old-type Labour politician.

Will Thorne had recognised the young Clynes as a speaker of ability, and had persuaded him to speak without any payment throughout Lancashire on behalf of the Gas and General Workers' Union. Clynes then became a union organiser and thereby easily won himself a Parliamentary seat in the 1906 election for North-East Manchester, which he represented till the constituency changed in 1918. Thereafter he sat for the Platting division. Clynes was therefore a trade union representative rather than a Socialist M.P.

It was inevitable that such a man would find disfavour with the new blood which entered the Parliamentary Party in 1922. On the grounds of prestige and reliability Henderson would have gained the majority of votes if he had been an M.P., but as was his custom he managed to lose the election and in his absence the only possible choice was MacDonald.

MacDonald had narrowly missed victory at the East Woolwich by-election in 1921 largely owing to the antics of the Communists and other extremist organisations, notably Horatio Bottomley's circus, who co-operated to make the fight one of the dirtiest of this century. The result of his defeat had been to create much sympathy for him, and he was gladly accepted as candidate for Aberavon and easily won the seat in 1922.

MacDonald had greatly impressed the younger members of the Party when, at the 1921 Conference, he had used a resolution of support for the miners, then suffering terribly from the prolonged lock-out, to speak on behalf of the Left section of the movement.

"My last words," he said, "are: Labour, do not regard the Left as mere talkers; remember that the Left is a Left of action and not of talk; remember that the Left is a Left of reality and not of imagination; remember that the Left is a Left of responsibility and not of irresponsibility."

This attitude encouraged the new M.P.s of 1922 to reject the tradition of the chairman of one session being automatically elected as chairman of the next one. They wanted to replace Clynes by MacDonald.

Ramsay MacDonald addressing the Labour Party Conference as Prime Minister, Queen's Hall, London, 1924.

Ramsay MacDonald, Arthur Henderson, and J. H. Thomas on their way to see George V, outside Buckingham Palace, 1924.

Ben Tillett, famous
Dockers' leader.

Tom Mann,
pioneer and one
of the great
Socialist orators.

The older M.P.s preferred to stand by Clynes, and a few others, notably Snowden, supported him simply because of their dislike of MacDonald. Maxton also disliked MacDonald: his influence among the I.L.P. members, however, failed to prevent MacDonald's nomination for leader. The reactionary trade union approach was typified by J. H. Thomas, at the time implacably opposed to Mac-Donald personally and the I.LP. in general.

When the Parliamentary Labour Party met in November, 1922, the expected break with tradition occurred. The formal proposal to support the officers elected in the summer was rejected. Clynes was then formally nominated. On behalf of the I.L.P. I nominated MacDonald, who won the subsequent vote-taking by 61 to 56.

More than a score of M.P.s did not attend the meeting, and most of them were of the old guard. Their presence might well have given Clynes victory, and the Party would have had a totally unsuitable Leader of the Opposition who would in little more than a year become Prime Minister.

By the spring of 1922 it was clear that the Coalition could not continue. That it had lasted so long was due to the fear of the Labour Party's emergence as the victorious Party if the schisms of the Liberal-Tory Coalition became too violent and widespread. So greatly had Lloyd George feared the spread of Labour into the middle classes that he softened the blow of the Geddes axe on teachers' salaries by cutting the proposed savings by nearly £12 million. This move was the result of a conversation with Philip Snowden, who had told the Prime Minister that because of the threat of salary cuts every teacher in the country would become a Socialist propagandist.

Churchill, preparing to return to the Tory Party after some twenty years, told a political meeting at Loughborough that the time had come for the nation's historic Parties to merge in order to circumvent the Labour Party which, he said, "was unfit to govern".

Retribution was in store for Churchill. He was one of two Tory candidates in the 1922 election who were defeated in Dundee, by E. D. Morel, who had exposed the Congo atrocities, and E. Scrymgeour, the prohibitionist.

H

8

H.M. OPPOSITION—AND MINORITY GOVERNMENT

1922–1924

MacDonald's vacillation and distaste for personal contacts marred his talents. As the most experienced M.P. he could have offered guidance to many of the new members. Their inexperience was the cause of brash and unwise speeches made by some of the tyros ignorant of the ritualistic procedure of Westminster.

The increase in numbers of Labour M.P.s in 1922, though considerable, was not enough to justify the belief that the revolution had arrived. The numbers had doubled, but in view of the shocking record of the Coalition, its failure to arrest the growth of unemployment and the decision to resort to economies in the social services, Labour should have achieved a greater success.

Most of the new M.P.s came from the depressed areas of South Wales, Durham, Scotland and Yorkshire. Few changes occurred in the marginal areas, though in London several seats were gained. More than thirty of the new M.P.s were sponsored by the I.L.P. and those from the Clyde and West of Scotland burst like a hurricane on the House of Commons at the beginning of the new session. For their supporters the revolution had come. The expectations of vast changes in social and industrial legislation promised during the election campaign would be sure to fructify.

In the first two weeks of the session nearly all of the new members had made their maiden speeches. All the election slogans were repeated. It became a chorus of park-gate and market-place voices. There was no attempt to follow Parliamentary procedure, or indeed to engage in debate with members of the Tory and Liberal Parties. Only a handful sought to adapt themselves to the rules of debate and were thus regarded by the Press and by the House as likely to become Parliamentary personalities. Scenes were frequent, and Mr. Whitley, the Speaker, probably one of the best occupants of the Chair in modern times, and certainly one of the most impartial, had his work cut out to maintain order.

Not many weeks had passed before a storm blew up which made Parliamentary history. The Tory Government sought to escape from its financial troubles by resorting to various devices such as cutting down the supply of milk to expectant mothers. This infuriated James Maxton, usually kindly disposed towards his opponents, and tempted him to describe the Tories as murderers, singling out one of the Tory diehards, Sir Frederick Banbury, for his attack. Immediately a demand was made for withdrawal of what was an unparliamentary expression. Maxton refused to withdraw and repeated the expression, whereupon the Speaker was compelled to name him and Maxton was asked to leave the House. Despite appeals by MacDonald, John Wheatley and myself to the Speaker on Maxton's behalf, the attendants forced the offending member out of the Chamber. Then Wheatley took the stage, followed by Campbell Stephen and George Buchanan, all Clyde members, and the same procedure was adopted.

By the rules of the House none was permitted to remain within the precincts or to return until in the opinion of Mr. Speaker, after several days, they had purged their contempt, and they were allowed to take their seats again.

Although criticism of Government policy was maintained, in particular by the I.L.P. section, the ebullience soon faded. It was soon discovered that scenes of the kind launched by Maxton missed fire for the reason that all the Tories had to do was to vote the malcontents out of existence in the division lobbies. MacDonald frowned on such scenes and on the use of language not consistent with Parliamentary custom. He made his views known, both in the House and at meetings of the Party. Admittedly his anger was justified. The language used then was far more forceful than is customary nowadays. In an attack on the Tories John Wheatley said:

"If there is one set of humbugs in the world, if there is one group of unadulterated hypocrites, it is the British ruling class. . . . I do not believe in your honesty at all. You are either knaves or fools. . . . You are the greatest enemies of the human race; I can see no hope for this country unless we can get the people to overthrow your system."

The result of MacDonald's annoyance was that several M.P.s associated with the I.L.P. became a faction, whose evident purpose was to make matters awkward for MacDonald. Nothing irritated the Labour leader more than what he described as sniping from the back benches. Even more he resented this from his comrades of the I.L.P. He also suspected that Maxton, who had never concealed his dislike, was anxious to promote the cause of John Wheatley for leadership.

All this led to trouble within the I.L.P. and the group split up into those who followed Maxton and Wheatley, and the others, who preferred to stand by MacDonald even though occasionally disturbed by his moderation.

Perhaps the only distinguishing feature of the 1923 period was the motion by Philip Snowden which referred to "the failure of capitalism" and called for its suppression "by an industrial and social order based on public ownership and democratic control of the instruments of production and distribution". This led to a series of animated debates, in which Snowden and Sir Alfred Mond, a well-known industrialist, played active parts. It brought the Socialist case before the House and the country. There is no doubt that Snowden was easily the most effective debater on the Labour benches at that time.

Labour's contribution to the record of the 1922 Parliament was undistinguished; so indeed was the Government's. The bogey of unemployment was increasingly menacing, and Baldwin, who had unexpectedly become Prime Minister when Bonar Law resigned on grounds of ill-health, decided to appeal to the country. This was intended to obtain a mandate for the introduction of tariff protection to safeguard existing jobs and possibly to create increased employment by a reduction in imports. The proposals made no appeal to the masses, reared on the theory of free trade, nor to any thoughtful person who could assess the economic situation both at home and abroad. Unfortunately, Labour found itself on the eve of an election without a challenging alternative to the weak and defeatist solutions devised by Baldwin.

Despite Labour's optimism about its political future nobody in the Party seemed to be aware of the change in the political climate in the first years of peace. That change was more generally accepted by the Tories, who were ready to concede recognition of the Labour Party as the second political group in Britain. For more than a decade this possibility had been suggested, more or less as a prophecy of disaster by Tories and Liberals during election campaigns. Now, in the words of Stanley Baldwin, "The future lay between the honourable Labour M.P.s opposite and ourselves, the Tories."

The dawn of Labour's real political advance coincided with the twilight of Liberalism. The coincidence of those momentous landmarks in modern political history was not, in fact, a natural outcome of events. The Liberals, even if divided, had nearly the same support in the country as Labour. But for reasons best known to himself Baldwin, as Prime Minister, deliberately risked the fortunes of the Tory Party in order to destroy the Liberals and in particular Lloyd George.

Baldwin's animosity to Lloyd George influenced him to ask the King to dissolve Parliament simply, as he put it, "to dish the Goat", his venomous description of Lloyd George. Lloyd George in retaliation, blamed his Party's misfortunes on Baldwin's intrigues. "Baldwin knifed me," he is reported to have said, "and I shall knife Baldwin."

The result of this squalid bickering was to prevent Lloyd George from ever again holding political office, while Baldwin involuntarily brought about the defeat of his own Party when the election returns came in.

Apart from Baldwin's personal vendetta with Lloyd George, this astute political tactician persisted in demanding that Parliament should be dissolved, despite George V's view that it was unconstitutional, because he considered both the Liberals and Socialists could not sustain another costly campaign so soon after the previous one. He was correct.

Enthusiasm in the Labour Party was not enough, and though 427 Labour candidates were nominated for election only 191 were successful: a check in the progress of the Party's Parliamentary representation. Nor did the vote increase as much as Webb had forecast. The increase to 4,347,379 was only about 100,000 over the previous poll. Many of the votes were not pro-Labour but were influenced by dislike of Baldwin's tariff proposals.

Yet on such shaky foundations of national support the Labour Party believed that the eve of momentous power, which had been long forecast, was imminent. Now that it had arrived the leaders were unprepared to grapple with the complex problems of Government. This applied to MacDonald as well as to the rest. The difference was that he had envisaged Downing Street as his future residence, ignoring the problem of who would be sitting round the table in the Cabinet room over which he dreamed of presiding.

This problem was the subject of avid discussion in the Webbs' house in Grosvenor Road immediately after the election. The guests were MacDonald, Clynes, Henderson, Thomas and Snowden. The morning papers had carried leading articles warning the nation that the virtual dead-lock produced by the election results meant that either Asquith must range his 158 Liberals alongside the Tories, an impossible proposal in view of the protection issue; that the King should ignore constitutional practice and invite Asquith to form a

Government; or thirdly the dreadful prospect of the monarchy and the nation facing a Socialist administration. That summer, at the annual Party Conference, Sidney Webb had forecast that Labour was on the brink of triumph.

This was not mere oratory or conference optimism. The delegates who assembled at the Conference were unaware of the schisms which meant that some M.P.s were hardly on speaking terms with one another in the Palace of Westminster. The cracks in the edifice were ignored.

Labour had the most active political organisation in the country, with vigorous constituency parties in all but a handful of remote areas. More than ten thousand Socialists were active in local government. The inference was that in some four hundred constituencies the majority of the electorate was Socialist. In every election the Labour vote had increased enormously, nearly doubling in 1922 as compared with the 1918 election. Mathematically it seemed certain that the 1923 election would mean that the gap of a million votes between the Tories and Labour would be filled.

Webb naturally found a willing listener in MacDonald as he insisted that the Labour Party must accept the challenge. Together they persuaded the other Party leaders that this was the right policy.

Little beyond the objective was discussed, so MacDonald immediately escaped from further discussions by going for an extended Christmas holiday at Lossiemouth, where he could brood in private on the candidates for office. His decisions he kept to himself, so that when the inevitable resignation of Baldwin occurred on January 18, 1924, MacDonald was able to go to the Palace with a completely free hand.

There were many Labour M.P.s who believed that the new Government should announce an intensely Socialist programme and then ask the country for a vote of confidence. This spectacular and admittedly dangerous move did not appeal to MacDonald. He had no intention whatever of practising Socialism in a country where five out of every seven voters were anti-Socialist. Whatever the technicalities of Parliamentary majorities inferred, the fact was that the country was not yet in a frame of mind to accept a Labour administration. The Tories had polled some $5\frac{1}{2}$ million votes against Labour's $4\frac{1}{2}$ million, leaving 4 million Liberal voters with no enthusiasm for either a Socialist or a Conservative régime. While therefore the 261 Tory M.P.s were in a minority in the House it was untrue to suggest that the attitude of the nation was constructively for any Party. The best that could be said was that it was anti-Baldwin, and that was, in the circumstances, an ominous foundation on which either the Liberals or the Socialists could construct a Government.

Baldwin went through the formality of continuing as Prime Minister until the inevitable amendment to the Speech from the Throne brought a vote of no confidence. By no means all the Liberals voted alongside Labour. Some abstained and a few voted with the Tories.

MacDonald, experienced in political manoeuvre, had calculated ever since the election that he was virtually certain of the Premiership. Asquith, whose influence was fading, had let it be known that he intended to support Labour's claim and thereby ensure that it took office.

The only voice implacably hostile to MacDonald and his Party was Winston Churchill, bereft of official impact. He was in the worst phase of his political life. He had been beaten at Dundee in 1922 when he stood as a Lloyd George Liberal, a defeat for which he never forgave the people of Dundee. Worse still, he lost again at West Leicester in 1923 to a Labour candidate, Pethick-Lawrence. The victory of his opponent and of a sufficient number of Pethick-Lawrence's colleagues brought about Churchill's change of heart. His dislike of Socialism enforced his break with Liberalism. A solitary battle in a by-election in the Abbey division of Westminster subsequently found Churchill fighting every Party, including the Tories, which managed to keep him out of Parliament. When he selected Epping as his future constituency he offered himself as a Constitutional and Anti-Socialist candidate, a description which was more honest than that of any Liberal and the majority of the Tories under Baldwin. More of the Churchill type in the 1924 Parliament might have enlivened the indolent Tory Opposition and possibly stimulated the Labour administration, which never really wrested itself from the feeling that it governed on sufferance.

The facts were that MacDonald, expert as he was in Parliamentary activity and in manipulating a Labour Conference by the sheer brilliance of his oratory, was without experience as a Government administrator. He had never held office and he was highly suspicious of the few colleagues who had.

Henderson, the self-effacing and industrious colleague in MacDonald's years of secretaryship of the Party, engendered groundless suspicions of rivalry for power. Henderson had experienced his invariable misfortune when it came to electioneering by losing what seemed to be a certain seat at Newcastle, but a Labour Government could, of course, easily arrange for a seat to be found for him. Thus it was universally expected that Henderson's wartime experience as a Cabinet minister would be eagerly exploited by MacDonald. In fact, MacDonald ignored him completely until, after some protests from his colleagues, he pondered on appointing him as chairman of the Committee of Ways and Means, then to the War Office and finally to the Home Office, which was Henderson's eventual sop as payment for running the Party's election campaign and was bestowed by MacDonald with as little grace as he could muster.

The final selections for Cabinet posts—after rather bizarre ideas such as J. H. Thomas for the Foreign Office—were reasonable if unimaginative. Considering the leader's own poor opinion of the available material, the array of talent and experience was certainly comparable to any of the post-war Cabinets.

Significantly MacDonald took the Foreign Office himself, believing that international affairs offered greater opportunities than the problems of the home economy. Clynes was inevitably appointed Deputy Leader and Lord Privy Seal; Thomas became Colonial Secretary in name and self-appointed adviser to the Prime Minister in fact; Webb was given a chance to put his statistical theories into action at the Board of Trade; Wheatley was Minister of Health; Trevelyan, President of the Board of Education; and Fred Jowett, First Commissioner of Works. Snowden, regarded by many in the Party as its ablest financial expert, virtually appointed himself to the Exchequer.

The appointment of Lord Chelmsford, a convinced Tory, to the Admiralty was a strange move. MacDonald was awed by Chelmsford's aristocratic lineage and seemingly grateful for his lordship's willingness to serve in a Labour administration. But it was a pointed insult to potential office holders by MacDonald who had preached pacifism at Labour conferences: he clearly had no faith in any Socialist at the head of the senior service.

Neither Lord Haldane, though a politician of varied talents, who became Lord Chancellor, nor Lord Parmoor, as Lord President of the Council, had Labour sympathies: they had, of course, titles and some political experience—adequate tesimonials in MacDonald's view. But the appointment of Sir Patrick Hastings as Attorney-General was in the circumstances a wise move. Hastings was a Socialist, albeit a new and not completely convinced one. He was also one of the great legal minds of the day, possibly the most brilliant advocate outside the Parliamentary arena.

Of great significance for the future were some of the minor government appointments. The Parliamentary and under-secretaryships during Labour's short tenure of office in 1924 provided invaluable training for future ministers. Among them were Clem Attlee and Jack Lawson, both at the War Office; Arthur Greenwood, at the Ministry of Health; A. V. Alexander, at the Board of Trade; Margaret Bondfield, at the Ministry of Labour; and myself as Secretary for Mines.

The Party supporters who may have unthinkingly expected the first Labour Government to pursue a Socialist programme were soon disappointed. Nothing could be done which would upset the Liberals. This meant, in the event, that nothing much was done at all.

Easily the best piece of legislation to reach the Statute Book in 1924 was the Housing Act, a triumph for the I.L.P.'s John Wheatley. It enabled local authorities to build houses for letting at controlled rents with the aid of a Government subsidy.

Otherwise the only progress of note was made in foreign affairs, where the triumph was a personal one for MacDonald rather than for his Government. To his credit he banished the avenging tone against Germany which had prevailed since Lloyd George's "Hang the Kaiser" attitude. The French agreed to evacuate the Ruhr. Reparations became realisitic instead of punitive. The Geneva Protocol provided a means of making the League of Nations work if its members genuinely wished it to do so. These activities were regarded as laudable by thinking persons of all Parties, and Mac-Donald's prestige grew considerably, both nationally and internationally, though an exception was with some sections of the Labour Party where he was regarded as either going too fast or not fast enough, according to the interests of his critics.

The Left he tried to placate by diplomatic recognition of the Soviet Union and by discussions to restore trade between the two countries, the stimulus to be a British loan. This satisfied a vociferous minority in his own Party, and upset the rest of the country. Russophobia was acute, and it was MacDonald's ostensible concern for the Bolsheviks—in reality a dislike motivated by horror of what they had done and what they intended to do—which spelled his doom. The Tories and the Tory Press were determined to discover some excuse for getting rid of him before it was too late. To many of them—and the parallel was made on some justification—MacDonald appeared to be a British Kerensky. His moderation annoyed his supporters. His inability to control the working classes, as evidenced by the interminable outbreaks of strikes, was precisely the defect of Kerensky which had enabled Lenin to take over the control of the striking masses of Moscow and Petrograd.

Nor did trade union leaders like Bevin view the record of the Labour Government's handling of industrial disputes with satisfaction. It was all too clear that the unions considered their interests were not identical with the policies of MacDonald's Government.

The Labour Government had at the outset relied on an easing of industrial tension, with the unions restraining their members from action which could embarrass the new administration. Tom Shaw, the new Minister of Labour, and himself a trade unionist, believed that an armistice in the industrial war was one of the strongest cards in the Labour hand, and one which no other Party could expect to hold. Under pressure to state his plans to reduce unemployment he explained, "I can't take rabbits out of a hat"— a remark met with derision by the Tories and dismay by Labour M.P.s.

The previous months had indicated that a steady deterioration in labour relations presaged major trouble. There had been several strikes during the year, including an unofficial stoppage in the docks. On the January day that Baldwin's Government was censured the locomotive engineers and firemen struck. Next Bevin called out the dockers when the Transport and General Workers' Union failed to obtain an increase of 2s. per day for them.

With every port in the country at a standstill the new Labour Government found itself in the anomalous position of making arrangements to use troops for the handling of essential supplies— a procedure which had been damned with unanimous vehemence whenever earlier Governments had resorted to such a move in an emergency. Fortunately for MacDonald, the employers gave way and the strike ended before he had to call on the military.

But the Government's troubles in the industrial field were not over. In March the London tram workers struck—a peculiarly delicate situation because the Minister of Transport was Harry Gosling, president of the Transport Workers' Union. Gosling fought hard to prevent the stoppage, managing to obtain some concessions from the private employers and the L.C.C., but the men were adamant, and they brought out the bus employees alongside them.

The situation focused the fact that Bevin and MacDonald were challenging one another for supremacy over employee-employer relationships.

MacDonald attempted to solve the difficulty by writing personally to Bevin with the full prestige of the Premier's office. Bevin was unimpressed. He retorted that the Minister of Labour, Tom Shaw, was a poor colleague and announced that he now proposed to bring out the underground railway workers in order to make the paralysis of London's public transport complete.

MacDonald accepted the challenge and set up a Cabinet Committee under Josiah Wedgwood to organise emergency services. To legalise this move the Emergency Powers Act, which Labour had attacked as one of the most vicious actions in Lloyd George's career when it was passed in 1920, was invoked. Whatever loyalty MacDonald had so far been able to rely on among the Rightist sections of the trade unions now evaporated. Both the National Executive of the Party and the T.U.C. General Council officially proclaimed their anger.

Behind the scenes MacDonald searched avidly for a compromise. A Bill was hastily introduced purporting to rationalise London's transport systems. On this promise the employers made a wage increase offer and the strike ended.

Although a prolonged and major industrial upheaval had been avoided the Labour Government did not emerge with much honour, as indeed was hardly possible in view of the pistol at its head, which had made any compromise which could be discovered something to grasp at all costs. The victor was clearly Bevin, whose words and actions proved his contempt for the Labour Government, despite the fact that there were seven trade unionists or ex-unionists in the Cabinet of twenty.

Bevin's attitude in the first few weeks of the 1924 Government encouraged other unions to ignore any truce to enable Labour to rule with a minimum of trouble. Strikes were always threatening or actually breaking out. It was said that in the brief life of this unhappy first Labour Government the only industrial success was averting a national coal strike, where, as Secretary for Mines, and left to conduct the negotiations myself, I was able to discover a solution.

The uncompromising hostility of the two most powerful men in the two movements—the Labour Party and the T.U.C.—sowed the seeds of future disaster, culminating in the General Strike and, indirectly, in the 1931 debacle.

The experience of both Bevin and MacDonald of the actions of the other during 1924 created a mutual pathological hatred. MacDonald called Bevin a "swine", and when this evidence of the Prime Minister's loathing was reported to Bevin by W. J. Brown, secretary of the Civil Service clerks, Bevin commented that everyone found out sooner or later the sort of man MacDonald was.

The injustice of Bevin's hostility was that he disliked MacDonald because he held political power but was not a trade unionist. Bevin had at that time a narrow view of what constituted the working class. He had no interest in supporting a Party which derived support from all classes, which to him meant including the intellectuals.

Worried by the Liberal trends of the Labour Government, G. D. H. Cole, by then emerging as a popular historian and thinker in the Labour movement, advocated a new organisation. It was to analyse the reasons for the Government's failure to pursue a Socialist policy and "to sit back and think out new purposes".

This was the sort of dispassionate and objective move which infuriated Bevin. He publicly lambasted factions which produced sets of rules for the workers "based upon such knowledge of the working class as were gleaned from the theoretical treatises in the university library".

No man could have weathered the storms of MacDonald's period as Prime Minister in 1924 without occasional misjudgment. He had a Tory Opposition determined to hamper his every move irrespective of the national welfare. He had to study every action in case the Liberals objected. Those were factors he knew about at the outset.

What he could not have envisaged was the constant sniping from his own colleagues and the outright disloyalty of the unions. Aloof and contemptuous of others, MacDonald's character did not encourage much friendliness or sympathy. Consequently, while he was at this time and for the rest of the nineteen-twenties probably the best-admired political leader ever appointed in peacetime, the admiration was principally from people who knew him only as a political personality in the Press and by reputation. Some who came to know him personally or worked with him were repulsed, although many who had known him in earlier days remained loyal to their one-time idol.

The downfall of his Government arose from a trivial situation which would never have happened if he had been on personal terms of friendship with all his Cabinet colleagues.

When J. R. Campbell, editor of the Communist *Workers' Weekly*, wrote to urge troops "neither in the class war nor a military war to turn their guns on their fellow-workers", the illegality was obvious enough, but the method of proving it absurdly pompous and intolerant. For this the Attorney-General, Sir Patrick Hastings, was to blame. MacDonald considered the prosecution, under the Incitement to Mutiny Act passed more than a century earlier during the Napoleonic Wars, was ill-advised but he refrained from throwing the subject into frank discussion by the Cabinet.

Consequently the ensuing uproar from the entire Party was not unexpected by him, but having authorised the prosecution he was ill-advised to withdraw it.

All the moves and counter-moves in the Campbell case took place during the summer recess. When Parliament reassembled the Tories were prepared for the kill, and unfortunately there were Labour back-benchers willing to assist them, notably Maxton, Lansbury and Jack Jones, M.P. for Silvertown. MacDonald was humiliated by Austen Chamberlain, who managed to get the Prime Minister to retract an earlier statement that he was unaware of the decision to withdraw the prosecution. But MacDonald's reputation was almost saved by a brilliant speech by Hastings justifying his action and citing precedents for it. The Tories had not yet gained their expected victory.

The Liberals, however, deserted their uneasy allies. They suggested a Select Committee. The Tories recognised the certainty of embarrassing MacDonald by this method in view of their own failure. They voted for the Liberal amendment. It was passed by 364 votes to 198.

The first Labour Government was over. Its record had brought very little besides disillusion.

9

THE 1924 ELECTION—THE
GENERAL STRIKE

1924–1931

Despite the fuss about the Campbell prosecution the Tories suspected that common sense could return long before polling day; at least five million electors might favour a new Labour administration. On virtually every domestic policy Labour could offer a more thoughtful proposal than its opponents. Consequently something was needed to turn the election into an hysterical rampage.

The bogy of godless Russia was displayed without much public reaction in the preliminary skirmishes. Then came the famous Zinoviev letter, allegedly sent by the President of the Communist Third International on September 15 to the British Communist Party. The letter harmlessly instructed the Party to support the Anglo-Soviet trade treaties, and less harmlessly ordered preparation for military insurrection.

MacDonald, who, incidentally, was condemned in the letter for being anti-Russian, was informed by the Foreign Office of the letter on October 16. He instructed the Foreign Office experts to examine it for authenticity and to prepare a complaint to be sent to the Russian Ambassador if the letter was proved genuine.

The *Daily Mail* had fortuitously obtained a copy of the letter and informed the Foreign Office that it intended to publish it the following morning—three days before polling day. Thereupon the Foreign Office issued both the letter and the draft reply, MacDonald not being consulted. He was at this stage of the election campaign almost prostrate with nervous and physical exhaustion. His tour had begun in Glasgow, and on his way south he spoke at every town and village, making more than twenty speeches a day. To that extent he can be condoned for failing to deal with the Zinoviev letter over the week-end following the Saturday morning when the letter was published. Even when eventually he referred to the subject his audience was completely mystified as to whether he regarded the letter as genuine or not. All over the country, at eve-of-poll meetings, Labour candidates were heckled and questioned. They could give no official answer.

When the election results were announced the effectiveness of the *Daily Mail* scare and the damage of MacDonald's silence meant that Labour had lost forty-one seats. But the total Labour vote had risen by more than 1,130,000.

Considering the anti-climax of the first Labour Government's roseate hopes, the 1924 election results were not as bad for Labour as they might have been. Neither disappointment with the Party's record nor the scare of the Zinoviev letter swayed the loyalty of the people. Indeed the number of votes cast for Labour candidates was a triumphant vindication for MacDonald's policy of compromise. The total was close on $5\frac{1}{2}$ millions, an increase of nearly $1\frac{1}{4}$ millions in a year.

The disaster of the election was the eclipse of the Liberals, who dropped more than $1\frac{1}{4}$ millions to a contemptuous total of under 3 millions. However, the switch-over had not been from Liberal to Labour, but to Tory, where the votes cast increased by nearly $2\frac{1}{2}$ millions. Labour's gain came mostly from new voters.

There were many significant swings to Labour. The Tory stronghold of Birmingham had been seriously challenged by the Socialists, and one of the dozen "safe" seats lost. In the Ladywood division Neville Chamberlain just scraped through—after three recounts—with a majority of seventy-seven over Oswald Mosley, who as a Tory had sat for Harrow after the war.

Despite the net loss of forty seats, which included Herbert Morrison at Hackney and Fred Jowett at East Bradford (the only Cabinet member to be defeated) there were many increased majorities and one or two gains, including Hugh Dalton at Peckham.

A brief boom in the coal industry had coincided with the tenure of the 1924 Labour Government, principally owing to the French occupation of the Ruhr. The miners not only got more regular work but the owners agreed to pay a higher minimum wage. This was probably due partially to the greater output, but also because the owners feared that the Labour Government would otherwise enforce a wage rise by legislation.

The boom ended when the French left the Ruhr. Exports fell, and both home and overseas prices with them. The owners insisted that a return to the wages of 1921 and an increase to an eight-hour day were essential. The pay cuts, on wages which ranged from £2 to £4 a week, would have varied between ten and twenty-five per cent. Churchill's return to the gold standard made a general depreciation in wage values inevitable.

The men who were looking after the miners' interests in 1925 were very different from Frank Hodges, whose ambitions for personal advancement had made him the sort of union official the owners regarded as pleasant and reasonable. When the Miners' Federation forced Hodges out of the secretaryship because he was devoting much of his time to Parliamentary work, the twin driving forces for the miners became Herbert Smith and A. J. Cook.

Both were remarkable characters, but of doubtful value in delicate negotiations. Smith, a dour, blunt Yorkshireman, distrusted practically everyone—in the Labour Party, among the mine owners, and even in his own union. His most frequent remark during discussions was "nowt doin'".

Cook, a younger man, had been a miner since childhood. He was a lay preacher and brought to trade union affairs the atmosphere of hysterical religious revivalism, which was none the less sincere for its violence. He was a near-Communist and his sole constructive interest was in the welfare of the miners. They in return worshipped him as someone akin to a Messiah.

Abortive conferences were held at which ministers attempted to negotiate with the miners and the mine-owners. Anyone with something to contribute was brought in, with the notable exception of Labour's political leaders.

In July the miners approached the General Council of the T.U.C. for help. The T.U.C. shouldered the responsibility of increasing its authority over its member unions, and the General Council formally issued an embargo on the movement of coal from July 31, the day when the mine owners' notice was to terminate.

Two days before this date a court of enquiry produced its report. It was in favour of a fixed minimum wage and criticised the management of the industry. The owners refused to accept the report, whereupon Baldwin was forced to agree that the Government would grant a subsidy until May 1, 1926. Baldwin bought this respite at a cost of £23 million. He had no illusions that it was a solution of the mining problem, but it was a method of buying time to prepare for a show-down.

Not unnaturally, the trade unions regarded the outcome of the negotiations as a tremendous victory, obtained by uncompromising resistance to the capitalist class. The day was hailed as Red Friday, banishing the bitter memory of Black Friday in April of 1921, and a milestone on the trade union road to political power, independent of all existing parties.

MacDonald showed something considerably less than pleasure in the miners' victory. He described it as a success for the "very forces that sane, well-considered, thoroughly well-examined Socialism feels to be probably its greatest enemy".

This remarkably frank glimpse of his real feelings about the trade unions brought about angry complaints from the miners, and MacDonald hurriedly elaborated on his views by saying that he really meant to condemn the Communist groups among the miners who had been most intransigent during the negotiations with the Government.

When, during the winter, the Government began preparations to run the country's economy on an emergency basis, notably through a national Organisation for the Maintenance of Supplies, hardly a word of enquiry or protest was made by the Parliamentary Labour Party. It was apparent that MacDonald tacitly agreed with the formidable plans being made.

Suspicious of Labour Parliamentarians and exultant in its new-found power, the T.U.C. pursued its own way. At the Congress in September, 1925, Swales, a prominent union leader, in the chair, made a rousing speech in favour of more militancy. In that month, too, the Industrial Alliance, in a sense a rival of the T.U.C., made more progress. The Miners, Foundry Workers, A.S.L.E.F., and the Electrical Trades Union joined it, thus ensuring that the Alliance could paralyse the heavy industries, transport and most of the public utilities.

But some of the smaller unions feared these ominous signs of a trend towards the syndicalist dream of "One Big Union", and they insisted on balloting their members. This effectively delayed the operation of the Alliance until the General Strike occurred; afterwards, of course, nothing more was heard of it.

The Labour Party was the only organisation which could possibly have harnessed and curbed the divergent union groups heading, eagerly in some cases, unwillingly in others, towards near-revolution. Instead, despite its knowledge of the ruthless plans the Government was making, it seemed to prefer to let the union extremists make fiery speeches and forget the need to organise for a prolonged and major struggle. Such plans as did emerge were quickly quashed. When extremist groups proposed formation of Workers Defence Units the Labour Party promptly condemned them. When Cook claimed that every Co-operative store in the country would be the victualling depot for the fighting workers, the secretary of the Co-operative Union speedily denied it.

Meantime a Royal Commission was studying the coal industry. Sir Herbert Samuel headed it. The other three members were Sir William Beveridge, a Liberal; Sir Herbert Lawrence, a banker;

I

and Kenneth Lee, a textile manufacturer. None had any knowledge of the coal industry and none had Labour leanings.

The Commission's report was released in March. It leaned
towards nationalisation in suggesting state ownership of mine
royalties. It advised amalgamation of small mines and government-
inspired research into coal utilisation. For the miners it recommended family allowances and profit-sharing schemes. These were
plans to be put in operation in an indeterminate future. For
immediate implementation were less pleasant proposals: a reduction in wages and no extension of the Government subsidy. The
miners therefore rejected the report. Most vehement of all was the
minority movement among the miners, Communist inspired, and
run by Harry Pollitt and Arthur Horner. Neither the T.U.C. nor
the Labour Party had the slightest control over this powerful and
growing faction.

Belatedly the Industrial Committee invited MacDonald and
Henderson to sit in on its meetings. Both politicians were reticent
in the presence of the trade unionists and still more reticent
when reporting to their colleagues in the Parliamentary Party.
Henderson's links with the trade unions ensured that he sat quietly
on the fence. MacDonald was deeply alarmed at the trend of
events. Whichever way the decision of the Industrial Committee
went he feared the result. A successful strike would make the
T.U.C. supreme in working-class interests; an unsuccessful one
would perhaps fatally damage the Socialist cause.

It was understandable that the public and the Government, knowing of the presence of the Labour leaders in the Industrial Committee negotiations, but over-rating their influence, believed that
a settlement would be found and a General Strike avoided.

In Parliament the Labour M.P.s remained silent. No one asked
any awkward questions and no one contributed to a forthright
debate. When, however, Ernest Bevin attacked them at a conference of trade union leaders on April 29, he was being less than
fair. If some M.P.s had kept quiet through timidity, as many had
obeyed the request of the miners that they should not interfere in
an industrial dispute.

Thomas, deeply involved both as a trade union and a Party
leader, worked hard to discover a last-minute settlement. He begged
and pleaded (his own description) that the Cabinet should insist
on the mine owners suspending the lock-out notices. He pleaded
in vain. The Emergency Powers Act had been signed. The Government had everything prepared. MacDonald caught the excitement
of the hour and said, "the sword is drawn, the sand in the glass

has emptied away". This flowery oratory did not go down very well among the trade union leaders, who suddenly realised they had a national stoppage on their hands and very little organisation to back it. The General Council clutched at the last straw of a further discussion with Baldwin.

This took place late on Saturday night. Three trade unionists conferred with three members of the Cabinet. No Labour leader was invited or wanted by either side. A formula was found, though it merely provided for a further fortnight to argue on a topic already argued to extinction. Whether it would have been accepted by the trade union movement at that late hour is doubtful. In any event when the negotiations dragged on into Sunday night Baldwin abruptly terminated them. The printers on the *Daily Mail* had refused to produce the Monday edition. The General Strike was not merely a Monday certainty. It had begun that Sunday evening.

Next day, in the Commons, the Labour leaders had a defeatist air. They understandably were alarmed and despondent at the ill-judged actions of the trade unionists so patently taken without consultation. But the anxiety demonstrably to wash their hands of the matter was regrettable at a time of crisis which might have justly inspired a gesture of solidarity with the workers who had voted them into Parliament.

MacDonald declaimed about his high regard for the Constitution and gratuitously explained to the Government that as regards "the discussion of general strikes and Bolshevism and all that kind of thing I have nothing to do at all".

Thomas, who had the day before been so deeply upset at the disaster confronting his union and his Party, had openly wept, vaguely pleaded (once again) for a last effort; this to members of Parliament who had walked or driven through streets where no buses ran and in a capital without trains, but with the Government's military precautions obvious on every side.

It was left to Henderson to make a valiant attempt at the impossible.

He approached Churchill outside the chamber.

"Have you come to say the strike notices are withdrawn?" Churchill demanded. When Henderson admitted that he had not, but wanted to take up Churchill's own promise that afternoon that it was the Government's duty to parley, Churchill turned away.

"There is no reason to continue this discussion," he said.

The bewildering and contrary records of the meetings which went on constantly during the General Strike agree on only one point: the Henderson approach to Churchill was the sole honest and open approach made by any Labour leader. The rest of the story is of trade unionist mishandling and internal suspicions, with Thomas flitting energetically and with conspiratorial air from the house of aristocratic friends to street-corner whispering with his T.U.C. colleagues. On the expectation that the Government would reopen discussions of the miners' case the strike was called off by the T.U.C., and in the face of bitter opposition from the miners. It was supposed to be peace with honour. The Tories regarded it as total victory. The miners found no gestures of aid. The trade unions heard the jubilant cry of "Back to Taff Vale" from exultant Tories.

The General Strike was thus a major disaster for trade unionism in Britain. Ten years of growth in membership was lost, and trade union funds dropped by £4 million in a matter of weeks. The savage and punitive Trade Disputes and Trade Union Act set back the workers' rights by more than a generation. Trade unionism by 1927 was without power, prestige or money.

Inevitably the eclipse of the unions dragged down the Labour Party with it. While a few working men accepted that the slow plodding of democratic negotiation was the only feasible course, despite the conviction in some circles of the Labour Party of faith in a General Strike as the ultimate and almost certain method of achieving victory, most turned to more violent ideas if they did not lapse into complete lethargy.

As a result a good many trade unionists joined the Communist Party, and a few others toyed with new ideas for unionism, the basis of which would be non-political and completely self-interested— a return to the middle of the nineteenth century.

The principal villains of the period were undoubtedly Birkenhead and Churchill, who swayed Baldwin from his innate tolerance and desire for peace. At least they were honest, self-proclaimed enemies of Labour and all its adherents, ready to smash Socialism whatever the cost.

In the T.U.C. the stupidity and obstinacy of men who found themselves with vast powers brought the inevitable penalties when cool organisation was required and still cooler attitudes in negotiation. They were fools, but not deliberately foolish.

MacDonald, with his fear of advancing anywhere which offered no retreat or deviation, must bear great responsibility. His prestige within the Labour Party and in the country was very great. It could have outweighed the suspicions of the unions. His genius for compromise could, if he had used it, have saved a disaster.

But the greatest harm to the workers, to the Socialist movement, and indirectly to the nation, was done by Thomas. A powerful figure in the trade unions and a man with close contacts in both his own Party and those of his opponents, Thomas above all others could have decided on a policy and thereafter seen it through. Instead, after having close knowledge of the strike proposals and being accepted as a leader who would help to organise the strike until its successful conclusion, he intrigued from the first moment of the strike to end it irrespective of the strikers' feelings and future.

He misled the unions, the Labour Party and the Government. If anyone wished to boast that he alone brought about the end of the strike and the total defeat of the strikers, Thomas had that right.

In hindsight the amazing fact was that Thomas remained in the realm of Labour politics and, moreover, rose with its slow and painful revival. But this he managed to do before 1931 took him with other of the Parliamentary leaders into oblivion.

The shock of the General Strike wore off only gradually. Labour was in the doldrums and the Tories were naturally revelling in their power. Hostility to MacDonald within the Party grew, and was the more implacable for its reticent and thoughtful nature. In the forefront of the critics were the I.L.P., now not so much a group of extremists but a channel through which ideas could be placed before large numbers of the rank and file.

Maxton, on behalf of the I.L.P., published *Socialism in Our Time*, which was an impatient plea for an end of the MacDonald policy of cautious compromise and was, incidentally, highly critical of trade union attitudes to political activity. MacDonald disliked the I.L.P. programme, whereupon the I.L.P. refused to re-nominate MacDonald as Treasurer, a post he had held since 1912 and regarded as the annual reward due in return for his long service to Labour.

Once again Henderson came to MacDonald's rescue. He spent the winter of 1927–8 formulating a careful policy, working in conjunction with R. H. Tawney, one of the intellectuals of the Socialist movement notable for an awareness of, and sympathy for, the working man. The result was the publication in 1928 of *Labour and the Nation*, a revised version of Henderson's 1918 policy outline. The electorate had some months in which to read and digest this sane if somewhat vague outline of Labour policy before they could record their reaction at the polls.

The Baldwin Government died by its own hand six months before the end of its Parliamentary term, disquieted by the deteriorating situation in the country at large, where unemployment was increasing, and within the Party, where by-election after by-election had gone against the Tories.

The Tory policy was summed up in the uninspiring slogan of the electoral campaign, "Safety First". The assessment on which Baldwin based his hopes of victory were that the Liberals were now wholly controlled by the despised Lloyd George and that the "flapper vote"—the women between 21 and 25 enfranchised by the Tories—would duly show their gratitude.

Despite an attempt at a Liberal renaissance—artificially contrived by Lloyd George with specious promises of ridding the country of unemployment within twelve months, and the array of more than five hundred Liberal candidates—no one really believed that the contest would be anything but a direct battle between Tory and Labour.

The result of the 1929 election was significant as the first of the modern polls. It was the first with a complete adult franchise, creating an electorate of 28½ millions. It was the first where broadcasting played a vital part: MacDonald's oratory came over far better than Baldwin's placidity, or Lloyd George's insincerity. And it was the first election where the issue between the two modern parties was in doubt until the final results came in.

Labour obtained 287 seats; the Tories 260; the Liberals 59, and there were nine others. The Tory total vote at 8,664,243 was still in advance of Labour at 8,362,594. The Liberals were poorly rewarded with seats for the 5,300,947 votes they obtained. The Labour Party had resumed their upward progress with an increase of more than 2,800,000 votes, compared with which the Tory increase of 809,000 was a technical defeat in view of the seven million additional voters.

The ominous fact that Labour was still without an overall majority was temporarily ignored while the Party made understandable celebration. MacDonald, always susceptible to atmosphere, promised that this time he would "rule without fear or favour".

As usual he had second thoughts. In the debate on the King's Speech, when the difficulties were in sight and the vagaries of power had to be translated into action, he showed—though few then realised it—that he was already envisaging the personal crisis which arrived in 1931. He advocated a termination of Party politics.

"I wonder how far it is possible," he said, "without in any way abandoning any of our Party positions, without in any way surrendering any item of our Party principles, to consider ourselves as a Council of State and less as arrayed regiments facing each other."

It was a thought dropped into a long and rambling speech, and was largely ignored, though it was not long before Labour M.P.s were recalling it as they followed MacDonald's timorous and placatory policies. It was all too obvious that he did not intend to put his own regiment in array against the enemy Party, and his regiment, incidentally, was not one to which MacDonald's long tenure of leadership meant very much.

The 1929 Labour M.P.s were very different from the cloth-cap idealists and quasi-Liberals of the Keir Hardie era. The majority were the nominees of constituency Parties. The sponsored trade unionists, though completely representative of a majority of their constituents, were a far less capable minority. Moreover, the working-class atmosphere was hardly noticeable in the thirty-six M.P.s who represented the London area. For the most part they were white-collar men representing a considerable proportion of white-collar voters.

Even in the industrial and mining areas many middle-class candidates had been successful. Dalton had transferred from Peckham to Bishop Auckland, one of the Labour seats which made Durham solidly Labour. In this county too MacDonald had found a safer berth; his majority of 28,794 at Seaham Harbour was one of the biggest on record.

In South Wales the miners remained protagonists of their own men, even if the last vestiges of Liberalism had been abandoned. Typical of the new M.P.s in the area was Aneurin Bevan, returned with a 11,000 majority for Ebbw Vale.

Jealousy and dislike coloured MacDonald's actions from the outset, influencing him to conduct which he must have known was morally wrong and, almost as bad, detrimental to his Party.

Henderson, as usual, was an undeserved target for MacDonald's spleen. Unwillingly MacDonald had appointed Henderson as Foreign Secretary, who had almost immediately gone off to Geneva. The co-operation that Henderson got via the diplomatic bag and by telegraph was so nebulous that he was aroused from his characteristic reticence to make a vigorous protest about the Prime Minister's lack of confidence in what the Foreign Secretary was doing."

Later Henderson became deeply disturbed by hostile articles in the Press about his negotiations on the Egyptian question. They had reached a critical stage and Henderson believed that the Press criticism might be misunderstood abroad. He invited the editor of the paper carrying the most vitriolic articles to send a reporter so that the official Foreign Office attitude could be explained.

Henderson was told by the reporter that he thought the Foreign Secretary should know that the article had been written at the request of the Prime Minister.

Snowden was of sterner stuff when he experienced the same sort of insidious disloyalty from his chief. He was fighting the European delegates at The Hague to enforce Britain's views on German reparations. MacDonald sent an uncoded telegram to the British delegation saying that he considered the situation was getting beyond Snowden's control and he should await discussion with himself before resuming negotiations. The telegram was of course read and circulated among the other delegates.

Snowden acted with all the vigour of a hot-tempered man beside himself with fury. MacDonald received an ultimatum that he should issue an official statement that the Government was giving Snowden and the British delegation full support. Needless to say, MacDonald hastily did as he was told.

It may be said that the Labour Government of 1929 tried to tackle the unemployment problem as its major task. It was no fault of the administration that the world was on the brink of economic disaster which far transcended anything which one nation —even a powerful nation—could tackle.

When the Government took office in the summer of 1929 there were 1,163,000 unemployed. The appointment of Margaret Bondfield as Minister of Labour was in reality an appointment to a Ministry of Unemployment: her job was to organise the welfare of the unemployed rather than to devise ideas for creating work.

That task was put in the hands of three ministers: J. H. Thomas, Lord Privy Seal; George Lansbury, First Commissioner of Works; and Sir Oswald Mosley, Chancellor of the Duchy of Lancaster. All three posts were sufficiently light or vague to enable these three men to devote all their time to the major problem of finding work for the masses.

Thomas, with his inevitable ebullient vanity, served the Government ill by taking every opportunity to promise publicly that the total of unemployed would be rapidly reduced. Lansbury was too parochial for a big task, seeking trivial palliatives like his Lido in Hyde Park and similar minor public works. Mosley offered grandiose ideas for roads and so on which would have been prohibitively costly to put in hand.

In less than a year the Big Three of the unemployment problem were confessing defeat. Mosley resigned and Attlee replaced him. Unemployment meantime nearly doubled its total since the three had begun work. Thomas was transferred to the Dominions Office, thereby confirming to the resigned and disillusioned electorate that no political Party had the magical touch for men of goodwill and energy to cure the universal evil of unemployment.

Drift was a world-wide government sickness, and the inability of the Labour Government to discover which way to turn was in line with the rest of the capitalist world. Unemployment in Britain rose to more than two millions. MacDonald appointed an Economic Advisory Council, thereby ensuring that the advice he obtained would be as reactionary and timid as economists and financiers, whose colleagues were by then leaping out of windows in the financial crisis of Wall Street, could make it.

The only avenue open to the Prime Minister appeared to be a dignified admission of defeat. But MacDonald had better ideas for the maintenance of his own prestige even if it would cost his Party infinitely more than the General Strike had done.

10

THE LONG ROAD BACK

1931–1935

MacDonald sprung a complete surprise on the Labour back-benchers when his scheme for the idea of a National Government was announced. Among the Tories it was not so unexpected.

Subsequent revelations indicated that as early as the beginning of July the Prime Minister dropped a hint to Lord Stonehaven that a government of all the parties might be the needed solution of the nation's financial problems. As Stonehaven was the Chairman of the Conservative Party this comment was, of course, immediately reported to Baldwin, who in turn informed his intimate colleagues; among them Neville Chamberlain, who was wholly against the idea.

It undoubtedly gave Baldwin much food for thought because a peculiar sort of intimacy had grown up between MacDonald and himself. They had found common ground in bemoaning the material with which they organised the life of a political Party; MacDonald grumbled about the poor quality of his back-benchers; Baldwin confessed he had little respect for the intellect of the old-fashioned diehards in the Tory Party.

The May Committee, created by Snowden to consider the economic crisis, conveniently issued its report twenty-four hours after Parliament went into the summer recess on July 31. Snowden told the House on its final day that when members obtained their copies they would see that it reflected a very grave situation. Many M.P.s, noting the signs of panic in the City, believed that the Commons would re-assemble before the scheduled date to tackle a major crisis. But virtually none suspected that MacDonald was about to throw in his hand.

During August the Cabinet regularly met. The May Committee's recommendations of cuts in public expenditure and increases in taxation to meet an expected Budget deficit of £120 million were not the source of great controversy. But the majority recommendation of the committee for a cut in unemployment relief brought a real split. Snowden's recommendation was a cut of ten per cent, which was half that advised by the May Committee. Twenty-one members of the Cabinet were present. The discussions remained secret, but the general view at the time was that the ministers implacably against any cut in unemployment relief were in a minority. The difference, however, was merely of one or two, so that resignations were inevitable. MacDonald requested resignation from each member in turn and received it. He then left for Buckingham Palace.

The King had earlier that day seen Sir Herbert Samuel and Stanley Baldwin. The Liberal leader (Lloyd George was ill) had hinted at a Coalition, with MacDonald remaining as Prime Minister. Baldwin, who had arrived at the Palace some hours later, had been asked by the King whether he would serve under MacDonald. He had agreed.

Thus MacDonald's evening audience produced advice from the Crown which had already been examined with the Liberals and Tories. His subsequent report to the Cabinet that he had advised the King to summon the three Party leaders to the Palace next day was accurate in fact but not in detail.

The news produced some encouragement for MacDonald among his colleagues. They universally believed his intention was to resign within twelve hours and that Baldwin would become Prime Minister of a Tory-Liberal Coalition.

MacDonald did not disillusion them. Shortly before midnight he conferred with Samuel, Baldwin and Chamberlain. The meeting the next morning at the Palace was really a continuance of the midnight discussion, except that Chamberlain was not there. The King, after expressing the hope that an all-Party Government would be formed, with MacDonald at its head, left his statesmen to go into details. It may be assumed that MacDonald felt safe in promising that half, and possibly a little more than half, of his Cabinet colleagues would serve in the new Government. This news was of some satisfaction to Baldwin and Samuel as evidence of a chance to avoid nation-wide controversy. But none of the three had any desire to utilize all the resigning ministers' services. The idea was for a very small inner Cabinet.

MacDonald returned to Downing Street and brusquely reported the decisions taken at the Palace. He invited no comment apart from a statement of willingness or otherwise to serve under his leadership. He then brought the meeting to a close, asking Snowden, Thomas, and Lord Sankey to remain behind. These were candidates for the inner Cabinet. They accepted. There were thus four

ostensibly Labour members in the Cabinet subsequently announced,
as well as four Tories and two Liberals. This, MacDonald explained over the B.B.C., was not a Coalition Government; he would
have no part of that.

It was, of course, a Coalition, but of Liberals and Tories. Only
a dozen Labour M.P.s sided with MacDonald. When Parliament
reassembled to pass the emergency Budget Labour was ranged on
the Opposition benches and Henderson sat as its leader. The
loyalty of more than twenty years, so often strained and so regularly
without reward, had been killed at last. But Henderson had no joy
in his position: he was grey-faced and ill-looking. He, above all
others, could assess the dimensions of the disaster which Mac-
Donald had brought on the Socialist movement.

MacDonald and his followers were formally expelled from the
Labour Party on September 28, a procedure urgently necessary in
view of the imminent general election. In this MacDonald asked
for a "doctor's mandate" to cure the country's economic sickness,
described as so nearly fatal under his own Premiership of a few
months earlier. The election was a shabby masquerade, with the
ex-Labour leaders outvying their Tory friends in denigrating the
Labour Party. Its programme was, according to MacDonald,
Bolshevism gone mad; in the view of Snowden, as fantastic
and impracticable. Nothing in it differed from proposals which
in the past both men had approved or, indeed, formulated.
These comments were less effective than the canard fortuitously
devised by Runciman that any administration formed by
Labour would raid the people's Post Office savings. It was disgraceful that this piece of electioneering had as its principal
enthusiasts MacDonald and Snowden, besides which Mac-
Donald's inferences in election addresses that the King had
encouraged him to take the patriotic steps he did merely caused
amusement.

Baldwin found it safe to retain some self-respect and allow his
ex-Labour colleagues to take the lead in alarming and misleading
the electorate. Their words, of course, fell on ready ears after the
profound shocks of the August crisis.

The ill-prepared Labour candidates could rave and declaim
about the perfidy of the Tories and the intrigues of the international
financiers to explain away the economic crisis. They gained some
respect as men loyal to their Party. But they could not brush away
the terrible truth which affected directly or indirectly one in three
of the electorate. When the Labour Government had taken office
in 1929 unemployment stood at just over 1,100,000. It had been

elected on the promise to cure unemployment, but when its leader went cap in hand to the Opposition for an alliance unemployment stood at more than 2,700,000.

Philip Snowden, in winding up the debate on the economic crisis, had been in his most vindictive mood. In language even more vitriolic than usual he launched a bitter attack on his former comrades, now sitting on the Opposition benches.

"I have noticed," he said, "during the last three days I have been sitting here the faces of my old associates. I have admired the way they have cheered to keep their spirits up, and I have admired that, knowing that only a few weeks remain before the place that knows them will know them no more."

His forecast was only too accurate. The election result was a Labour tragedy. The remnants of a great Party numbered fifty-two. There had been 213 seats lost and not one gained. Nearly two million voters had turned from Socialism.

But National Labour had no more cause for rejoicing. The thirteen successful candidates who had stood with the blessing of the Liberals and Tories gained election with a total of only 343,000 votes. They meant less than the Liberal Nationals and the National Liberals. And none of the three subservient parties was worth more than a moment's notice by the victorious Tories. With 471 seats there was little need for the support of the eighty-one votes of the Samuelites, Simonites, and MacDonaldites.

In the sorry if valiant squad of Labour M.P.s there was only one who had held Cabinet office—Lansbury. He was over seventy and unsuitable for the forays ahead, both in the House of Commons and in the Party. But it was inevitable that he should be elected chairman.

The attitude of the rank and file of the Labour movement towards the National Government arose from two motives. The first, and strongest, was the feeling of disillusion that all that they stood for had been betrayed by MacDonald. The second was the policy which the trade unions immediately adopted.

Although MacDonald, at Henderson's urgent request, had consulted the T.U.C. because Henderson saw more clearly than any of the Cabinet the dangers of a major split if the unions had no voice at all in the proposals for tackling the economic crisis, the meetings were fruitless.

The first meeting did not take place until August 20, three days before MacDonald went to the Palace. The General Council held a short conference before members of the Party's National Executive and the Cabinet Economy Committee joined in.

MacDonald was supercilious, telling the meeting, in Walter Citrine's view, no more than they had read in the papers. Snowden supplied some financial statistics which were even more alarming than those in the Tory Press. The meeting quickly broke up, but it was resumed at Downing Street in the evening. Both Bevin and Citrine were highly critical of Snowden's proposals. The conference ended, like the afternoon one, in total disagreement.

Bevin's subsequent campaign against the National Government was on grounds of personal dislike of MacDonald as well as for the principles he believed in. He used the *Daily Herald* to attack MacDonald and urged the Labour M.P.s to go into vigorous opposition without delay. This was largely rhetoric, for he did not trust many of them, and indeed, at a joint meeting of the General Council, the Party Executive, and the Consultative Committee of the Parliamentary Party, he taunted the M.P.s for compromising the workers' movement by agreeing to even some of the proposed economy measures.

The failure of some Labour M.P.s to stand true to Socialist precepts tempted Bevin into more direct political activities. At the T.U.C. Conference at Bristol, held as the newly formed Government presented itself to Parliament, he demanded a programme of economic planning. The details he omitted, excusing himself on the grounds that rigidity and a doctrinaire approach were both dangerous.

But this speech, though vague, did make some impression. Henderson, seeking a new master, seems to have already believed that he had found one in Bevin and had suggested that Bevin should oppose MacDonald at Seaham when the election came.

Bevin was flattered, but wary. He told Henderson that he was being pressed from many quarters to place himself at the disposal of the Labour Party, but he did not want to contest Seaham. "If I ran at all, I should endeavour to get a seat near London to make things as easy as possible," he wrote.

At the Labour Party Conference at Scarborough, held a few days after Henderson's first approach, Bevin was again asked to stand as a Parliamentary candidate. By that time an election was certain. Bevin agreed, though determined not to sever his trade union connections. He stipulated that he would stand only if he remained general secretary of the union. The seat offered him was the apparently safe one of Gateshead.

The news of his tentative agreement immediately made him an important personality at the Conference. His principal speech was on a resolution concerned with monetary policy.

He found satisfaction in recalling the sins of the Labour Party over the years and his constant reproofs about its activities:

"I have been trying as a trade unionist to get our people and several Labour Conferences to abandon the policy of hoping to achieve Socialism by taxation, and trying to achieve Socialism by socialising the sources and real tools of industry. . . . You can talk about socialising your railways and other things. But socialise credit and the rest is comparatively easy."

He preached this at Gateshead, but it was useless. There were four candidates: National Liberal, Labour, National Labour, and Non-party. The Government nominee won by a majority of nearly 13,000 over Bevin.

Before polling day Bevin suspected that he would lose. This feeling, and the confirmation of it, convinced him that the unions must participate more closely in politics for which more power in the Labour Party was to be the method. He was impressed with the fact—which was true enough—that the battered remnants of the Labour Party still comprised a coherent force, and there had been no break between it and the unions. The nucleus was there to start rebuilding.

Typically Bevin set about to learn the rules of the political game but to obtain power in the way that had taken him to the top in trade unionism. The old contempt for the intellectuals and theorists was suppressed, at least temporarily.

He became chairman of the Society for Socialist Information and Propaganda, founded that winter by G. D. H. Cole. It brought him into close contact with other members such as Cripps, D. N. Pritt, Attlee, and Arthur Pugh. He believed that he could find a way of bridging the gap between the intellectuals and the workers. He was at first impressed with the lucidity and knowledge of his fellow-members, and the experts they employed to draft papers and pamphlets, but he soon tired of them. The ultimate result was to increase his dislike of the intellectuals, instead of finding how to co-operate with them.

The I.L.P. had also become impatient with the theorists. At their special conference at Bradford held in the autumn of 1932, the decision was taken to disaffiliate from the Labour Party and pursue an independent, militant line. A minority, headed by Frank Wise, regarded this as a disastrous policy, depriving the I.L.P. of its traditional rôle of a ginger group within the Labour Party. Wise took his adherents with him and formed the Socialist League.

Wise was therefore able to attend the annual Conference of the Labour Party at Leicester and obtain considerable notoriety for himself and his new League. He criticised the Party's financial proposals, largely the work of Hugh Dalton, because they omitted the taking over of the joint stock banks along with the Bank of England. He was supported by Stafford Cripps and an amendment was carried.

The Conference had an atmosphere of enthusiasm about it, born of recovery from the election shocks. It was optimistic in its belief that by passing resolutions it could achieve its ends, even though Labour was not in power and unlikely to obtain power. It cheerfully passed a resolution advocated by Cripps committing a future Labour Government, whether it had a majority or not, to passing Socialist legislation immediately on taking office even if such a move would result in instant defeat.

More thoughtful and sensible was the Conference's attitude to Herbert Morrison's plans for nationalisation of electricity and transport. On the principles involved the Conference was agreed. Where controversy lay was in the composition of the Boards to run the industries. Morrison, and the Executive, desired Board members appointed solely on grounds of ability and irrespective of their political outlook. This entirely realistic approach ignored the emotional factors involved, as has been shown in the hostility of many workers in the nationalised industries to the Boards since 1945.

In 1932 the union delegates were already voicing it. To them the stipulation of ability seemed an obstacle which would effectively bar a worker from membership of a Board. It was a strange attitude perhaps, only understandable by men whose lives were coloured by the conviction that they were not paid to think but to serve.

So strong was the reaction against Morrison's report that he offered to withdraw it for further study. At all costs he wanted to avoid rejection. The contents of the report, and the scheming which occurred to save it from complete destruction, infuriated Bevin. He saw nationalisation of industry coming, but nationalisation without workers' control. He hated the idea as much as he hated Morrison, the man responsible; the source of needless strife and misunderstanding when both men in the 1945 Government were of Cabinet rank.

The emergence of trade union ambitions to utilise and influence the political machinery of the working classes coincided with a fundamental change in the problems confronting the nation and the individual.

Within a few months of the end of the Great War social and economic problems had come to the fore. They became more

E. Shinwell, D. Kirkwood, and J. Muir. Three of the "Clyde Group" rebels in 1922.

The Reverend Campbell Stephen, Jimmy Maxton, and John Wheatley, three I.L.P. M.P.s suspended from the House in 1922.

Ramsay MacDonald in Court dress.

David Kirkwood in the House of Lords.

Arthur Greenwood in Levee dress.

J. R. Clynes in Levee dress.

formidable as conditions got worse; for years they preoccupied the minds of people of every political colour almost to the exclusion of everything else, particularly as international affairs presented even greater problems than internal difficulties of employment, trade and finance.

But exterior factors were about to enforce a fundamental change in the political life of the nation. The world economic depression began to ease by 1933. In the same year Hitler came to power, and if the possibility of war was not regarded as worth much thought the danger of the new ideologies certainly was. Early victims of the Nazi régime were the German trade unions and the German Social Democratic Party. The warning was noted by the T.U.C.

The mass of the population, grateful for the easing of unemployment and the general improvement in economic life, continued to ignore the danger signs in Italy and Germany. Encouraged by the Tory Press, which tended to praise Mussolini for transforming a feckless and happy-go-lucky nation into one which ensured that trains ran on time, and to endorse Hitler as the saviour of Germany from the Red menace, the average Briton now feared Communism more than he did Fascism during those birth-months of the coming holocaust.

In the Labour movement awareness of the dangers implicit in European trends was considerable. The I.L.P. and the Communist Party appealed for the formation of a United Front against Fascism. The I.L.P., since its disaffiliation, had sought valiantly for notoriety by making such calls, but it was by now an unimportant organisation, losing many of the 17,000 members it had at the time of the break. The Communist Party probably had more card-carrying members, but only a minority were active.

Both the Labour Party and the T.U.C. avoided the trap set by the United Front appeal. Pointedly the National Joint Council issued a statement which condemned Fascist and Communist dictatorships on equal terms.

But there was a strangely ambivalent attitude—typical of the whole nation—which enabled both the union and Party leaders to call for resistance against undemocratic ideologies on one hand and to declaim about defence measures on the other. Thus at the annual Conference of the Party in 1933 Dalton spoke on behalf of the Executive in favour of a general strike if war became imminent, and the resolution was passed unanimously.

Policies of this kind were very like the anti-war resolutions of undergraduates and peace pledges of the general public of the

K

period. They were a gesture of hatred against war, emotional rather than realistic. Later events rendered them meaningless.

A practical move at this time was the discussion about the Party programme. At the 1933 Conference the new programme was presented under the title of *Socialism and the Condition of the People*. The debates, both at the Party Conference and at the T.U.C. a month earlier, were largely concerned with the composition of the Boards for nationalised industries, the question shelved the previous year. The trade union vote eventually ensured statutory guarantees for direct trade union member representation on the Boards. Discussions were amicable and constructive. No crisis developed in these debates.

But real trouble arose through the antics of Sir Stafford Cripps and his Socialist League. Cripps was impelled by two beliefs, not uncommon in the Socialist movement, which have all too frequently caused trouble and brought little benefit. A deeply religious man, he considered the Labour Party could be uplifted into a sort of religious crusade. A highly intelligent man, he believed his mission was to educate and re-educate everyone else in the Party: the supremacy of the intellectual.

Cripps was forty-four when he made his attempt to direct the fortunes of the Labour Party in 1933. Public-school educated and very English, Cripps had by this time amassed a considerable fortune as one of the most successful barristers of the late twenties. His interest in Socialism had been tenuous, mostly derived from conversations with Beatrice Webb, whose nephew he was. The information he gleaned from visits at the Webbs' house had aroused no enthusiasm for political life. Indeed, he told friends that if he changed his career it would be to enter the Church.

It was Morrison who persuaded Cripps to join the Labour Party, after he had handled some L.C.C. interests at the Railway Rates Tribunal. The paucity of legal luminaries in the Party thereupon ensured that he was appointed Solicitor-General in the 1929 Government and a seat found for him. As he was one of the few M.P.s to retain his seat in 1931 he inevitably had to intervene in Parliamentary debates and quickly formed ambitions which he had previously denied.

At the 1933 Conference he spoke in favour of any future Labour Government immediately taking to itself emergency powers. These were principally the abolition of the House of Lords and Government by decree, the decrees being confirmed by the Commons at its leisure.

Such proposals at a time when Hitler was adopting similar measures were, of course, extremely ill-judged. Strangely, he found allies in Attlee and Frank Wise, but general objections, of which Bevin's was the most formidable, got Cripps's amendment shelved for a year. The harm was done, however. Cripps's dictatorial and revolutionary words received far more publicity than the general opposition of the Conference which they engendered.

The struggle in the thirties for power between the unions and the political groups was sporadic but never absent. Occasional incidents caused a flare-up. There was, for example, the significant affair of the by-election at Clay Cross, caused by the death of Charles Duncan, a former union leader. The local Labour organisation had been almost wholly financed by the T.G.W.U., and they chose Ben Smith as the union candidate. But the Labour Party was anxiously seeking a safe seat for Henderson and he was nominated as candidate without any discussion. Bevin was furious and thereupon withheld his union's Party affiliation fee, and the National Executive had to humble itself with a formal apology for getting the Party secretary a seat.

That was a minor union defeat. A big and deserved victory occurred in February, 1934, when the National Executive met to consider the previous Conference decision about calling a general strike if war should be imminent. The Conference was also attended by the General Council of the T.U.C. whose delegates effectively smashed this out-dated, woolly-minded and unrealistic proposal.

The outcome was a pamphlet *War and Peace*, presented to the 1934 Conference by Henderson. It contained the traditional propaganda of the Labour movement that war was a capitalist activity and that in most wars the masses were duped into patriotic enthusiasm; that was Henderson's contribution. But the meat of the report was trade union inspired. It stated that any British Government might have to resort to force in support of the League of Nations in restraining an aggressor, and it called for unflinching support of the Government undertaking such action. Cripps complained in vain. Pacifists, like Lord Ponsonby, were ignored. The report was adopted by a big majority. Cripps suffered a further defeat when his notorious amendment for a future Labour Government taking emergency powers was also rejected.

The Party, prodded by the T.U.C., was by 1934 determined to protect itself from mutinous groups, both within the Party and among those which, though disaffiliated, were synonymous with Labour in the public mind. The Executive's chief move was to request the Conference to give it powers to discipline individual members who took part in United Front and similar activities.

Aneurin Bevan, who had been making a name for himself by eloquent though vituperative speeches in the Commons during debates on the Special Areas and on unemployment pay, had found much to admire in Cripps. He now tilted a lance on behalf of the Socialist League by claiming that the Executive's proposal was just a heresy hunt, designed to disguise their own shortcomings.

He was attacked so bitterly by Bevin that he appealed to the chair for protection. Bevin contemptuously asked if he was so thin-skinned that he could not take his own medicine. "In this Conference you aren't going to enjoy the flattery of the gossip columnists you get in London," he said. "You are going to get facts."

The facts impressed the delegates. Bevan suffered ignominious defeat. Yet another private war among future Cabinet colleagues had broken out.

When 1935 began there were many who regarded it as a year of decision both for the country and for the Labour Party. The National Government was stumbling towards its end, with little in its record to praise. The organisation on which both pacifists and non-pacifists in the Labour movement pinned their hopes—the League of Nations—was failing on every side, the Government preferred that old-type diplomacy should be used either to safeguard peace or select who were to be the country's allies when war came. There was the Anglo-German Naval Treaty, and there was the much-publicised Stresa Conference. On the other side of the coin were Hitler's vast rearmament plans and the looming crisis of Abyssinia. Almost unwillingly, because of the national alarm the economic crisis—still vivid in their minds—had caused, the nation's Tory leaders made some gesture towards a rearmament programme.

Prior to the debate on the Government's expansion plans for the Royal Air Force, the Parliamentary Labour Party met the T.U.C. and the National Executive to shape a policy. It is some indication of the manner in which Hitler had by then gained supremacy in the field of international propaganda that all but the most confirmed pacifists agreed to await a speech by Hitler the next day before making up their minds.

Hitler duly told his accustomed lies and assured the nervous world that he regarded the Locarno Pact as sacrosanct. This was sufficient to influence the Parliamentary Party to decide to vote against Air Ministry estimates. Attlee was selected to explain to an indulgent House that the Labour Party's policy was to "seek security through disarmament".

The incubus of treachery still remaining from a situation where the most prominent Labour personality of the age was Prime Minister of a predominantly Tory administration disappeared completely in June, 1935, when Ramsay MacDonald resigned as Prime Minister. For months his speeches in the House of Commons had been prolix and incomprehensible. Little comment accompanied his going beyond the fact that he refused an earldom.

His succession by Baldwin was merely a formal acknowledgment of a situation which already applied. For some time MacDonald had been the willing tool and the wordy mouthpiece of Baldwin, and nothing more. But Baldwin wanted a free hand to go to the country, freed from the awkward ties of the 1931 alliance.

His preparation for the election was masterly. Foreign policy swung round to support the League of Nations, and in the League of Nations Assembly at Geneva the Foreign Secretary, Sir Samuel Hoare, changed from a policy of isolation to support for collective security.

This was designed to find favour in the minds of the majority of the eleven million people who had signed the Peace Ballot and more especially to gain the confidence of the working classes. That this was highly successful was shown at the 1935 T.U.C. Conference which followed immediately after the Hoare speech at Geneva. Support for the Government, while it followed the policy of carrying out obligations under the League Covenant, was promised with enthusiasm. It remained for the Labour Party to follow the T.U.C.'s lead.

Lansbury, as leader of the Parliamentary Labour Party, had already formally pledged his Party's support of a stand for League principles to Hoare during July.

Then some Labour leaders had second thoughts, instantly preparing the way for a violent split at a time when the whole Labour movement—and indeed the whole country—seemed to have reached agreement on the methods of resisting Fascist aggression and of avoiding war.

A fortnight after the T.U.C. resolution was passed by an overwhelming majority Ponsonby resigned from leadership of the Labour Party in the Lords. Next, Cripps resigned from the National Executive. Third, Lansbury publicly stated that he disagreed with the Party's policy. It was as if the Labour Party wished publicly to confess, prior to the election which everyone knew must be imminent, that it was indeed too divided to govern.

The trouble arose on the eve of the annual Conference which itself took place as Italian troops massed on the Abyssinian frontier.

Dalton introduced on behalf of the National Executive the formal resolution pledging the Party "to support of any action consistent with the principles and status of the League of Nations to restrain the Italian Government and uphold the authority of the League".

It was not a new conception, and in principle and similar terms it had been approved periodically since the League was founded, but it had, of course, a new urgency.

Cripps spoke against the resolution, falling back on his familiar theme that the League was the tool of capitalist-imperialists. He gained some applause from the pacifists and Left-wing elements, but on the whole his speech made no impact.

Lansbury, who had dissented from the Executive's resolution, was by then ageing and disillusioned. He had from the outset disliked his tenure of office as leader but he did not regard the occasion as the opportunity to resign to the sound of sentimental applause. He was sincere in his pacifism and in his statement of personal faith.

His words produced a wave of highly emotional sympathy, for Lansbury had been expressing sentiments which were held by many of the delegates not confined to the old guard.

But the Lansbury line was not practical politics in 1935. It was left to Bevin to point this out, and he did so with all the considerable brutality at his command.

Amid considerable uproar he made his famous charge, while he turned to face Lansbury directly, "It is placing the Executive and the movement in an absolutely wrong position to be trailing your conscience round from body to body to be told what you ought to do with it."

Bevin's subsequent rhetoric destroyed all the hostility which had existed when he insulted Lansbury. When he dealt with Cripps and the Socialist League in similar forthright fashion, there were only 102,000 votes in support of Cripps, compared with 2,168,000 against him.

Bevin's surgery had been cruel, but it was effective as a cure. In a matter of an hour he had saved the Labour Party, moving towards a mild renaissance, from a repetition of the disastrous situation of 1931, when the leader had one policy and his lieutenants another, with the rank and file bewildered and disillusioned.

Lansbury resigned a month later, within two weeks of Arthur Henderson's death being announced. Time and events were producing a complete severance with the past. Attlee, as deputy leader, automatically succeeded Lansbury despite suggestions that Herbert Morrison, increasingly active on the National Executive, should be found a safe seat and appointed leader.

Baldwin adjudged the controversies within the Labour movement as bigger than they actually were. He promptly decided the time was ideal for an election. Polling day was fixed for November 14, 1935.

11

PRELUDE TO WAR

1935–1940

There was no clear-cut issue in the general election of 1935. All three Parties professed support for collective security organised under the aegis of the League of Nations. The timing of the appeal to the country was entirely Baldwin's estimate of the ideal opportunity for his Party, and his assumption of an occasion for profit due to schisms in the Labour ranks. The electorate was bewildered and therefore wary of leaping from the frying pan into another Party's fire.

The agreement on the need to prepare defences against aggression by Germany and Italy led to different theories as to method. The Tories, after considering a campaign based on a bold programme of large-scale rearmament, temporised by promising that on re-election they would repair the gaps in defence.

The Liberals, encouraged by Lord Snowden (who used the opportunity for gratuitous and vicious aspersions on his erstwhile colleague MacDonald), criticised the outgoing Government's League policy but supported rearmament. Labour, convinced that the Tory support of the League was insincere, refused to support a re-armament programme which could be used to further a repugnant policy.

Thus, while accepting the unpleasant truth that potential enemies were arming themselves to the teeth, the Labour leaders rejected defence measures they believed to be fraught with danger. Morrison, for example, claimed during his election campaign that a vote for the Tories was a vote for war. This negative attitude was suspect to a nation which was of finer calibre than to prefer butter in the "guns or butter" question borrowed from the speeches of the German Nazi leader Herr Goering.

Wishful optimism as well as the absence of a realistic approach to the problems of the day did the re-born Labour Party ill service in the 1935 campaign. Attlee, thrust into the difficulties of speaking as the Party leader, made prophecies of a great electoral victory.

His advisers at Transport House estimated that two hundred Labour victories was the least that could be expected.

The results indicated the weakness of the Labour leadership in the eyes of the electorate. Labour gained only 154 seats, to which could be added the four I.L.P. M.P.s for Clydeside in the calculation of anti-Tory opposition. But these four had, in fact, been opposed by official Labour candidates, all of whom were soundly trounced and lost their deposits. Nor was the result an indication of any substantial progress by the Party. It was true that the total vote of nearly 8½ million represented an increase of 1.8 million over 1931, but when compared with the 1929 election, thus ignoring the abnormal situation of 1931, the increase was a mere 105,000.

The Tories enjoyed an overall majority of 159, and Baldwin could with reason plan his retirement, assured both of his Party's own strength and his opponents' weakness. But within a matter of days of the new Parliament meeting in December, 1935, his reputation for honesty and wisdom was jeopardised in a manner which indicated that faults in political judgment were by no means defects unique to Liberal and Labour. A crisis arose through the publication of the terms of the Hoare-Laval pact proposed to settle the war in Abyssinia. The national outcry which ensued was so great that Baldwin was compelled to drop the plan and to ask for the resignation of Sir Samuel Hoare.

In the censure debate in the House Attlee questioned the honour of the Prime Minister, an unprecedented charge which had the effect of closing the wavering ranks of the Tories and ensuring that the Government defeated the motion by 232.

Although the Parliamentary Labour Party's handling of the first major controversy of the new Parliament was ineffective, the general approach was encouraging and impressed the country. Baldwin soon discovered that the onrush of foreign disasters had made the nation uneasy about Tory policy. Early in 1936 Hitler occupied the Rhineland, and by May all the intrigues, hopes and promises to make the League of Nations effective had been nullified with the announcement that the King of Italy had assumed an additional title as Emperor of Ethiopia. And in July civil war broke out in Spain.

The changes in Labour policy resulting from the 1935 Party Conference provided cause for some satisfaction among Labour's adherents, but little for the uncommitted voter. Attlee was re-elected leader of the Parliamentary Party on the tacit understanding that this was a temporary measure until the result of the general election clarified the Party's future. Most people outside Parliament considered that the quarrels and indecision rampant in the Labour Party presaged little future at all for it.

The death of Arthur Henderson, occurring soon after the Brighton Conference, was a symbol of the end of one chapter of Labour's history and a suggestion that there was no one big enough to write the next one. Henderson had contributed magnificent service to the cause of British Socialism over a period of more than thirty years. Self-effacing, cautious, and sometimes narrow-minded, he had quietly enforced discipline within the Party which minimised one crisis after another. It was probably Henderson who virtually alone achieved the salvation of the Labour Party after the debacle of 1931, collecting the remnants and making them a foundation for something sounder and stronger. There was something paradoxical about his political diligence, because he was never an ardent Socialist and the theories of Marx were largely repugnant to him. His inborn loyalty was to the trade union movement; his adopted devotion was to the Party which employed him. The result was that he brought the T.U.C. and the Party closer together and consistently smoothed out major difficulties between them.

As was expected by everyone except the MacDonald clique itself, the election brought about the final erasure of the disgrace of 1931. The handful of men who had sided with MacDonald were either dead, retired or had recanted. Some who wished to make amends were told that it was up to the constituency Party to decide on the question of their re-admission to the Party. Only MacDonald continued to believe that immunity from criticism was his divine right. His contempt for all but his friends in the National Government— men who had long since come to regard him as of no profitable use —was typified in the fact that he visited his constituency only on two occasions during the life of the 1931–35 Parliament. It was generally believed that the 1935 Birthday Honours would see him elevated to a peerage, thus avoiding the generally expected disgrace of his defeat at the election. MacDonald's vanity had, however, by this time reached a point of near-mania, and he insisted on standing again. I was chosen from a large number of candidates to oppose him.

The National Government, alarmed at the inferences which his defeat might create, applied themselves with zeal to propaganda on his behalf in Seaham, in contrast to MacDonald himself, who continued to neglect the constituency. Despite the convoys of Tory-owned cars, the monopoly of halls which forced me to hold most of my meetings at street corners in November weather, MacDonald was defeated by 21,000 votes. He did not trouble to be present when the result was declared.

Despite the huge Tory majority, the 1935 election result was a welcome signpost to Labour's future. It had brought back to Parliament Alexander, Greenwood, Morrison, Dalton, Tom Johnston, who, with myself, were to remain in the House of Commons for many years and provide experience of previous office for a future Labour Government.

Several of the prominent members, who were elected in the fateful election of 1931, were returned, including Attlee, George Lansbury, Josh Wedgwood, Nye Bevan and Stafford Cripps. Notable reinforcements were Tom Williams, a miner and a future Minister of Agriculture; Creech Jones, an authority on Colonial affairs; George Hall and Jack Lawson, who were to become Service Ministers; Arthur Henderson, the son of "Uncle Arthur"; Fred Montague, a veteran Socialist who had attended the first meeting of the Labour Representation Committee in 1900; George Hardie, the brother of Keir Hardie; Ellis Smith, a forthright and typical representative of the workers; Ellen Wilkinson, and Sydney Silverman. In two by-elections in the following year Jim Griffiths and Noel-Baker were returned.

The comparatively small Labour Opposition of 154 M.P.s were then as united as any which had ever sat in the Commons. The I.L.P. had obtained only four seats, and the election of one Communist, Willie Gallacher, in West Fife, was of no particular significance. Gallacher was an effective advocate of Socialist policy. His victory was due more to his popularity than to belief in Communism.

Behind the scenes there was, however, some immediate difference of view on future policy. On the whole the rank and file M.P.s approved of Attlee as leader. Though his introduction to Socialism had been via the Fabian Party, which he joined in 1908, his diffident character ensured that there was none of the lofty and didactic manner so often found in members of the intellectual groups. Further, as M.P. for Limehouse without a break since 1922, his Parliamentary experience was not merely invaluable but almost unique at the time.

These facts tended to engender an almost sheeplike docility among the new M.P.s so that they were ready to vote for Attlee as leader without thought or discussion. Mindful of the dangers which the wrong type of leader could bring to the Party solely through his personal defects, I suggested at an early meeting of the Parliamentary Party that as the majority of M.P.s were either new or had been out of Parliament for some time, the election of leader should be deferred, while confirming Attlee's temporary leadership, which was a continuance of the position he had held in the previous Parliament.

Attlee was in the chair and he did not, of course, contribute to the discussion, but the meeting was wholly in his favour and my motion for some delay was heavily defeated.

The formal election of the Parliamentary Party's leader, which came later, was far from unanimous. It inevitably involved Attlee, Greenwood, and Morrison. Attlee could be assured of the loyalty of all the M.P.s of the 1931 Parliament. Greenwood had achieved an excellent reputation for his activities in the 1929 Government and was confident of the support of several M.P.s. Morrison enjoyed considerable prestige as the architect of Labour's spectacular triumph in gaining control of the L.C.C. in 1934.

Surprisingly, Greenwood's nomination came first, in preference to Attlee, with Morrison third. The first voting, however, gave 58 votes to Attlee, 44 to Morrison, and 33 to Greenwood.

It had been agreed that the third candidate should stand down and a second election would then take place. In this Attlee received 87 votes and was duly elected. Morrison, presumably piqued by the result, refused to become deputy leader, his stated reason being that political work with the L.C.C. made the office unsuitable. This was the start of a quiet rivalry and not-always-concealed dislike between the two men which was to jeopardise Party unity for the next twenty years.

Attlee, in his speech of acceptance of the leadership, stressed that he believed it to be an office of brief duration. It was then difficult to forecast, as events later proved, that he would remain at the helm for many years. In the first months of his long tenure of that office it is probable that he would have been willing to stand down, for his was a thankless task. The formidable Tory majority in the Commons made any and every Labour move a gesture of little practical value.

Outside Parliament as well as in it, Labour spokesmen periodically made the task of a leader whose duty it was to maintain unity heartbreakingly difficult. Oswald Mosley, still remembered as a brilliant if temperamental political figure in the public mind, was stirring up trouble with demonstrations and what seemed to be anti-Semitic propaganda. Cripps, Strauss and Bevan were forcing the Labour Party to consider expulsion because of their Socialist League propaganda, and Cripps's subsequent United Front, copying the French pattern of Leon Blum, while formed with the object of

uniting Labour, I.L.P., and Communists in one anti-Fascist organisation, merely achieved isolation: Labour, I.L.P. and the Co-
operative Party rejected any kind of amity or affiliation with a body
which included Communists.

Cripps, if only because of his immense powers as a controversial-
ist, did the most harm to Labour's unity in the pre-war years. By
1936 the National Government's policy of appeasing the dictators
was completely out of touch with public opinion, as indeed was
Labour adherence to non-intervention in the Spanish civil war. To
that extent the nation had lost faith in both Parties, but it was the
ceaseless efforts of Cripps to stir up class strife which caused the
most dissatisfaction. In a speech in March, 1937, he had called on
workers to refuse to make armaments, and on other workers to
refuse to use any that might be made. By that time there were many
millions of ordinary peace-loving people becoming deeply worried
at the strength of potential enemies and the weakness of Britain's
defences.

If Cripps could be branded an outlaw—though this did not
officially occur with expulsion until the annual Conference in 1939
—the attitude of the Parliamentary Party towards rearmament as
approved by Attlee, in the light of subsequent events, merited no
such excuse. This was "playing politics" with a vengeance. The
need for meeting an imminent challenge from the dictators was
recognised; the chance to attack the foreign policy of the Government by voting against even timid moves to build up our defences
was too tempting.

Controversy in the Parliamentary Party came to a head when
on March 3rd Attlee explained that very shortly the Party would
have to face the estimates for the fighting services. He outlined the
position and reported on recommendations made by the Parliamentary Committee. They included opposing the motion that "Mr.
Speaker do leave the Chair"; in effect opposition to either men or
money for defence, because neither could be voted upon except in
Committee of Supply. Token votes against the estimates should
be supported, but on the main question the Party should abstain.
These recommendations sparked off a heated discussion. One
section demanded that, in view of the tension created by Hitler,
defence measures must be encouraged; another group was in opposition to any defence expenditure, their attitude being based on
pacifist sentiment; probably a majority were in favour of demanding from the Government assurances of support for the principle
of collective security before accepting the policy of rearmament.
Finally the Party, with only one dissentient, accepted the executive

recommendations. Thus, in the following weeks most of the Service estimates were opposed, and the performance was repeated in March, 1938.

That maladministration, waste, and incompetence were rampant in almost every part of the defence programme in the four years before World War II was proved by events. These faults Labour M.P.s may have pointed out; but the criticism became impractical in the anxiety to score a Party point over the hapless if arrogant Party on the Tory benches. Rarely has the traditional pacifism of Labour, in theory a noble and desirable virtue, been so ill-advisedly practised to the detriment of the movement. That the Tory opponents were even more culpable does not minimise the tragedy of the policy pursued by the Parliamentary Party after 1935.

The attitude of Labour to the question of rearmament at this time was, however, to some extent forgivable. In the first place there was the traditional respect for pacifism. In the second the Party was not taken into the confidence of the Government so that the real situation could be explained.

Baldwin's memorable comment, "Supposing I had gone to the country and said that Germany was rearming and we must rearm? Does anyone think that this pacific democracy would have rallied to that cry at that moment? I cannot think of anything that would have made the loss of the election more certain" was typical of the secrecy maintained by him even in the case of the leaders of His Majesty's Opposition.

Attlee during this period was himself more pacifist than the nation and many of his colleagues. His broadcast on the 1937 Budget, for example, was seriously out of tune with the national feeling when he condemned it as putting guns before butter. Nor did his personal dislike of Baldwin's successor, Neville Chamberlain, who became Prime Minister in May, 1937, help Attlee to bring his views into line with public opinion.

The result was his technical defeat as the Party leader at a meeting of the Parliamentary Party in July when the official policy on the defence estimates came up for discussion. Attlee, along with the majority of the Executive, favoured voting against the estimates. Dalton led the group favouring abstention. In the subsequent voting Attlee, along with his colleagues Greenwood and Morrison, was defeated by six votes at a meeting which seventy M.P.s had not troubled to attend. It was a major defeat of the leadership which might in other situations have brought about the leader's resignation. Instead, Attlee accepted the democratic principles of the Labour Party and bowed to its orders. This decision had the two-

fold result of avoiding yet another sensational split in the Party
and also of strengthening Attlee's position as a leader who was
amenable to suggestion from the rank and file.

In fact the slight change of attitude from one of opposition to
abstention which this meeting forced on Attlee was long overdue.
The Parliamentary Party's policy of opposing defence measures
while calling for resistance to the aggressions of Hitler, Mussolini
and Franco was in contrast to the views of the National Council
of Labour about arms-supported collective security, a feeling endorsed and backed by the T.U.C. This policy had found favour at
the Labour Party Conference in 1936, and the general attitude
there was such that opponents of the Government's rearmament
policy, such as Morrison, who had steadily opposed it during the
early months of 1936, remained silent at the October Conference,
thereby ensuring that the resolution in favour of support of the
arms programme was easily carried.

Most of this quietly conducted revolt against the leadership and
against the Parliamentary Party was the work of Dalton and Ernie
Bevin. They found it advantageous to work in amicable co-
operation to this end, but those two ambitious men had little in
common by temperament or background. The agreeable alliance
was severely strained in 1937 when Dalton began his campaign to
permit constituency Parties to elect their own representatives to the
National Executive. One reason for this was to minimise the likelihood of non-union members of the Party joining with the splinter
groups such as the I.L.P. or the Socialist League in order to find
a useful outlet for their energies. Another was, of course, to
minimise trade union influence.

While Bevin was in favour of the former, any erosion of the
latter, no matter how small, aroused his immediate hostility. However, Dalton had his way, and at the 1937 Conference (held at
Whitsun in order that it would precede, instead of follow, the T.U.C.
Conference) the number of seats for constituency Parties became
seven. This enabled the intellectuals without Parliamentary seats
to join the Executive; typical of them were Laski and D. N. Pritt.
These ostensibly independent thinkers, usually strongly to the left,
were safer within the National Executive than out of it. For one
thing they could always be outvoted; for another they usually
appeared amenable to majority opinion. When the question of the
expulsion of Cripps and his National Front adherents came up for
decision, Laski made no objection, while the objections of Pritt
and Ellen Wilkinson carried no impact and caused no Press reports
of rumours of a split.

Despite the stream of evidence both at Party Conferences and in the constituencies that Labour's rank and file were resigned to the need for rearmament, and despite the almost universal belief that the European dictators were untrustworthy and would be amenable only to force, a majority in the Parliamentary Party continued their gestures of opposition to practical effort.

One reason was that Attlee distrusted anything that Chamberlain proposed or did, but this personal view hardly justified opposition of conscription which was voiced in the House in April, 1939, when Hitler occupied that part of Czechoslovakia which the appeasement of Munich in the previous September had not given him.

It must be admitted that Attlee and the Parliamentary Party were in line with the general opinion of the Labour movement in opposing conscription. At the Southport Conference held at Whitsun it maintained that Chamberlain had erred in failing to go to the country for endorsement of such a fundamentally revolutionary interference with the liberty of the subject.

But the big talking point of that Conference was the conduct of Cripps and his followers, notably Aneurin Bevan, by then making a name for himself in the House as a master of invective and on occasion a brilliant orator. The Executive had little difficulty in getting the Conference to confirm its decision to expel members of the United Front, but the mere fact that it engendered debate gave the public the impression of yet another fissure in the Labour edifice. With Cripps the matter was definitely one of principle, and it was to be six years before he could be persuaded to return to the Labour fold. Bevan gave the impression that his defiance was at least partly motivated by a desire for publicity. He was repentant and forgiven by the end of the year.

During the August days preceding the outbreak of war the Labour Party achieved a unity very different from the doubts and indecisions of July 1914. All but an insignificant fraction of pacifists were agreed on, or resigned to, the fact that war was inevitable. Morrison, Dalton and Citrine were appointed by the National Council of Labour to confer with Chamberlain. Attlee was not included because he was undergoing an operation. His deputy, Arthur Greenwood, was in charge of the Parliamentary Party.

After Hitler's invasion of Poland was launched on September 1 the National Executive and the Parliamentary Executive held a joint meeting at which it was decided that Labour should not participate in the Government. This decision was made without direct consultation with the T.U.C., at the time holding its Congress

Reunion of ex-prisoner M.P.s includes, left to right sitting: Morgan Jones, J. H. Hudson, Emanuel Shinwell, Charles Dukes, R. C. Wallhead, Miss Susan Lawrence, John Scurr. Left to right standing and including: W. H. Ayles, E. D. Morel, Pethick Lawrence, James Maxton, David Kirkwood. The photograph was taken at a dinner given on January 10th, 1924, in honour of members of the new Parliament who had been imprisoned on political or religious grounds.

The Labour Cabinet, 1929. Front row, left to right: J. R. Clynes, Lord Parmoor, J. H. Thomas, Philip Snowden, Ramsay MacDonald, Arthur Henderson, Sidney Webb, Lord Sankey, Wedgwood Benn. Back row, left to right: George Lansbury, A. V. Alexander, Sir Charles Trevelyan, Maggie Bondfield, Lord Thomson, Tom Shaw, Arthur Greenwood, Lord Noel-Buxton, William Graham, William Adamson.

The Labour Cabinet, 1945. Front row, left to right: Viscount Addison, Lord Jowitt, Stafford Cripps, Arthur Greenwood, Ernest Bevin, Clement Attlee, Herbert Morrison, Hugh Dalton, A. V. Alexander, J. Chuter Ede, Ellen Wilkinson. Back row, left to right: Aneurin Bevan, George Isaacs, Viscount Stansgate (Wedgwood Benn), George Hall, Pethick Lawrence, Jack Lawson, Joseph Westwood, Emanuel Shinwell, Edward Williams (minister not in Cabinet), Tom Williams.

Herbert Morrison in action.

at Bridlington, though it was known from informal discussion that
the T.U.C. was in agreement with the decision.

That resolution was passed on Saturday September 2. Parliament remained in session over the week-end and the general feeling
of Labour M.P.s was that Chamberlain was still hoping to discover
a way to avoid war, despite the pact to aid Poland if she were
invaded. In the debate Labour was virtually unanimous for a
declaration of war while the Government still remained indecisive.

It was left to a Tory M.P. to present the Labour Opposition with
its great moment. Leopold Amery shouted across the floor, "Speak
for England!"

Greenwood did so, in a restrained but splendid speech which
destroyed for ever any lingering beliefs from the past that the
Labour Party was unpatriotic. He indicated that he and his
colleagues were horrified at the idea of war, even against the Nazis,
but he believed that there could now be no other rational or honourable means of curbing Hitler.

Labour remained in Opposition both in fact and theory. The
only truce was agreement that in by-elections candidates in opposition to the previous M.P.'s Party would not be sponsored, and
subsequently it was agreed that the general election due before
November, 1940, should be postponed.

During the months of the "phoney war" Labour performed the
useful tasks of a ginger group, stirring the Government out of complacency, and there were vigorous debates on production delays and
shipping losses, and on the bizarre situation of serious unemployment during a breathing space when every worker should have
been engaged in preparation for a prolonged struggle.

The invasion of Norway and Denmark on April 9, 1940, inevitably forced a vote of censure on the Government. It was moved
by Morrison. The House was almost full and the Government could
in theory rely on a majority of 247. In fact its majority was 81—a
symbolic defeat. Labour had rallied the dissident Tories and had
thereby ensured Chamberlain's downfall. With some justification
the Party can claim to have thereby paved the way for Churchill to
save the country from ultimate defeat.

Curiously neither Attlee nor Greenwood appeared to have
envisaged this situation; at least no open discussions were held
prior to the debate on the Norwegian situation to enable the
Parliamentary Party to formulate any policy. With the change
of Prime Minister, and perhaps of Government, it dawned on
the Labour leaders that some policy of future action was urgently
required.

L

Chamberlain was grimly hanging on to office, and on the day after the censure motion vote he invited Attlee and Greenwood to participate in a reconstruction of the Government. Attlee reported the conversation to the Parliamentary Committee and then told Chamberlain that Labour would not serve in any Coalition while he remained Prime Minister. This was the final blow, and Chamberlain resigned forthwith.

It was Whitsun, and the Labour Conference was about to start at Bournemouth. The delegates went there with the knowledge that momentarily the Party leaders would be invited by the new Prime Minister, Winston Churchill, to participate in his administration.

The high expectations of the Party after the election of 1935 that within three or four years the Baldwin-Chamberlain combination would have failed in both economic and international affairs, and that another general election would bring victory to the Labour cause, was now to be frustrated by war. It was true that there had been much dissension in the Party, and precious little achievement with which to encourage the electors, but the Party organisation was now in a stronger position than ever before. Membership and affiliations had increased. There was undoubted reason for optimism. The Party spirit was strong enough to shoulder responsibility even at such a time of crisis. Certainly it deemed itself capable of contributing usefully, and perhaps vitally, to any Coalition based on arrangements it could approve.

12

COALITION

1940–1945

Clem Attlee and Arthur Greenwood conferred in London with Neville Chamberlain, Winston Churchill and Lord Halifax at the historic and decisive conference on May 9, 1940. The meeting ended with Attlee assuring the other side that there could be no question of a Coalition under Chamberlain but reasonable certainty of agreement with "someone else", which left no doubt in anyone's mind that he meant Churchill. While this meeting took place the delegates were assembling for the Labour Party Conference at Bournemouth. They were in solemn mood. It was realism rather than defeatism to speculate on the possibility of invasion, and it was not unreasonable to query how that invasion could be successfully resisted. Delegates who were M.P.s and were aware of the nation's lack of preparedness, or had first-hand knowledge of the muddle and delays in armament production because they came from the factory floor, were unlikely to display any false optimism about Britain's invulnerability.

After the initial shock of Nazi successes in the Low Countries, reported almost hourly, there developed a sense of having an almost impossible job to do—and to achieve success—which was soon to encompass the whole nation. By Friday, therefore, when a meeting of the Joint Executive took place, there was virtually unanimous agreement that Labour should serve under Churchill, who that morning had begun the task of forming a Government.

Attlee went to London to see Churchill at the Admiralty, and over the week-end there was considerable excitement as rumours swept the Bournemouth hotels about likely appointments. Attlee was still absent when the Conference assembled, and I was asked to reply on his behalf on the Parliamentary Party's report. Most of the ministerial appointments were made in the first few days and I received a message to telephone Churchill, who invited me to join the Government—an honour which I felt unable to accept.

The national emergency was such that unquestioning discipline by those who accepted office was just and reasonable. Nevertheless, both the terms under which co-operation would be forthcoming and the policy for which the rank and file would have to give a mandate to the Labour members of the Government were vague.

Attlee and other leaders were moved by a natural sense of patriotism, and they were impressed with the generosity of Churchill's offers to the Labour Party. Considering the size of the Labour Opposition in the Commons the chance of having two out of five offices in the War Cabinet was extremely good, especially as Attlee, in effect Deputy Prime Minister, and Greenwood, as Minister without Portfolio, could inevitably be the leading personalities in the Commons' day-to-day business.

Other Labour posts were those of A. V. Alexander at the Admiralty; Hugh Dalton, after a short period of suspense and insistence about his claims, became Minister of Economic Warfare; Sir William Jowitt, who had joined MacDonald in 1931, but had recanted, as Solicitor-General; Herbert Morrison, as Minister of Supply (later to be transferred to the Home Office and Ministry of Home Security); and finally, and significantly, Ernest Bevin, as Minister of Labour.

Tory critics of Churchill—and they were still numerous at the time—regarded the appointments as over-generous. In fact they were proof of Churchill's common touch: he realised that Labour support in the country was far larger than its representation in the Commons. His appointment of Bevin was a master touch, though he could not know how it was to affect the future history of the Labour movement. At the time the close friendship which later developed between Attlee and Bevin was little more than mutual respect between two leaders of powerful groups.

The Labour members of the Government found it comparatively easy to assert their exalted position. Criticism was sparse. The Chamberlain Tories were all too anxious to make amends for their years of denigration and sneering about all that Churchill had said and done in the thirties. On the Labour side mild criticism came only from Pethick-Lawrence, Arthur Woodburn, and James Griffiths, with rather more forceful criticism from Aneurin Bevan and myself.

The House gained the impression that most of the Labour members of the Government were in office as a sop to the electorate, and that most decisions were made without much consultation on their views. Bevin evinced proof of his tremendous energy and powers by what he did outside the House, but in debate and at

question time he cut a poor figure, still having to learn that the
Commons was a very different place from Transport House. He was
reminded more than once that Parliament was a democratic
assembly.

By August, when invasion was expected in a matter of days, I
spoke in a debate on the country's economic policy. Greenwood, in
defence of the Government, made a vague speech full of promises
akin to those of the Chamberlain régime. I asked about priorities
and planning, arousing the anger of both Bevin and Greenwood so
that their replies gave the impression of our being on opposite
political sides.

In May, 1941, Churchill asked for a vote of confidence. I was
one of the speakers who protested at the insinuation that criticism
was censure and demanded to know whether the Prime Minister
preferred a collection of yes-men.

These were pin-pricks which were not unhealthy proof that
Britain, even with her back to the wall, was still a democracy. The
only serious attack Churchill ever experienced in the Commons was
the censure debate in the summer of 1942, when a few Labour and
Tory members demanded an immediate second front. Nye Bevan
came to the forefront in that debate and aroused a hatred in
Churchill's mind which never lessened. But the censure vote was
rejected by 476 to 25 votes.

It will be realised that as a political force in its own right the
Labour Party merely ticked over for most of the war years. One
reason was that the Parliamentary Party became virtually leaderless.
It was agreed soon after the Coalition Government took office
that Labour ministers could not be expected to serve on the Parliamentary Executive. Instead a committee was formed of private
members, to which Attlee and other ministers could come as of right
but not of duty. The acting leader appointed by the Parliamentary Party was H. B. Lees Smith, selected on account of his
seniority rather than the possession of exceptional ability—indeed
the appointment was in the view of many deliberately made to
reduce criticism of the Government to a minimum.

Within a year the National Council of Labour, through which
the T.U.C. had been able to exert strong political influence, was
augmented by the inclusion of delegates of the Co-operative Union
on an equal footing with the Labour Party and the T.U.C. This
had the effect of weakening the T.U.C. influence—which, in its
current lack of interest in politics, it did not greatly mind—and
also of making the body so unwieldy that its decisive power was
minimised.

Periodical reshuffles of the Government took place without serious consideration of the Labour Party views. In addition to Morrison's promotion to the Home Office, other changes included Tom Johnston to become Secretary of State for Scotland, Dalton to the Board of Trade, Attlee to have the additional responsibility of the Dominions Office, and Bevin and Morrison included in the War Cabinet. Two other notable events were the resignation of Greenwood, which mystified the Opposition, and the appointment of Stafford Cripps as Lord Privy Seal and Leader of the House of Commons, with a seat in the War Cabinet.

The last appointment caused many misgivings among Labour adherents. Cripps had done more than most to destroy Party unity in the years before the war, and his expulsion had been far longer and for more serious reasons than Bevan's. Few Labour M.P.s, or for that matter their Tory opponents, were much impressed by Cripps's work as ambassador to Russia, where increasing friendliness was inevitable when the Nazi enemy became common to both. Nor did M.P.s regard Cripps as a born House of Commons man. This was quickly proved and his Leadership of the House was probably the lowest point in a distinguished career. Churchill soon realised the fact and moved him outside the inner circles of the Government to the Ministry of Aircraft Production at a time when Beaverbrook had got the industry running at something close to perfection.

Conference matters during the war years reflected the standstill atmosphere. In 1942 Laski, on behalf of the National Executive, moved a motion calling for a planned democracy after the war, and Frank Pakenham (now the Earl of Longford) made a plea for a programme of nationalisation of all major industries and services, asking at the same time if there was going to be more Socialism even before the war ended. This militant call, which may be contrasted with the more genteel views expressed by the speaker since, brought no decision. The Conference was content to pass resolutions requiring no action till the war was over.

In view of the personality in charge of the nation's affairs and remembering the dangers to the nation's very existence which prevailed until the last weeks of the European War it is surprising that as much legislation of a purely Socialist nature was passed as was the fact. The White Paper of 1944, while not, of course, legislation, committed any future Government, either Labour or Tory, to a policy of taking Government action to ensure full employment—even to the acceptance of the principle of public ownership where a case on its merits could be made out. This was a fundamental change of Tory heart for which the Labour ministers must be solely credited.

Other items of progress, if minor, were useful. Bevin's Catering Wages Act cleaned up one of the most ill-paid trades in the country. Johnston's Highland electric power schemes have since transformed Northern Scotland. Dalton's Location of Industry Act helped to focus attention on the misery of the depressed areas of pre-war days. But no real effort was made to accelerate or approve the Beveridge Report, though it served as the blueprint for the post-war Labour Government. Here the suspicions of the trade unions played their part. A resolution for family allowances, one of the Beveridge proposals, was debated during a wartime Labour Conference. It was opposed by several trade union delegates, including Arthur Deakin. Their fear was the old and outmoded one of the trade unionist that a family allowance would be taken into account in wage negotiations.

A significant feature of wartime emergence was the independent attitude of the T.U.C. When war broke out the T.U.C. had been meeting at Bridlington. Fewer than 500 of the 659 delegates were able to attend, but the trivial contrary vote of two delegates on a resolution pledging the Government full support on the war effort was an accurate reflection of the general attitude among the organised workers at the time.

The Government, anxious to avoid the industrial troubles which broke out sporadically from the beginning to the end of the 1914–18 war, approached the T.U.C. to ensure industrial peace. Chamberlain instructed all Government departments to consult direct with the T.U.C. on all matters affecting the interests of trade unionists, thus raising the status of trade unionism to a peak and coincidentally depriving the Labour Party of some prestige as the sole watchdog of workers' interests.

As a result of this move the complicated and on the whole effective network of boards, committees, and councils which were organised to handle industrial matters was dominated by the T.U.C., with the other two parties concerned, the Government and the employers, accepting that T.U.C. policy took into consideration national interests as well as workers' welfare.

Once again, the Labour Party was somewhat in eclipse in these important developments, though the arrangements followed closely the ideas of Socialists of the past who had often found the unions obstructive during debates on Socialist policy. It was thus the T.U.C., and not the Labour Party, which could be semi-seriously described by a journalist addressing the T.U. Congress, "You have no longer any need to thunder; you have only to whisper, and ministers tremble and Field Marshals bend their knees." It was power which, to the unions' credit, did not corrupt, but it weakened the bonds with the political body.

The discipline which the T.U.C. was able to impose on its unions during the second world war weakened only in the case of the miners. By tradition the miners were a law unto themselves, while memories of the alleged treacheries of the 1926 General Strike and the years of unemployment of the thirties were still fresh. In addition, mining was perhaps the only depressed industry once the war potential was harnessed. The fall of France and the occupation of almost the whole of Europe meant that coal exports almost ceased, and this brought serious unemployment in the exporting areas of Durham, South Wales and parts of Yorkshire. Men sought work in arms plants and younger men joined the forces. Experienced colliers were tempted away by the high wages of the factories on war work. Belatedly the creation of the Ministry of Fuel and Power in 1942, with operational control of the mines, eased the situation, and a year later a national minimum wage lessened the growing discontent. The failure to secure the retention of miners in wartime had a serious effect when the post-war Labour Government nationalised the mines.

The smooth and conciliatory atmosphere prevailing in most other industries never emerged in the mining industry during the war. A National Negotiating Committee set up in 1943 had the doubtful distinction of never finding means of agreement on any question it was asked to consider. Neither the Labour Party nor the T.U.C. did much to help solve the fundamental impasse which existed. Bevin was never particularly interested in the miners, and the Labour leaders, more than necessarily anxious to observe the terms of the Coalition, refrained from siding with causes which on any just assessment would be considered as anti-Government and anti-employer.

Strikes and lock-outs were, of course, illegal after 1940 unless the Minister of Labour failed to take action within three weeks of a dispute being reported to him. In fact unofficial strikes were quite numerous during the war years, and an annual average of two million working days were lost, compared with more than four millions in World War I. Invariably, due to the official position of the T.U.C. in Government affairs, these disputes were condemned by the union leaders, and one had the bizarre situation that the strikers' only champions were the few Labour M.P.s taking an independent and Socialist line.

Underlying the uneasy relationship between the T.U.C. and the Labour Party during the period of the wartime Coalition Government was something deeper than the unionists' sense of power. Ever since Morrison had indicated in 1933 the trend of Labour's thought about the public ownership of "industries ripe for socialisation" both Bevin and Charles Dukes, the only names which really mattered in T.U.C. affairs, had resented the Labour Party's lack of enthusiasm for trade union direct participation in the management of a nationalised industry. By 1943 the T.U.C. felt strong enough to insist on its point, and it issued a *Report on Post-War Reconstruction* in which it was recommended that the governing boards of nationalised industries should include members with wide experience in the trade union movement, with the proviso that membership of the board would automatically result in the surrender of any trade union post or responsibility. The report was unanimously adopted by Congress in 1944. Willy-nilly the Labour Party had to agree to it; the principle was in fact followed in the nationalisation of the mines, the first industry to come under public ownership after 1945.

Wartime power tempted the trade unions towards an examination of policies which were traditionally narrow, but attractive purely because of the advantages to the union concerned. Thus there was a strong movement to regard favourably a manifesto of 120 large-scale employers advocating industrial self-government. This scheme lauded the advantages of capitalist monopolies in which the trade unionists concerned would have some kind of partnership with the employers as regards control. This was highly satisfactory to some reactionary trade union leaders who, like their ancestors of the early days of the movement, were solely concerned with the well-being of craftsmen and uninterested in the fate of other workers less well organised and less skilled. Quiet pressure and advice from Labour M.P.s dissuaded the T.U.C. from ever promoting this as a subject for serious discussion, and the T.U.C. 1944 report condemned control of industry by private groups. This was a service to the community and to the trade union movement for which the Labour Party has been insufficiently thanked. It is, unfortunately, one of the few examples of the development of trade union thought and policy during World War II.

The facts of the political situation in the closing months of the war were that none of the leaders of either Party realised the changing temper of the nation. Members of the Government had little time or inclination to get about the country, but M.P.s such as myself, who addressed large and enthusiastic meetings more and more frequently after the beginning of 1944, knew that the people had become more Socialist-minded than since the early nineteen-twenties. At the Labour Party Conferences of 1943 and 1944 delegates were preoccupied with ideas on post-war reconstruction on thoroughly Socialist lines, and despite the advice of the leaders to defer definite decisions until the war was won the Conferences rejected delay and insisted on some gesture.

The most important result was the formation of the Central Committee of Reconstruction with various sub-committees to consider and report on future policy. I was appointed chairman of the principal committee and of two of the sub-committees, and it may be justly claimed that their recommendations produced the framework of policy on which the 1945 election was won and the 1945 Government succeeded in putting through a massive programme of Socialist legislation.

The 1944 Conference marked a turning point in Labour Party affairs. By the time it ended the Party leaders were given a blueprint of the policy they could confidently present to the nation. It cannot be said that many of those in the Government showed great enthusiasm for it. Churchill's personality dominated them, and they were ready to leap to his defence as well as to infer that the nation would be best served by a continuance of the Coalition.

Ernest Bevin was a notable example of this. In a Conference debate on British policy in Greece, where the monarchy was supported by Britain in preference to the republican factions, Benstead, the able leader of the railwaymen, claimed that this was characteristic, not of the Churchill of 1940, but of the Churchill of 1926. He added that the union movement had stood loyally by the Minister of Labour throughout the war, but "we are not going to be hamstrung always; that is the negation of democracy".

Angrily Bevin sprang to the defence of Churchill, claiming that the decision on Greece was a Cabinet responsibility and not the Prime Minister's.

Nye Bevan was among the speakers who attacked Bevin bitterly, and although the Executive escaped defeat the mood of the Conference gave it ample warning that a continuance of the Coalition could easily split the Party quite as seriously as it unfortunately had been in 1931.

The leaders seemed unwilling to test the optimism and confidence of the rank and file. Herbert Morrison took the opportunity on four separate occasions to warn the House of Commons that the electoral register was imperfect, as indeed it was, but his subsequent comment was opinion rather than a reflection of fact. He said,

"There will be no difficulty about the Government and Parliament living happily together for a few months more."

Those extra months would have had to terminate before the end of November, 1945, because in October, 1944, the Prime Minister had stated that there would be no further prolongation of the Parliament Act. His acceptance of a minimum of three weeks' notice of an election instead of the normal seventeen days was purely a gesture, and did nothing to confound the general impression among both Tory and Labour M.P.s that there was every likelihood that Churchill would imitate Lloyd George after the 1918 Armistice and capitalise on victory with a snap election.

With the news of Hitler's death and the meeting of the Soviet and Allied armies on the Elbe it was clear that an early election was probable. Attlee, whose loyalty and patriotism had enabled him to accept without question that, although Deputy Prime Minister, he should work under Anthony Eden at the San Francisco Conference on the formation of the United Nations, took the precaution of extracting a promise from Churchill that Parliament would not be dissolved during his (Attlee's) absence in the U.S.A.

This was a wise precaution, for Churchill was under heavy pressure from a section of the Tories, encouraged by Lord Beaverbrook and Brendan Bracken, to announce victory in Europe and the date of the general election more or less simultaneously. The idea was to go to the country as a Social Reform Party, where a façade of social legislation culled from the milder proposals of the wartime Labour Party Conferences would augment the general enthusiasm for rewarding the victorious war leader and his Party.

When Attlee returned from San Francisco on May 18 a letter from the Prime Minister awaited him. It confirmed the suspicions of the Labour rank and file that the Labour Ministers were very ready to continue the Coalition.

"From talks I have had with you and your principal Labour colleagues," Churchill wrote, "I have gathered the impression that the Labour Party, instead of leaving the Government on the defeat of Germany, would be willing to continue the Coalition until the autumn. I have given the most careful and anxious thought to this suggestion and I regret to say that in its present form I cannot feel that it would be in the public interest."

The letter went on to suggest that the Coalition should continue until Japan was defeated. Churchill, aware that the atom bomb was ready and would be used on Japan, could reasonably estimate that the suggestion he put forward might mean an extension of the Coalition for a shorter period than the autumn date-line acceptable to his Labour ministers. To Attlee, with no knowledge of the existence or probable success of the atomic project, the proposal appeared like an extension of the Coalition for a year or more.

Churchill's letter came to Attlee on the eve of the 1945 Conference at Blackpool. During the week-end preceding it the proposals were discussed by the National Executive. Bevan and myself were among the minority convinced that Labour could win an election and that any extension of the Coalition was undesirable.

The majority, including Hugh Dalton and Harold Clay of the Transport Workers, one of Bevin's principal officers, evinced uncertainty and forebodings about the consequences of rejecting Churchill's proposal. Will Whiteley, the Labour Chief Whip, sensed the restive nature of the workers and servicemen. Commenting on the Churchill letter he said, "The lads will never agree. If you adopt his suggestions there'll be a split."

Attlee, who placed great reliance on Whiteley's judgment, was swayed by this terse comment as much as by the views of some of his more prominent colleagues. The Executive meeting ended with the resolve to decline Churchill's offer, although it could not be regarded as a decision altogether consistent with some of the views previously expressed.

In contrast, on the following day, the Party Conference was full of enthusiasm and confidence. Delegates showed no reluctance to enter the struggle, and a motion that the Coalition should be continued until Japan was defeated was overwhelmingly rejected. By this decision the Party was probably saved from a disaster similar to that of 1931. Attlee thereupon informed Churchill that "a fair and just solution would be an election in the autumn".

This surprised Churchill, who had by then read reports of pre-Conference speeches made by Morrison and Albert Alexander, both of whom claimed that an early election was unwanted and unlikely. Dalton and Ernie Bevin had also let the Prime Minister know that they were in favour of a continuance of the Coalition. Both men were confident that they were influential enough to mould the views of the rank and file. Militant speeches from delegates at the Conference must have tardily convinced them of their inability to sense the change in public opinion which had been in evidence since 1944.

Before the Conference ended, news arrived that Churchill had seen the King and tendered the Government's resignation. Parliament was to be dissolved on June 15 and polling day was fixed for July 5.

The Conference immediately went into private session to discuss the financial situation. Money was short, and £250,000 had to be found in a matter of a few weeks. Membership of the Party had dropped to 265,000 as compared with a pre-war total of 447,000. About three out of four trade unionists had not troubled to "contract in" to the Labour Party.

The facts were not reassuring. But the spirit was inspiring. The cheering which followed Ellen Wilkinson, the Conference chairman, when she said forcefully but quietly, "The Labour Party will fight— and fight for power," was as great as anything ever experienced in the history of the Labour movement. It was inspired by the scent of victory rather than any evidence of its practical probability. But it impressed even the solemn-faced leaders on the platform. They were having greatness thrust upon them.

13

THE PINNACLE OF POWER

1945–1950

In the final hours of the 1945 Labour Party Conference enthusiasm for the coming election had encouraged some of the delegates to demand a programme of sweeping legislation in pursuance of Socialist aims. On behalf of the Executive I was asked to speak against a Yorkshire resolution that, in the event of the Party winning the election, it would nationalise land, banks, all large-scale financial undertakings, fuel and power, large scale building, heavy industry, and all major forms of transport.

It was difficult to restrain the advocates of unrealistic and over-ambitious schemes of this kind, though eventually I succeeded in convincing the Conference that we should restrict our first schemes to coal and transport.

Nye Bevan, despite his rebellious activities before 1945, and insisting that his differences with the leadership no longer existed, whipped up the fervour with emotional views. Our aim, he said, was the complete political extinction of the Tory Party and twenty-five years of Labour Government.

Bevan was elected to the National Executive, coming fourth in the constituencies' poll after myself, Morrison, and Dalton. His election had the effect of qualifying his criticisms and kept some of his adherents under control.

An involuntary electioneering ally of Labour in 1945 was Churchill himself. His correspondence with Attlee over the question of the future of the Coalition, published before the election, gave the impression of indecent hurry to return to Party politics and to dispense with the services of colleagues who had so loyally served under him during the war.

Presumably his genuine dread of a Labour administration pre-siding over the destiny of the British Empire, recalled by his charge that Labour was unfit to govern, discoloured his judgment and moved him, in a broadcast on June 4, 1945, to say:

"I declare to you that no Socialist system can be established without a political police. They would have to fall back on some sort of Gestapo, no doubt very humanely directed in the first instance."

In the public mind a possible candidate for the rôle of a British Himmler might be the man responsible to Parliament for the police forces during most of the war: Herbert Morrison, the Home Secretary. The vision of the man known to millions of Londoners and blitzed provincial towns as "Our 'Erbert" strutting around in jackboots was too much for the electorate. The Churchill warning became subject for mirth. In Britain a political pronouncement which sounds ludicrous is a verdict of political suicide by the speaker. So it proved for Churchill, who in those few seconds of a foolish outburst undid much of the honour he had attained as the nation's champion.

Churchill's tactical policy again was misjudged when he publicly announced his alarm about the influence of Harold Laski on the Parliamentary Labour Party. Laski was chairman of the Party Executive. Perhaps he regarded the position as carrying advisory duties greater than this essentially formal office justified. He stated that though Attlee might attend the Potsdam Conference with Churchill nothing decided there would necessarily be ratified by the Labour Party. It would have to come before the Executive for approval or disapproval.

Whether Churchill genuinely feared a potential weakening of Parliament's supremacy or had devised a personal query of political innocence the result was the same. His series of grave and ominous letters of enquiry to Attlee were answered by clever and cogent replies which once more made a Tory canard seem absurd.

But errors of judgment by Labour's opponents were merely fortuitous aids in a campaign won before it began. An overwhelming proportion of the country was anti-Tory, and a sufficient number of them were ready to be pro-Labour.

The declaration of the 1945 election results was a unique occasion. Because of the necessity to include the forces' vote from all theatres of war the votes were not counted for three weeks. Then, on July 26, the flood of results began. Salford South was the first result declared—a Labour gain. Within minutes more Lancashire results came through: with more Labour gains. Soon the first of the ministers in the Caretaker Government knew he had suffered defeat. Harold Macmillan was one of the thirteen ministers to experience defeat that day. He had lost Stockton by 8,664 votes. Before midmorning, when the eagerly awaited results for Birmingham came through, with ten seats won there by Labour, the nation knew that

Labour had gained a striking victory and obtained the largest number of votes for a single Party in British political history.

Churchill tendered his resignation to the King that evening. Fifteen minutes after he left the Palace Attlee was Prime Minister. He had spent most of the day at Transport House, listening to the results along with Bevin and Morrison. All three had been elected with resounding majorities for London constituencies. Attlee, as was his invariable custom at times of crisis or historic moment, remained quiet and poker-faced. Morrison was understandably elated that his forecasts had been proved true. Bevin was dazed, and later told the Press, when asked for a comment, that he was speechless.

Labour received more than 12 million votes as compared with the 9.2 millions of the Tories. Liberal Nationals were dismissed with a contemptuous 750,000, and the Liberals had 2.2 millions. The Labour poll was, in fact, within 100,000 or so of the grand total for all other Parties. In terms of House of Commons strength Labour, including the three I.L.P. members, had 396 seats, compared with 200 for the Tories. The rest were of no significance for either Party. There were sixteen Independents, thirteen Liberal Nationals, a dozen Liberals, two Communists, and one Commonwealth member.

Behind the scenes, controversy in Labour ranks began even while the victory celebrations took place.

The acerbities centred around Attlee, though he had no part in them. Attlee had returned from Potsdam on the eve of the declaration of the election results. The growing belief that Labour had won aroused discussion of who would hold office and in particular who should be Prime Minister. The latter was a theoretical and wholly academic discussion, for there was really no alternative to Attlee. Nevertheless, there were those who required, for personal reasons or for the more understandable one of safeguarding the Party against another MacDonald régime, to be the arbiters on leadership.

The other candidates named by these critics of Attlee were Morrison, Greenwood, and Dalton. It is doubtful if any of them was anxious to contest the issue with Attlee, but this had not prevented Laski and his friends from proposing that in the event of a Labour victory Attlee should defer an audience with the King for forty-eight hours while the Parliamentary Party debated the leadership question. Bevin, who had always disliked Laski intensely, was furious and named the persons he described as the trouble-makers.

Stafford Cripps as
Chancellor of the
Exchequer, 1949.

Nye Bevan at his
most persuasive.

Prime Minister Clement Attlee at vesting ceremony, nationalisation of the Coal Industry. Emanuel Shinwell in the chair, and from left to right: Herbert Morrison, Arthur Greenwood, Ernest Bevin, Nye Bevan, Stafford Cripps, Hugh Gaitskell, and Sir Donald Ferguson.

New York meeting on American proposals for German re-armament 1950–51. Left to right: Ernest Bevin, Emanuel Shinwell, Morris Schuman, Jules Moch, Dean Acheson, General Marshall.

In the event nothing came of the Laski manoeuvre, but Attlee could not fail to note the situation. It was noticeable that he studiously avoided consulting Laski in any way on the selection of his Government.

So far as Attlee consulted anybody, he relied on the judgment of Ernie Bevin and Will Whiteley, the Chief Whip. Decisions were made quickly, because Attlee was due back at Potsdam. Attlee's experience of the effectiveness of the small War Cabinet influenced him to appoint an unofficial inner Cabinet within the larger body— the latter totalled nineteen—an effective means of maintaining a firm grip on the reins of Government.

This inner group consisted of Herbert Morrison as Lord President, in charge of co-ordination and the programme of legislation; Arthur Greenwood as Lord Privy Seal, supervising the social services; Hugh Dalton as Chancellor of the Exchequer; and Ernest Bevin as Foreign Minister. Attlee held the office of Minister of Defence as well as Prime Minister.

It was a curiously ill-assorted group yet paradoxically one of potential efficiency as a team. Morrison was hardly an intimate friend of the Prime Minister. Greenwood's record was not a testimonial to his ability to face a busy session: indeed Attlee dismissed him in 1947 on the pretext of Greenwood's age and re-placed him by Addison, ten years older than Greenwood himself. Bevin, though a loyal and admiring friend of Attlee, was ill-tempered because his ambition to be Chancellor of the Exchequer was thwarted. Dalton, whose declared ambition to be Prime Minister had been tempered with modest dreams of the Foreign Office, was similarly rebellious. Yet Attlee recognised that under supervision the Government would succeed and rivalries among the ministers might well enhance their personal effort, while guarantee-ing that his personal position was secure and he could remain the sole, unassailable manager of affairs.

There were few appointments to cause alarm among those who feared that the "wild men of Blackpool" would destroy the British way of life, neither did any create dissension in Labour circles. Perhaps the least expected appointments were of Nye Bevan and myself in view of our unofficial opposition during the war years.

The "Red Flag" was sung on the first day of the new Parliament: expressing the natural exuberance of 396 Labour M.P.s, and a challenge to disgruntled Tories who had half-heartedly struck up "For He's a Jolly Good Fellow" when Churchill entered the Chamber. For the Government the honeymoon was soon over. The Cabinet was gravely embarrassed when, on August 21, Presi-

M

dent Truman abruptly terminated the Lease-Lend agreement. They
had to find sufficient currency to purchase food and raw materials,
fulfil commitments for the rehabilitation of Europe, to maintain
occupation forces costing more than £200 million a year, while
many ships on the high seas with Lease-Lend grain had to be
diverted from the United Kingdom and ordered to India, Burma,
and Malaya where famine was imminent.

In the circumstances Dalton advised the Government to apply
for a substantial loan from the United States. The nation would
have been staggered at an abrupt acceleration of rationing so soon
after the end of hostilities. Dalton was an economist of the conventional Keynesian school and regarded a loan as essential in
what he mistakenly believed would be a temporary shortage of
liquid finance. Nye Bevan and myself argued that a year or eighteen
months of belt-tightening would in the long run be more acceptable
to the people than a temporary relaxation followed by further
austerity but this view was rejected. Unfortunately the loan was
all too quickly expended and the austerity we had envisaged
occurred and redoubled in force by 1947.

In the House the new Government had a surprisingly easy
passage. Not only did the large Labour majority ensure the smooth
handling of the Government's programme, but the Tories were
demoralised and incoherent. The early nationalisation legislation
for the Bank of England and the fuel and power industries caused
little trouble. The Tories were remarkably acquiescent about the
Bank. As regards the coal mines, they knew that the owners, who
had neglected the mines for six years and had exploited many to
extinction, were relieved to abandon private ownership of enter-
prises which could only be run at a loss.

Electricity and gas, nationalised later, were public utilities already
under partial public control, as were the cable and wirless companies
and the airlines. Nationalisation of transport only created difficulties because it included control of road haulage, the only section
which showed any profit. The iron and steel industry was the final
item in the nationalisation programme, but members of the Government were not unanimous about the scheme, and only the desire
to finalise the nationalisation programme for which the Government
had a public mandate saw the legislation, but not the complete
operation of the Act, carried through.

The 1945 Government's other historic contributions to the modern
state were the varied developments and innovations in the social
services. James Griffiths piloted through the National Insurance
Act which was basically the plan of the Liberal Lord Beveridge.

Bevan, after much argument with the medical profession, scored a great triumph with his National Health Service legislation, but was not so successful with the housing programme.

Blemishes on this otherwise satisfying picture of Labour's fitness to govern were in the sphere of foreign affairs and defence. Bevin, who originally had preferred the Treasury, soon created the image of the great negotiator. His reputation in the field of trade unionism was, of course, second to none, but his success was attained because of numerical strength and his dictatorial authority. The requisite diplomacy needed in foreign affairs was not in evidence. Faced with the obstinacy of the Soviet Union and recognising that Stalin was impressed only by big battalions Bevin turned from patient diplomacy to an alliance with the only nation whose power was commensurate with Russia—the U.S.A.. His readiness to adopt General Marshall's Plan to aid Europe, and the eventual birth of N.A.T.O., is to Bevin's credit, but it also ensured the inevitable East-West split and the deterioration of Britain and her Commonwealth into satellites of America.

Foreign Office policy eventually aroused widespread criticism in the Party. Bevin's Middle East activities brought matters to a head. He had for years been preoccupied with the misery of the Egyptian fellaheen and deprived classes throughout the Arab countries. He regarded these unhappy people as ripe for organisation, whereupon they would be everlastingly grateful to the man and the country which had organised them. Thus Bevin's policy evolved into support of the masses in the Middle East, and automatically he became anti-Israel because of his failure to solve the Palestine problem.

In the autumn of 1946 criticism of Bevin was pin-pointed when twenty-one Labour M.P.s sent a manifesto to Attlee, asserting that the Government had lost the initiative in foreign affairs which was expected by British democracy.

In tone the manifesto was largely anti-American, claiming that the Government was unduly concerned about Soviet zones of influence in Europe but unconcerned about the extension of U.S. military bases. There was criticism of the recognition of Franco Spain, of military support to the reactionary forces in Greece, of encouragement of capitalistic reconstruction in Germany, of the continuance of conscription, and of our dependence on the U.S.A. both economically and as regards defence.

It was a Left attack of the kind that occurs periodically, but the signatories included moderates like James Callaghan and Woodrow Wyatt, as well as the more expected ones of Michael Foot, Jennie Lee, and Richard Crossman.

Within a month of this attack the assaults on Bevin were transferred to the Chamber. In a debate on the King's Speech Crossman moved an amendment demanding "Socialist planning on foreign affairs, collaboration with all nations (including the U.S.S.R.) and groups, in order to secure a Socialist policy". There were some speeches in support, and although no attempt was made to force a division, the incident was a warning to Attlee not to ignore Party sentiment on foreign policy or about Bevin, a formidable trade union leader rather than an experienced Labour politician.

Bevin's own attitude to the M.P.s ranged on the benches behind him became less tolerant. He failed to understand Morrison's purpose in giving Labour M.P.s increased independence by suspending the Standing Orders which had prohibited votes against Party decisions. He was suspicious of the new style Labour M.P.s, many of them middle class and professional men. Most of all he deprecated the fact that only 120 M.P.s—less than one third—were sponsored by the unions. He regarded this as a poor return for the £52,000 contributed to the Labour Party's 1945 income of £83,000, and the £111,000 given for the 1945 election campaign.

Bevin's genuine bewilderment at the way a democratic Party conducted its affairs was shown in a speech defending his foreign policy at the 1947 Conference. He referred to the criticism by Labour M.P.s while he was in the United States and unable to answer. He insisted that his purpose in Washington was not to discuss foreign policy but to obtain cereals and to help Dalton to ease the dollar bill for our occupation zone of Germany.

"On the very day I was trying to get the agreement with the Americans to stop the bread ration going down, on that very day I was stabbed in the back," he shouted. "I am emphasising this because those concerned never went to the Government to find out what it was they were asking me to do, and I do say that if you are to expect loyalty from ministers, the ministers—however much they may make mistakes—have the right to expect loyalty in return. I grew up in the trade union, you see, and I have never been used to this kind of thing."

The trade union mass vote at the Conference would have assured Bevin that he had nothing to fear so far as Conference discussions were concerned. Although much of the criticism, whether based on motives of pacifism or genuine alarm at the policy Bevin was pursuing, was troublesome, Bevin could rely on his "stab in the back" protest calling most of the recalcitrant M.P.s to heel. The result was that the *Keep Left* movement retired to brood and consider the next move.

Its dilemma was increased with the more militant tone of international Communism, symbolised by the formation of the Cominform, from 1947 onwards. While the Labour Party was content to ignore crypto-Communists in its membership, the unions, prodded by Bevin's admirer and disciple, Arthur Deakin, began a soul-searching analysis of the danger within their own ranks. The General Council warned all unions and many heeded it, either dismissing Communist officials or exercising strict discipline over them.

The result was not only a remarkable era of obedience and self-sacrifice by the majority of the unions in the austerity period of wage restraint and steady inflation, but an easier time for subsequent Tory governments. The activities of the Electrical Trades Union, one of the few which ignored the T.U.C.'s advice after 1947, indicate the sort of industrial strife which might have been more frequent right up to the present time.

Bevin's prestige and power which he enjoyed among the trade unions and in the country misled some ministers to consider him a desirable replacement for Attlee, against whom there were periodical but secretive plots of revolt.

Dalton and Cripps, facing the economic crisis of 1947 which necessitated an autumn Budget, preferred to ignore their own defects in failing to forestall the crisis by laying the blame at the feet of the Prime Minister, who was not, in Cripps's view, granting sufficient authority to the economic departments, or appointing a powerful Minister of Economic Co-ordination. Together they launched a scheme to replace Attlee with Bevin, ignoring the fact of Bevin's loyalty to Attlee, save only, perhaps, to prevent Morrison being installed in 10 Downing Street.

Bevin's foreign policy was again under attack at the 1948 Conference, from the leftists, whose major spokesman was Koni Zilliacus. He moved an amendment to a resolution approving the Marshall Plan, and added his conception of a Socialist foreign policy. Although the amendment was overwhelmingly rejected the number of abstentions, representing a million and a half votes, indicated that in both the unions and the constituencies Bevin's position was by no means unassailable. Soon afterwards Zilliacus, along with L. J. Solley, was expelled from the Party for extreme leftist sympathies, an action in harmony with the increasing suspicions of fellow-traveller factions when the cold war intensified. By 1949 the attacks on Bevin were weakening. Several motions demanding positive action by Britain to minimise the threat of war, including the fostering of trade with the Iron Curtain countries, were swept aside by overwhelming majorities.

Thus almost all the points of controversy which spread beyond the confines of the Commons and Government circles were concerned with foreign affairs and defence—the traditional ingredients of Party controversy for reasons either of conscience or political theory. Underlying both was the fundamental schism between the unions and the political body, accentuated in this instance by the fact that a prominent trade union leader was responsible for political action.

On the domestic front, despite the enormous problems of re-organising a bankrupt country for peace-time effort in a world short of food and everything consistent with civilised life, the nation showed wonderful self-discipline, and evidence of discontent was sparse. The fact that the Government was tackling its huge election programme efficiently and in a practical manner was recognised. The characteristic sense of fair play influenced most people, even those opposed to Labour, to wait and see. Even with this tolerance, few people could appreciate the dimensions of the difficulties which arose. The facts behind the fuel crisis of 1946-7 are typical.

Nationalisation of the mines became the prototype for subsequent legislation on public ownership. The miners were exerting strong pressure for urgent action, and it was clear that without urgent implementation of this particular election promise the discontent in the coal industry might become serious.

It was immediately apparent, as in the case of other industries, that though the principle of nationalisation had been advocated for half a century there was little but generalised ideas on how it should be achieved. As Minister of Fuel, and informed by Attlee in a personal statement to me that my immediate task was to transfer the mines to public ownership, it was impossible to arrange for vesting day in under eighteen months. The target day was set as January 1, 1947, and this, of course, was met.

The coal crisis, which reached its peak during the abnormal winter conditions of January 1947, existed from pre-war days. The war years accentuated the problem. By 1945 men were leaving the pits at the rate of 70,000 a year, while industrial demand for fuel, principally from the electricity generating stations, was increasing at a phenomenal rate.

Attlee was advised in October of 1946 that a coal shortage was likely. He thereupon appointed Dalton to preside over a committee consisting of George Isaacs, Minister of Labour; Alfred Barnes, Minister of Transport; myself as Minister of Fuel; and permanent officials of the Ministries involved.

Dalton, for reasons known only to himself, did not consider it necessary to call a committee meeting for ten days, by which time the shortage had become acute. The problem was not one of production—though this was far below estimates, and in contrast with assurances of increased output by miners' leaders—but of lack of transport. At the end of November 309,000 tons of coal were stocked at the pitheads and the disposal areas of the open-cast sites. Frozen stocks continued to rise, while supplies at power stations and factories dropped alarmingly. Promised fleets of lorries proved to be non-existent; much railway rolling stock was unworkable through shortages of manpower and locomotives, and railwaymen refused to work at week-ends.

By the New Year coal stocks awaiting transport had risen to over 700,000 tons, while supplies at the power stations continued to decline.

The Government lapsed into a phase of indecisive action. Vague plans for getting locomotives back from France, locating fleets of lorries and bringing men for the mines from Northern Ireland were of no value for the immediate crisis. Ruthless plans such as clearing the railway system for coal traffic in a similar manner to that organised for troops and munitions prior to D-day were shelved as unworkable. Cripps, who had inaugurated a national campaign for increased productivity in the House during November, advised cutting coal to industry by 40 per cent (except in the case of coke ovens and steel works) and severely restricting electricity and gas supplies to industry. Meanwhile, he insisted on an increase of electricity equipment and open-cast plant for export. Dalton wanted the B.B.C. to close down at 11 p.m. to send the nation to bed.

By the time the severe blizzard of January 30 burst upon the country close on 900,000 tons of coal was "in the pipeline". It was literally frozen there, and the climatic disaster became an economic and social catastrophe.

Whatever individual responsibility existed, there was no doubt that defects in co-operation at the top level weakened the efforts of those ministers in the departments concerned. Morrison, officially responsible for co-ordination of Government effort, was ill in hospital with thrombosis. Attlee, having appointed Dalton, no doubt expected his committee to operate effectively. Cripps, in complete charge of the economy, might have selected an alternative to ruthless deprivation of supplies as the negative solution of a coal shortage which did not, in fact, exist.

Cripps, however, fortified those who appeared blameless for the fuel crisis, thereby avoiding any blame for the nation's general

economic situation through his own policies. His remedy was a
change at the Ministry of Fuel, resisted by Attlee. But when the
legislation on coal and electricity supply for which the Ministry
of Fuel was responsible was completed, Attlee decided that the
minister would no longer be in the Cabinet. He asked me to accept
the post of Secretary for War, and left me in no doubts that he
was being hard pressed to remove me from the Ministry of Fuel.
Reluctantly, and only after persuasion by several colleagues, I
accepted the War Office, whereupon Hugh Gaitskell, who was
Parliamentary Secretary in the Ministry, became the minister.
Ostensibly this was, in the opinion of Attlee, no longer a major post
in the Government, but it was significant in advancing the career of
a Cripps protégé. As later events indicated, it was also an early
move by Attlee to sift through the recruits for the succession. He
had not forgotten his fortuitous progress to the leadership, suddenly
opened up by Lansbury's resignation. After fifteen years in office
there were indications of contemplated retirement. But he was
resolved that his successor should be of his own choice.

Both Bevin and Cripps were ailing men and unlikely to be
available for leadership extending for years ahead. These men he
respected, though confessing that Cripps's judgment was sometimes
at fault, but there were others whose capabilities he questioned: he
was determined they should not succeed him.

One whose high ambitions were no secret was Hugh Dalton, who
had foolishly spoiled whatever chances he had. His indiscretion
on the eve of the interim Budget of 1947 had the important sequel
of elevating Sir Stafford Cripps to the Exchequer. Though Dalton
was, after a period of repentance, appointed as Chancellor of the
Duchy of Lancaster his disclosure of Budget secrets had finally
terminated all his hopes and the several intrigues associated with
them. The incident also enabled Cripps to run the national economy
in his own fashion, and with little regard either for Conference
decisions, his own election promises, or his colleagues' views. Because of the vital part economics played in every facet of the
country's internal and external life at the time, the date of the 1950
election, and the policy on which it was fought, were really a reflection of Cripps's policies.

At the Conference of 1949 a new policy statement, *Labour Be-
lieves in Britain,* was produced and approved. It was mainly a
continuance of the 1945 programme—the unfinished business. But
the election manifesto was entitled *Let Us Win Through Together*
—virtually an invitation to the electorate to approve the Cripps
economic policy. Attlee appeared to make the decision on the

election date without consulting others, though he undoubtedly enjoyed the advice of Cripps. He went to Sandringham during the New Year holiday period and the result was the surprise announcement of a general election on February 23, 1950—more than six weeks ahead.

Such long notice was a calculated risk. The new Representation of the People Act, which altered all but eighty of the old constituencies, was a gamble, which in the event proved unfortunate for the Labour movement.

14

DEFEAT AND DISSENSION

1950–1955

The 1950 election was a subdued and rather colourless affair, the only notable event being the Tory Party's new façade with its image more to the left and bringing a semblance of social reform into its programme.

The electorate was confused by the sober attitude of both Parties and showed little enthusiasm for the campaign. The candidates, however, by sheer weight of numbers created more clamour than in any election of the century. The 1,868 candidates seeking election in 625 constituencies made it a record for a British general election.

For the first time since Keir Hardie sat in Parliament the I.L.P. had few candidates and no hope of victory. James Maxton, the I.L.P.'s most brilliant orator, who had led the organisation in its last years of effective life, had died in 1946. No prominent personalities remained to carry the banner of revolt. Several advocates of the I.L.P.'s special brand of Socialism had already joined the Labour Party.

Labour candidates enjoyed a more favourable position than in any previous election. It was to be fought on fairer terms; legislation had come into force which controlled campaign expenditure and restricted the numbers of cars to be used on polling day.

Although the Parties had carefully prepared their election programmes the contest was fought on the slogans of the two principal leaders. Attlee's theme was "Fair shares for all"; Churchill's, "Set the people free." Despite the apparent clash of policy inherent in these slogans both leaders seemed aware of the close identity of view embodied in their respective foreign and domestic policy statements which might lead to a stalemate. Both Attlee and Churchill frowned on those unwanted candidates who were regarded as embarrassing allies. Attlee attacked the Communists and near-Communists who were contesting many seats. Churchill indulged in a series of captious letters to Clement Davies, then leading the large army of Liberal candidates, complaining that Liberal intervention on this scale was a policy of "fantastic vote splitting".

The fears of stalemate were confirmed when the results were known. Labour won 315 seats with 617 candidates, the Tories 299 with their 624, and the Liberals suffered a most shattering electoral defeat when only nine of their 475 candidates were returned. Two Irish Nationalists made up the Commons total.

The Labour Party could find a modicum of satisfaction in the results. On a higher percentage poll and a larger electorate their total vote was 13.2 millions, which was ahead of the Tory and National Liberal total of 12.5 millions. But the increased vote could not disguise the probable embarrassments that a tiny overall Parliamentary majority of six would inevitably create. Not only would the Labour Government be hamstrung, but the situation was fraught with danger for the democratic system of traditional Parliamentary administration.

When the barriers of Party politics were weakened both Attlee and Churchill were capable of finding a statesmanlike identity of interest. But when motivated by an anxiety to woo the electorate, the policy of one Party becomes a rough replica of the other, and when the strength of the Government is merely a fraction greater than that of the ostensibly defeated Parliamentary Party, democracy is obviously facing danger.

The result of the 1950 election, reflecting the political view of a society in which the classes were believed to be slowly merging, was a phenomenon recognised as a danger signal to a political system admired throughout the world, and copied, more or less, by much of it. Of course, even with a bare majority of six, Attlee had to accept the responsibility of accepting the country's mandate. But unlike the Liberals in the early years of the century there were for Attlee no allies, no Lib.-Labs. to call upon in an emergency; not even the situation of the minority Labour Governments of the inter-war years. Labour was on its own and without the Parliamentary strength the responsibilities entailed.

In the event, the formidable difficulties of the task were increased by spectacular and violent disagreements among the Party leaders. With an overall majority of six, such dissensions, however genuine the motives of the disputants, inevitably courted disaster.

The task which faced the new Government was aggravated by a world situation of considerable gravity. In the previous autumn news of an experimental atomic explosion in Russia was announced, thus minimising the sense of security that American monopoly of the weapon had created. Communist domination of China was completed. The birth of the Republic of India had been accompanied by serious upheaval through racial and religious differences with Pakistan. The impact of the N.A.T.O. Treaty, which came into force in the previous August, was forcibly conveyed to the British people with the arrival of U.S. bombers at their Norfolk bases—a relief to those who appreciated the deterioration in East-West relationships but an ominous sign of the possibility, even the probability, of war—a situation which was threatened when North Korean troops advanced into South Korea in June, and when United States forces went into action.

The external problems which beset the Government, bedevilled by its small majority and the furious activities of the Tory Opposition, which abandoned all gestures of statesmanship in its endeavour to score Party points, were emphasised by internal troubles.

Attlee had lost two colleagues he regarded as among his ablest ministers. Cripps resigned as Chancellor of the Exchequer in October, 1950, and, seeking in vain an amelioration of his illness, soon retired from public life. Bevin, who, with obstinate courage and tenacity, struggled with his Foreign Office duties at a time when they would have sorely tried the fittest of men, left office in February, 1951, shortly before his death.

Hugh Gaitskell succeeded Stafford Cripps at the Treasury as "an experiment"; the words Attlee used when he asked me to discuss the subject with him. I had suggested Morrison on grounds of his seniority and because such an appointment would cause less resentment among those colleagues who considered themselves capable of tackling the nation's financial problems. The "experiment" was undoubtedly based on assurances by Cripps that Gaitskell was the one most likely to succeed. He had previously advised his appointment to the Ministry of Fuel and later on as Economic Secretary. The appointment produced a formidable result, affecting the Party's future. It profoundly disturbed Nye Bevan, who, in length of service and as a minister senior to Gaitskell, considered he was due for promotion. In the view of a considerable section of the Party, Bevan was regarded as a probable heir to the leadership when Attlee decided to retire.

Bevan realised that the Chancellor of the Exchequer would be a key figure in the new Government, for finance had become an even more important factor in Government policy than in the difficult years from 1945 to 1950. Shortly before Cripps resigned the Government announced that expansion of the defence programme, prepared at the Ministry of Defence, would cost £3,600 million—

a figure which, Attlee told the House, represented the maximum which could be found without resorting to the drastic expedients of a war economy.

The programme, involving what was then a substantial figure, was based on the result of discussions with the service chiefs: Sir William Slim, Chief of the Imperial General Staff; Lord Fraser, the First Sea Lord; and Sir John Slessor, Marshal of the Royal Air Force. At the Ministry of Defence it was considered unreal to estimate defence expenditure on an annual basis, and so the figure was envisaged on a three-year plan. Members of the Government had misgivings about an increase in military strength but the programme was strongly supported by Ernest Bevin, who as Foreign Secretary had with myself attended the Conference of the North Atlantic Council in Brussels in December, 1950. A decision to ask President Truman to appoint an American as Supreme Commander carried with it an agreement that Britain must increase its divisions in West Germany in order to convince the U.S.A. that Britain was pulling her full weight.

The British decision to increase her military strength directly resulted in the appointment of General Eisenhower to take over the control of European forces as a barrier against Communist penetration. American setbacks in North Korea had meanwhile caused the United Nations to endorse Allied action in that area, and Britain prepared to honour her commitments. In consequence defence estimates had to be revised. Service chiefs were requested to prepare plans, based on what were considered to be calculated risks. In their view a minimum arms programme to provide adequate defence came to £6,000 million for the three-year period.

Shortly after the issue of a White Paper describing the revised defence programme, Attlee made his Cabinet changes on January 17, 1951. The most notable was the transference of Bevan from the Ministry of Health to the Ministry of Labour. By any standard this was demotion for one of the outstanding personalities of the Labour movement, who had patently proved his abilities in the administration of the National Health Service. Not only was Bevan being sidetracked into a post hitherto handled by George Isaacs, a reliable, though not spectacular, minister, but it was evident that in the Budget proposals already being formulated by Gaitskell essential items in the social services must be abandoned in favour of defence expenditure, and that Bevan's social services might be a leading victim if he no longer held a senior Cabinet post where his views could predominate.

The combination of divergent views on policy and of personal dislike was fertile ground for quarrels among the two ministers which would almost certainly cause a split throughout the Party. Forebodings among their colleagues were minimised in the early weeks of 1951 when it was remembered that in the previous Government Bevan had eventually admitted that the country's defences would have to be increased. In conversations with his colleagues he had indicated tolerance about the problem by saying that rearmament should be approached with restraint, not with enthusiasm.

But Gaitskell, residuary legatee of Cripps's policy, realised that he must now find an additional £38 million for the health services, which was one of the largest items of increased civil expenditure, offsetting his hopes of meeting most of the increased defence expenditure by varied prunings and economies.

Bevan's principal ally was Harold Wilson, President of the Board of Trade, who preferred to cut expenditure on defence rather than on the health services. Bevan freely ventilated his opinions about Party principles, and poured contempt on Gaitskell's excuse that his proposed charges for dentures and spectacles would help to finance a modest increase in pensions.

When the dispute came into the open Attlee was not available to exert restraint. He was in hospital. Bevan, abandoning any pretence to moderation, gave fair warning that he would carry the controversy to the point of resignation.

The Budget was duly presented to Parliament in the form originally planned by Gaitskell. Morrison reported to Attlee of the imminent trouble when the Budget debate was due to take place, and the Prime Minister, from his sick bed, did his best to forestall the crisis.

He sent a message expressing the hope that ministers would bear in mind the effect on the fortunes of the Party before any of them took a serious step, and he added that it was most unusual for a minister to resign on a Budget issue. He recalled that one minister who had done so, Lord Randolph Churchill, had never recovered his political fortunes thereafter. His final words were a serious warning, and an accurate forecast. He stressed that Labour could hardly hope to win the subsequent election if a split occurred; as a result the Tories might remain in office for a very long time.

The uneasy waiting period lasted until April 19, when Bevan warned his colleagues that if the second reading of the Bill amending the National Health Service led to a division he would not vote in favour of it, and if it were carried he would resign. On April 23 Bevan and Wilson announced their resignations. Attlee had done his utmost to discover some method of compromise. Even an offer of modifying the notorious charges on spectacles and dentures failed to mollify Bevan.

Nobody in the Party gained from this dispute, though Bevan's loss was not as serious as it might have been. Unlike the example of Lord Randolph Churchill, Bevan's fortunes steadily recovered. Within a short time he was undisputed deputy leader of the Party. Without much doubt, exercising restraint, and with his undoubted ability, Nye Bevan would have attained the leadership if he had lived.

In a surprisingly quiet and rather ineffective speech on his resignation Bevan made no criticism of the policy of increased defences. He merely denied the possibility of the envisaged programme being implemented. His real sentiments were in evidence to the Commons when in debate he stabbed an accusing finger towards the back of Gaitskell, who was, of course, sitting on the Front Bench, and said, "There are too many economists at the Treasury, and now we have the added misfortune of having an economist in the Chancellor himself."

Considering the dramatic impact of the resignation of two senior ministers (as well as one well-known if minor minister, John Freeman, Parliamentary Secretary to the Ministry of Suppy) the practical effects were surprisingly small on the Party and the country.

There was the gesture of one letter of protest, signed by four members of the Executive—Mrs. Barbara Castle, Tom Driberg, Ian Mikardo, and Nye Bevan—complaining about the alleged slant of opinion in an official statement issued by the Executive which was said to favour a Government, rather than a Party, view. A few Labour M.P.s abstained when the spectacle and dental clause came before the House; only three members voted against it. In the trade union movement confirmation of which side the unions were on came from the Scottish T.U.C. Bevan was due to address their Congress at the end of April. The invitation was sent to Gaitskell instead.

The effect on Party morale was, of course, serious. Parliamentary duties were difficult enough, with the Tories sniping and harrying at every opportunity, and the tragic farce of sick M.P.s being brought by ambulance in order to avoid Government defeat. It was clear that another election could not long be delayed.

More troubles were imminent. Early in May, Persia announced that the oil industry was to be nationalised and the refinery at Abadan taken over. The Persian leader, Mossadeq, was not the type of man to heed normal diplomatic negotiation, and it was realised that British lives were in danger. Morrison had shortly before taken over the Foreign Office from Bevin, and was not proving completely at ease in his new post. The Foreign Office experts considered military preparations advisable as a precaution, but the service chiefs advised the Ministry of Defence that it would take at least six weeks to mount an adequate force off Abadan. All the Government could do was play for time and ensure that sufficient craft were available to evacuate British subjects should danger be imminent.

The State Department of the U.S.A., by then examining the Soviet Union's proposals made in the U.N. for the ending of the Korean War, was anxious to further the easing of international tension that this Russian gesture symbolised. The British Government was left in no doubt that Washington did not favour military action by us against Persia, and though they offered to help solve the problem, it was stressed that they would act only as mediators, not as allies.

Under this sort of pressure, both from allies and potential adversaries, and demoralised by the Bevan-Gaitskell dispute, the Government vacillated and hesitated, showing little strength of purpose. Not unexpectedly Attlee made up his mind to go to the country.

There can be little doubt that one practical consideration was the view of Gaitskell at the Treasury that the economic situation was deteriorating. The haste with which Attlee came to his final decision was indicative of the fact that he was personally tired, and officially weary of the difficulties imposed on him by a Parliament without a real majority, and with a Government perpetually on the verge of internal dispute.

Both Morrison and myself were returning from the U.S.A. when we were told that Attlee was planning to ask the King to dissolve Parliament. We cabled to the Prime Minister suggesting he delay a public announcement until there had been time to discuss a suitable date. But before we reached Southampton the election had been fixed for October 25.

Attlee had made no effort to cause the expulsion of Bevan and his followers from the Party, nor did he at any time express any official reprimand. Tolerance in face of internal opposition undoubtedly lost Labour many votes, either through abstentions or by transfer to opposing candidates, simply as an anti-Bevanite gesture.

On the other hand, expulsion might well have brought about the emergence of Bevanite candidates in some constituencies, caus-

Hugh Gaitskell leaves the Treasury for the House of Commons to present the 1951 Budget.

Forty years on. Reunion of colleagues who entered Parliament in 1922. Left to right: George Oliver, Lord Alexander, Emanuel Shinwell, Lord Attlee, Lord Tom Williams, Lord Lawson.

Hugh Gaitskell:
"Fight, fight, and
fight again."

The Party Leader,
Harold Wilson.

ing disastrous vote-splitting and a further general decline in Party morale.

Neither in speech nor in actions was there any justification in the charge that Attlee wished to lose the election in order to end an impossible situation and to teach an effective lesson in defeat which has proved efficacious to the Party in previous times. There were good reasons to believe that the rank and file in the Labour movement were loyal, and that many who had not troubled to vote in 1950 saw to what danger their lethargy had brought the Party in which they believed.

In the event, this belief was not far wrong. With a vote of 13.9 millions, Labour gained the greatest total ever recorded by a single Party in electoral history. But the 13.7 millions recorded for the Tories and their National Liberal allies represented a swing to them of 1.1 per cent. Due to the number of marginal victories in 1950 and the "wastage" of enormous majorities in Labour strongholds, the fact that about one person in a hundred swung from Liberal or Labour to Tory was sufficient to produce an overall majority for the Tories of sixteen seats, hardly a workable majority but sufficiently larger than the 1950 Labour majority to avoid an impasse. The new House consisted of 321 Tories and their supporters, 295 Labour, 6 Liberals, and 3 Irish Independents.

Experience would indicate that Labour's defeat, honourable in view of the increased vote and the small decrease in the number of seats, could have provided encouragement for the Party.

After six years of exhausting and not unsuccessful administration, a change of Government in a democracy, whatever the political extremists may say to the contrary, is no disaster. It could have been a reason for dispensing with any feeling of complacency and for a resolve to close the ranks to make an effective Opposition. Instead, the subsequent dissensions and changes in leadership weakened the organisational force of the Party.

The signs of the Bevanite rift being carried into the constituencies were in evidence before the election. In July, 1951, Bevan was abroad in Yugoslavia, but a pamphlet bearing his name, *One Way Only*, attacked both Attlee and the trade unions. This statement of the faction's policy was supported by practical action. Bevan's supporters began forming a definite group which, after the election, became virtually a second Opposition to the Shadow Cabinet.

On the eve of the election the annual Party Conference took place at Scarborough. Bevan rather surprisingly agreed very amicably to a statement supporting defence, but he ensured that it omitted any details on the amount of expenditure. This gesture

N

towards unity was made easy because of the Bevanites' increasing influence. They gained four out of seven of the constituency seats on the Executive and were successfully threatening the Old Guard. As Minister of Defence—in the Labour Party a most unpopular post—I was their primary target for attack. Morrison and Dalton lost their seats in the following year. In the Parliamentary Labour Party Attlee was re-elected leader without any question of ascribing the election defeat to him or implying criticism of his handling of ministers.

Circumstances played into the hands of the Bevanites, who found it profitable to capitalise on emotional factors. In October, 1952, Britain detonated an atomic bomb in the Monte Bello Islands, thereby revealing what few ministers had known—that Britain had engaged in atomic armament for years. A month later the U.S.A. detonated a hydrogen bomb at Eniwetok. Russia soon followed with a similar device.

The atomic arms race became a far more potent source of propaganda than protests about the economic factors of an increase in conventional arms. In March, 1952, the Commons and the nation saw the growing dimensions of the conflict between the leadership and the Bevanites during a debate on rearmament.

The Parliamentary Party decided not to oppose the Government motion, but to move a reasoned amendment. Despite this decision fifty-seven Labour M.P.s voted against the motion, something they could safely do without risk of expulsion because of the tolerance allowed, through the suspension of Standing Orders, in 1945. Although the Press described this incident as a Bevanite revolt it was less sectionally organised than such a description implied. Among the fifty-seven rebels were motives of great variety. There were the Bevanites, the Keep Left adherents, and the pacifists. In fact, this revolt was of precisely the pattern of similar qualms about defence which had existed in every such crisis since the Party had achieved Parliamentary representation.

Reimposition of Standing Orders was effective in curbing gestures of defiance in the Commons because withdrawal of the Whip and possible expulsion could be virtual condemnation to defeat at a subsequent election. The record of what had happened to candidates standing as Independent in the post-war elections was an effective warning to the malcontents. While the Parliamentary Party enjoyed calmer days, at least in public, the dissidents continued to stir up trouble—principally through the Press, where the journalistic talents of several Bevanites made expert propaganda easy. Indeed, professional writers on Labour topics were almost

entirely in the Bevanite group, and the official view got little air-
ing outside the *Daily Herald*, which was read principally by trade
unionists, already strongly convinced of the menace of the Bevanite
movement.

The most vigorous attacks on Bevan and his followers came,
not from the Party leadership, but from Arthur Deakin, described
as more of a politician than a trade union leader. As fraternal
delegate from the T.U.C. at the 1952 Labour Conference he lashed
out at those causing dissensions, describing their activities as
deplorable antics.

He asked "those within the Party who have set up a caucus to
realise that the ordinary rank-and-file Party member or trade
unionist has no time for their disregard of those principles and
loyalties to which our movement has held so strongly through the
whole course of its existence".

His alarm was justified. The Bevanites had just taken six out
of seven constituency seats on the Executive and were heady with
the vision of victory. Deakin attacked the *Tribune* faction and
hinted that if its activities continued he would see that the T.U.C.
formed a group to work against it.

With thoughts of this support behind them, Attlee and Morrison
quickly ordered the ending of all organised groups within the
Party unless they were officially approved. They gained the support
they needed in the Parliamentary Labour Party with 188 votes, but
104 members either voted against, abstained, or were absent. These
positive and tacit oppositions to the leadership were comparably
reflected in the subsequent votes for the deputy leadership of the
Parliamentary Party. Morrison was secure with 194, but the 82 for
Bevan were highly significant, because of the accepted fact that the
election was a forecast of who would be leader when Attlee retired.

His seventieth birthday would fall in January, 1953, and he had
expressed the opinion that the occasion was one when retirement
should be considered. Morrison was seeking to consolidate his
position, though he had suffered some serious setbacks. His few
months as Foreign Secretary were unfortunate as they tended to
overshadow the rank and file's high regard for his devoted service
to the Party and his success in other ministerial positions from
1940. Not only had he suffered defeat in the elections for the
Executive at the 1952 Conference, but he had shown himself
indecisive in the following days when the trade unions, determined
to find a right-wing personality to offset the Bevanites' influence,
suggested to Morrison that he should stand for the office of Party
Treasurer in opposition to Greenwood. The office of Labour Party

Treasurer is largely a sinecure, but ever since it was awarded to MacDonald in gratitude for services rendered it had earned a position of respect and inferred high sentiment for the holder. Morrison was flattered by the proposal, but on consideration turned it down when he learned that the Conference would agree to giving the deputy leader of the Party an *ex-officio* position on the Executive. He undoubtedly regarded this move as an effective method of keeping his hand closely on all facets of Party activity, making the eventual position of leader little more than a formal change of name.

Morrison failed to consider the intentions of the trade union leaders and their Bevanite adversaries should the office of Treasurer fall vacant. When, because of Greenwood's death, this situation had to be faced at the 1954 Conference the trade unions ensured Gaitskell's victory by four million votes to Bevan's two millions.

The old bogey of defence now became a heated source of controversy. The Government had accepted, at the behest of the U.S.A., the principle of German rearmament. Officially the Parliamentary Labour Party was not against this, but many M.P.s, correctly claiming their right to vote according to conscience, refused to adhere to the policy of Attlee. Bevan, estimating that the issue was one on which he could carry the majority of the Party at the next Conference, resigned from the Shadow Cabinet in April, 1954; Harold Wilson, Bevan's closest ally, surprisingly accepting the vacancy caused by Bevan's resignation.

Bevan came within an ace of winning his case against German rearmament at the 1954 Conference. The actual occurrence of a split and the defeat of the leadership was avoided thanks to the hasty rallying of some trade unions, and Attlee got a majority of 250,000. The fact that the union block vote had achieved this result served to convince Bevan that he had won a political victory, while the fact that the movement was almost equally divided on the question, and equally divided on the case for obedience to the leadership, was only too evident.

When the Government announced in February, 1955, that it had been decided to make an H-bomb, Bevan demanded restrictions on its use. The comparatively mild amendment to the motion approving the Government H-bomb policy which the Parliamentary Party decided on was not pleasing to Bevan, and he announced that he and his friends would abstain from voting.

The fifty-seven varieties of 1952 had now grown to sixty-two, and when the leadership, rankling under the jibes of the Bevanites during the debate which paraded the dissensions before the whole country, decided to withdraw the whip from Bevan, the vote in favour was 141 to 112. Attlee was reluctant to do more, though he knew that the right wing of the Party and the trade unions were calling for Bevan's expulsion. A way out of the trouble was devised by requesting Bevan to apologise for his behaviour which had, incidentally, included studied rudeness to Attlee during the Commons debate. An apology, it was inferred, would obviate the need for expulsion. With the National Executive of the Party manned strongly by Bevanites Attlee was fortunate in once again scraping through to a nominal victory with a vote in his favour of 14 to 13.

The Tories, like the rest of the country, had watched Labour's schisms grow, change and develop. Eden had succeeded Churchill on the latter's retirement. Not unnaturally the Conservative Central Office deemed the demoralisation of the Labour Party as an appropriate reason for a general election as soon as possible.

15

HUGH GAITSKELL AS LEADER

1955–1962

Apathy and cynicism in 1955 were the inevitable fruits of dissensions in the previous months, and they infected both the electorate and the Labour Party machine. Audiences at meetings were a mere trickle compared with former proportions. Nor was television the sole reason for this decline. As vital a factor was the weakness of the constituency organisation. Full-time agents in the constituencies had dwindled by almost seventy since the 1951 election. Virtually no impact was made on the minds of the younger generation, in contrast to the Young Conservatives who were flourishing and gaining in membership.

The swing from Labour was again trivial—under two in every hundred votes. But abstentions on all sides were striking. Labour's poll fell nearly one and a half millions, and the Tories' by more than 400,000 on an electorate total up by nearly a quarter of a million. The election results were not so much a rejection of Labour's programme, which stressed nationalisation plans, as well as the peace aims common to both parties, but a vote of no confidence. Nor could the Tories claim a triumphant victory, though for the Party of the outgoing Government to increase its majority was notable. In terms of seats the Tories and their supporters had 345, Labour 277, the Liberals six and Sinn Fein two. The increase of five seats in the Commons as compared with 1951 was beneficial to the Tories in helping to give them an effective overall majority of fifty-nine.

An inquest on Labour's failure commenced immediately, with Harold Wilson appointed by the National Executive to preside over a committee to investigate the Party machinery. It reported its findings at the October Conference, mentioning as the more obvious faults the shortage of voluntary canvassers, and inadequate remuneration of full-time constituency officials. It was emphasised that the highly centralised organisation, effective enough when the experienced and vigorous hand of Herbert Morrison was in control in 1945, had failed to match the task entailed. In future the Party organisation was to be regionalised, marginal seats were to be carefully nursed, and general publicity was to be maintained at a high level between elections. These were all reasonable and practical suggestions; they ignored the fact that if the causes of disillusion were eradicated the traditional zeal of voluntary Party workers would revive.

The air was charged with an indeterminate and largely unspoken dissatisfaction with the status of the Party as it began a further period of Opposition, and with a weaker force. It was inevitable that critics from a variety of motives should suggest that the image of the Party was outmoded, and that leading personalities were resting on past achievements, now rapidly fading into the limbo of history.

Of the many episodes marking internal crisis in the Labour Party's history those between December 7 and 14, 1955, are particularly significant. On the 7th Clem Attlee announced his retirement. This, though long expected, caused surprise when it actually occurred and it found the Party bewildered and undecided on his successor.

Attlee had remained in office long after his anticipated retirement as Party leader. His motives were doubtless to await an easing of the Party's internal tensions and to reach a personal decision on his successor. To some extent his hand was forced by the pointed comments of Hugh Dalton who, realising that a Tory administration was virtually certain for at least five years, finally accepted the fact that the office of Party leader for which he had always yearned would elude him. Dalton, having decided to seek political refuge in the Lords, publicly criticised the fact that nine members of the Shadow Cabinet were over sixty-five. He excepted Attlee on the score of "Party unity", but inferred that any member of the Shadow Cabinet in his middle sixties was politically expendable. This was doubtless a blatant gesture of support for Hugh Gaitskell, and only coincidentally, and perhaps regretfully, approval of Bevan, then fifty-eight years old.

Some senior members of the Party hierarchy, irrespective of Dalton's criticism, had previously announced their intention to withdraw from the Shadow Cabinet, but Herbert Morrison, 67, treated Dalton's suggestion with marked contempt. Chuter Ede, a highly respected member, with long service, whose activities in the House had never diminished, went much further than Morrison. He launched an attack on Dalton, accusing him of being senile, intolerant, and suggesting that Dalton was actuated by only one motive: he could not bear any of the Old Guard remaining in the

House of Commons when he had reached the stage of being unfit to continue his duties.

Whatever Attlee himself felt about the age question as regards himself and his contemporaries he undoubtedly considered that vigorous leadership demanded a man who could shoulder the burden for at least a decade. This was the source of his misgivings quite as much as any feeling that Morrison was unsuited for the position of leader.

Attlee's view was not reflected by several Labour members with long years of political experience. Not only did Morrison deserve the leadership on the score of long service to the Party, but the situation made it a commendable policy to appoint a leader to hold interim office, while the Party had a breathing space for putting its house in order with an experienced and steady hand guiding its actions. Two years' healthy self-examination would be sufficient; after that there was likely to be time enough for a younger man to succeed.

Unfortunately, personal ambitions were as strong a factor as an objective regard for the Party's future, and none of the three expected contenders for the Attlee succession—Morrison, Bevan, and Gaitskell—suffered from any sense of false modesty. Nevertheless Bevan was ready to stand down in favour of Morrison provided Gaitskell did the same. Bevan was prepared to wait a little longer for the culmination of his ambitions. Gaitskell might personally have wished to withdraw had it not been for the insistence of his friends in what was known as the Hampstead Set—a typical cabal of the kind that has frequently attempted to denigrate the fundamentally democratic rule of the Labour Party—that the Party needed a young intellectual to drag it to its feet once more.

By December 8, 1955, the three nominations were official and the Party was thereby thrust into further controversy—far deeper than that implied by a routine internal election. On December 14 Morrison was administered a harsh rebuff with only 40 votes; many of the M.P.s and junior ex-ministers he had trained and encouraged in the London County Council and Parliament had abandoned him. The trade union M.P.s' vote, which Morrison could have well estimated as his, surprisingly swung over to Gaitskell, helping to give him 157 votes. Bevan obtained 70 votes.

Although Arthur Deakin, general secretary of the Transport and General Workers' Union had collapsed and died suddenly in May, the influence of his implacable hostility towards Nye Bevan still had its impact on his own union and the majority of others of the T.U.C. Like Ernest Bevin before him, Deakin had the traditional trade unionist's belief in the essential rightness of the views of the big battalions, translated into the more respectable policy of acquiescence to the view of the majority. Deakin had been vociferous in his charges against Bevan and the *Tribune* caucus, undoubtedly because he was deeply worried at the threat to the unity of the Labour movement which could result.

He described the Bevanites' activities as the antics of disruptionists, and at the Conference in 1952 had denounced those who disregarded principles and loyalties to which the Labour movement held so strongly throughout its existence.

Deakin was unconcerned with the finer points of political policy, and still less with the struggles for personal influence and the advancement of individual careers which were inextricably mixed with the controversies based on ideologies. His aim was to safeguard the political interests of trade unionism. Nothing else mattered. On this basis of attitude (an inheritance of the Bevin approach) the unions might have been expected to support Morrison, but Morrison's attitude to the composition of the boards of nationalised industries which had infuriated Bevin years before rankled. Nor had Nye Bevan, despite his mining background— a factor which rarely impressed the miners themselves—any chance whatever of inspiring the trade unions to prefer him to the equally unsuitable (from a trade union viewpoint) Gaitskell. In the opinion of the T.U.C., and almost as strongly in the constituencies, Gaitskell was the least of three evils.

Morrison's defeat in what had been a most successful career in the sphere of British politics caused him much offence. It wounded his feelings and was an affront to his integrity. Consequently, when asked to stand for the deputy leadership, he declined. Nye Bevan was nominated and was opposed by Jim Griffiths, himself an old servant of the Party, and one who seldom, if ever, caused offence either to the right or left sections. He was, however, in the view of the hierarchy, the most likely candidate to attract moderate votes and keep Bevan out. Griffiths won with 141 votes compared with 111 for Bevan. The dimensions of support for Bevan indicated that, in view of Griffiths's age, Bevan could assure himself of the deputy leadership in due course, and thereafter, with normal expectation of life, become the leader should the somewhat right-wing attitude of Gaitskell produce an untenable situation.

The new chapter of the Party story thus began in ominous circumstances. Friends and foes alike of Labour estimated that the views of the two top men were irreconcilable and their personal attitudes implacably hostile.

Gaitskell's speeches and activities during the 1955-9 period of Opposition served to contradict the view that his leadership would not restore the coherent front of Labour. Bevan, perhaps on account of the first effects of the illness which was prematurely to destroy him, showed fewer signs of fiery revolt than were expected.

One reason was that the Party soon found cause for unity in contrast to the disunity of its Tory opponents, as the result of the controversy over the Suez campaign. The near-fragmentation of the Tory Party over this operation and its implications served to conceal the contradictory actions of the Labour leader as the Egyptian crisis developed.

Originally Gaitskell had shown sound judgment in his objective treatment of the Suez affair. A few days before Nasser announced the nationalisation of the Canal company Gaitskell referred to Nasser's conduct as arbitrary and considered that Britain was justified in reacting sharply, and taking precautionary measures. He also advocated more favourable consideration regarding the supply of arms to Israel. By the time military action had begun his opinion changed markedly, and in his anxiety to destroy public confidence in the Government he weakened public belief in the Labour Party's sense of patriotism in a crisis. Considering that Gaitskell was projected as on the right of Labour philosophy the charge of putting country last was a wry triumph for the Tories, usually reserved for those on the extreme left.

But the vital need for unity prevailed, largely owing to the loyalty of Bevan to his chief. Gaitskell's broadcasts and speeches in the House were more or less forgotten in the sense of optimism which swept the rank and file as they watched the schisms grow in the highest circles of the Tory Party.

The National Council of Labour organised a thoughtful campaign based on the slogan of "Law not War" and, while views on the Suez affair split the private thoughts of Labour adherents just as they split opinion in the nation as a whole, there was a greater sense of hope than at any time since 1945. By-elections confirmed that Tories were abstaining while Socialists were returning to the polling booths. Bevan was able to stand for the post of Treasurer at the 1956 Conference and obtain not merely the vote of the constituency Parties, but also that of some of the unions, while his growing prestige persuaded Gaitskell to appoint his rival to the position of Shadow Foreign Secretary which Bevan had coveted since 1947.

Bevan's public attitude to the question of atomic defence steadily changed. By 1957 he was ceremoniously shaking hands with

Gaitskell for the benefit of Press photographers at the annual Conference and could abandon the hostile gestures of the past. He spoke during a debate on a resolution in favour of abandonment of the H-bomb. "There is no member of the Executive who is in favour of the H-bomb," Bevan told the delegates. "But if you carry this resolution you will send a British Foreign Secretary (whoever he may be) naked into the conference chamber."

The Bevanites and other leftist groups were thus left without a leader. Its residue became the Victory for Socialism Group, a vociferous body led by Sydney Silverman and Stephen Swingler, two able Parliamentarians but incapable of making an impact on the majority of Labour M.P.s. Its lack of influence was partly due to the fact that none of its adherents was pursuing personal power. As a group without a figurehead the unilateralist Left made no impact, and its pristine leader, Bevan, harshly told them, "It is not in your power to enforce nuclear disarmament. All you can do is pass a resolution."

Bevan's change of attitude dramatically influenced the unions' support for him. Union block votes helped to defeat by more than five millions a 1957 Conference resolution that a future Labour Government should refuse to test or use nuclear weapons. In the 1958 Conference resolutions for total nuclear disarmament, opposition to H-bomber patrols and rocket sites, and demands that a Labour Government should promote international agreement on banning nuclear weapons within one year of taking office or do so unilaterally thereafter, were all easily defeated.

In the period 1956–8, therefore, the Labour Party's future appeared more rosy. Gaitskell and Bevan had dropped their personal controversies. Both Bevan and Harold Wilson had purged their offence of Cabinet resignation and were back in the Shadow Cabinet. The political machine was refurbished and augmented. A new policy promised planned economic expansion, sensible financing of the social services, a better educational programme, and a restrained if vague approach to the thorny problem of nationalisation and re-nationalisation.

Unfortunately, the programme required careful examination to discover any fundamental difference from that of the Tory Party. Labour's opponents had shown infinitely greater powers of recovery after a major internal crisis than Labour had ever done. With the resignation of Anthony Eden, Harold Macmillan had taken over and adroitly rehabilitated the Party. On the domestic front the Tory economic policy was correctly dubbed Butskellite because Butler's policy as Chancellor of the Exchequer differed only slightly from that of Gaitskell in the previous Labour administration. In foreign affairs Macmillan presented himself (or was presented by the expensive and skilful services of a commerical advertising agency) as a man who could persuade America and Russia to come together at a summit meeting. The unions seemed not unhappy with the conditions under the new Tory image personified by Macmillan and Butler, and improved economic conditions aided their satisfaction.

A significant development in the ceaseless efforts of the Labour Party to live with its fundamental divergencies of opinion occurred in February, 1959, when Sydney Silverman put forward a motion in favour of British disengagement in Germany, the isolation of Germany as regards military alliances, and the recognition, *de facto,* of East Germany. This had all the ingredients of another major conflict, for the motion was in direct contravention of the leadership's policy. The potential crisis was heightened when John Hynd, one of the Party's experts on German affairs, as far to the right as Silverman was to the left, advocated an amendment which obtained considerable support from his friends. All the material for a serious split was prepared.

But on this occasion the bickering faded away when both left and right worked out a compromise which enabled a new resolution to be composed. Instead of dissension it suggested unity, for its sponsors were from both sides, and deliberately the signatures alternated with names from left and right: Sydney Silverman, John Hynd, Koni Zilliacus, Arthur Henderson, and some sixty other M.P.s of normally opposing views on the German rearmament question, appearing in a sequence presenting a façade of unity despite difference of opinion.

This was a testimony to the growing prestige and wisdom shown by Gaitskell, learning how to overcome problems through somewhat bitter experiences. His efforts, particularly in 1958 and 1959, to strengthen his grip on the Party were very marked. He began to create a solid group of loyal if rather unspectacular friends in the high echelons of leadership. Men like Denis Healey, an expert on international questions; Gordon-Walker, an ex-Oxford tutor; and George Brown, the trade unionist, were given their due rewards for services rendered.

When the October, 1959, general election was announced both parties could with reason estimate that their chances of victory were improved. Both were, in fact, making much the same appeal, and while the electorate might well be bewildered by the similarity of the programmes neither of them offered much cause for existing adherents to abstain or change their politics. Lord Hailsham's call for no mud-slinging during the campaign was superfluous. Neither Party had a rival target to smear.

The election therefore created little enthusiasm in the country. Macmillan's fortuitous appearance on television with President Eisenhower as a sort of introduction to the coming summit conference (provided the electorate gave Macmillan the mandate to ensure world peace) was regarded by Labour as sharp practice, but the unfortunate attributes of bribery with which Gaitskell embellished his final appeals were equally condemned. Increased old age pensions, no increase in income tax, a reduction in purchase tax, all airily suggested to be taken care of by increased productivity, were promises which aroused the suspicions of the electors. Even in Labour circles, not hostile to Gaitskell, it was claimed that Labour lost the 1959 election in the last few days, thanks to the lack of judgment of political campaigning on the part of its leaders.

The result was that the Tory Party, which had been in office for eight years and should have by all precedents lost the election, found itself back with an increased majority. There were 365 Tories, 258 Labour, and six Liberals and one Independent. Labour's proportion of the vote had dropped to 43.8 per cent with a total of 12.2 million, 200,000 fewer than in 1955 and a million down on 1950. The Tories, despite the burden of the Suez debacle and the difficulties of obtaining a mandate on a third occasion, polled 13¾ million votes, higher even than their 1951 record.

The cold statistics of the election results were highly demoralising to the Labour Party, which had become more convinced of victory as polling day drew nearer. The Conference which came on the morrow of the election was not so much an inquest on defeat as a burial ceremony of many items of policy the Labour Party had advocated in the first half of the twentieth century.

Strident claims by several of the so-called intellectuals of the Party that preoccupation with working-class interests were responsible for loss of votes were reasonable enough on the assumption that the original demands of Labour pioneers were now meaningless, but the majority of Labour M.P.s who had not forgotten their working-class origin denied that the condition of old age pensioners, of millions of low-paid wage earners, of countless slum dwellers, were in tune with what was now described as the "Affluent Society".

The claims of the pioneers had not been implemented; the fundamental principles of the Party must not be profaned. In the view of many Labour members the 1959 election was as much lost by the New Guard who had intrigued steadily and resolutely to rid itself of veteran leaders of the Party, and with them a good proportion of their policies, as by reliance on basic Socialist principles.

Determination to eradicate the old concepts without unduly worrying about positive principles to replace them marked Gaitskell's approach to the task of leading a Party in Opposition for the third time. His strong line was to revise the Party's objects in order to bring them up to date, and he regarded Clause Four, the main plank of the Labour policy since 1918, as the first to merit attention. It had to be finished and done with.

The very vagueness of this clause, the product of Sidney Webb's fertile brain, with its demand for the common ownership of the means of production, distribution, and exchange, was its strength, for it permitted flexibility in any Labour Government programme. The alleged damage done to the Labour Party's prospects by its electoral nationalisation "threats" was not due to the existence of Clause Four, but to the anxiety of the bright young men of the Party to itemise a vast number of trades and industries convenient, profitable, and simple for the State to take over.

Inevitably, controversy was revived, and Gaitskell suffered a technical defeat when the National Executive not only advised retention of Clause Four but confirmed the established principles in a more up-to-date form. This was a new and ominous phase in the relationship between Party chairman and the movement as a whole. Despite the appearance of a democratic and genuine Conference, where the leaders come to listen as much as to talk, only exceptionally has a Labour Party Conference done other than the leader, or the sub-leaders who are engineering a change of leadership, intended that it should.

Gaitskell's defeat over Clause Four was concerned with a technicality. The next setback was on a topic of much greater touchiness —a problem which affected the emotions as well as the mind. It was, as usual in Labour's history, the question of defence.

The Party's statement on its defence policy issued in the summer of 1960 was in many respects a responsible effort, and due testimony must be paid to Gaitskell's probity in formulating a programme which he could follow in the event of his becoming Prime Minister.

But the factors involved—the genocidal implications of nuclear war, the use of Britain as a front-line rocket base by an alien power (albeit a staunch ally), and the encouragement of a renascent Germany as a military power—would have created dissension whoever the Party leader might have been.

The genuine protests of pacifists, adherents of the far left, and the theoretical militarists, were augmented by others whose object was to use the defence controversy as a means of ousting Gaitskell from the leadership. The period was the nadir of Gaitskell's fortunes. Bevan, his recent ally, had died. Morgan Phillips was unfortunately ill. The T.U.C., though following its usual procedure of supporting the Labour Party so long as it pursued a rightist policy, was in the throes of its own internecine strife. At the T.U. Congress complete bewilderment was ingeniously achieved when the Congress approved not only the Labour defence statement but also a resolution of the Transport Workers disapproving of it.

The situation which had now emerged indicated that Frank Cousins, the leader of the Transport Workers, had shattered the traditional union block vote on which the National Executive relied since the National Council of Labour was created in 1932.

And so it happened. The Labour leaders suffered defeat for their defence statement when a resolution for unilateral disarmament was carried, due to the minority unions on the left plus the Transport Workers. The fact that the decision involved only a small majority was cold comfort for the Party leadership. Doubtless Gaitskell engendered some respect by his obstinate claim that he would "fight, fight, and fight again" to ensure that the decision was reversed, and thereby probably saved his own political career. When Parliament reassembled he was re-elected to the leadership of the Parliamentary Labour Party with 166 votes. Harold Wilson, who could do no more than offer a vague compromise in an endeavour to meet the wishes of the Party Conference and also retain the basis of the official defence statement, obtained 81 votes.

The fact that Conference decisions are not binding on the Parliamentary Party, and that a well-organised and vigorous campaign had brought about a reversal of the 1960 decision, created an odd situation for the Party. What was the official policy? Was it the policy carried at Party Conferences, or that decided upon by members of the Parliamentary Party?

This dilemma has not as yet been resolved, nor is it likely to be in the foreseeable future. It remains, however, as a persistent subject of controversy, both in the Parliamentary Party and in the local constituencies. Clearly, if after debate on resolutions submitted by affiliated organisations decisions on important items of policy are carried by majority vote and thereafter ignored, the question may arise as to whether the annual Party Conference is anything more than an occasion for a reunion of delegates seeking relaxation in a series of academic debates.

16

THE FUTURE

As the foregoing survey has sought to show, the Labour movement attained some coherence and sense of purpose nearly a century ago. Since the name, The Labour Party, was adopted by twenty-nine M.P.s in 1906 tremendous advances, eclipsing anything ever achieved over a similar period by other political Parties, have been recorded. In such a brief chapter of a nation's history, to have formed two minority and two majority governments is no mean triumph.

Labour's potential strength has always alarmed the other Parties and has paradoxically been one cause of Labour's recurrent weakness. Lloyd George's policy of social reform stole some of Labour's thunder in the years before the first world war and influenced some of Labour's adherents to support the Liberal administration as well as enhancing the influence of the Lib.-Lab. members, most of whom represented mining constituencies. Since the second world war the Tories have moved towards social reform, imitating both Liberals and Labour in adopting and adapting policies where convenient and beneficial to the Tory Party's future. The record of the Labour movement as the Party of progress and of the people has thereby been unjustly dimmed and distorted.

The pressure of events and of political rivals has been the principal cause of dissension within the Labour movement which is the recurrent theme of this history. Generally, ultimate benefit has accrued from such clashes of opinion. They are inevitable in a Party which is progressive, and gains by the presentation of new ideas.

A Party which accepts democratic principles cannot expect to achieve more than a moderate regimentation of its rank and file. Nor can cohesion occur automatically when the movement is in reality a loose federation of many groups, the individual interests of which are frequently in conflict. The trade unions proudly and rightly claim that they founded the Labour Party, but their original objective was not Socialism. As Thomas Burt, the miners' leader in the 1880's, explained, it was the "reconciliation of the interests of Labour and Capital".

Except for a minority of militant unions, the trade union movement has continued to follow a policy of negotiation within the
existing industrial pattern, a policy which can with equal justification be described either as a steadying influence on the malcontents
or a reactionary brake on progress.

The political side of the movement has had to wage a constant
struggle to change the outlook of a predominantly trade union
membership. The task of broadening the outlook of the trade
unionist, to induce consideration of issues less parochial than the
day-to-day conflicts within the capitalist system, has been ceaseless,
and complete success has yet to be achieved.

Progress has always stemmed from the pressure of forward-
looking and militant sections of the Party—whether typified by
middle-class Fabians, political malcontents, or intellectual theorists.
Doubtless they often lacked wisdom and judgment, but their
opinions served to inspire a movement which would otherwise
have become as reactionary as any rival Party.

The differences existing among the various sections forming the
Labour movement have often led to compromise in the selection
of a Party leader. The safe and reliable chairman was more
capable of ironing out obstacles and effecting compromise than
the extremist, whether on the right or left, whose purpose was to
exercise authority rather than to be a representative spokesman.

Keir Hardie was a founder member of the I.L.P. and a visionary.
His prestige as a Socialist pioneer was enormous, but this reputation
did not prevent the Parliamentary Labour Party giving equal
support to David Shackleton, the textile trade union leader, who
never concealed his antipathy to Socialist theory. It was only with
MacDonald's casting vote that Hardie became chairman, and then
only on the understanding that the Party chairman should not hold
permanent office. Hardie did not ignore the lesson and replaced his
visionary ideas with practical moves to strengthen the trade union-
political alignment.

Even Hardie in this more restrained guise was too extreme for
some M.P.s, and he was replaced by Arthur Henderson, in his
early days not a Socialist but a trade unionist. He in turn was
succeeded by George Barnes, the engineers' leader. Ramsay Mac-
Donald's turn came fortuitously when Barnes fell ill in 1911. The
progress of the Party for the next twelve or fourteen years under
MacDonald's direction indicated the value of a leader with ability,
forceful opinions, and ambition. But MacDonald soon discovered
that both wings of the Party were equally ready to criticise, and
gradually his forcefulness was replaced by caution and reaction,

o

until the persistent sniping from his own Party brought about the tragedy which was personal as well as almost disastrous to the Party he had brought to maturity.

George Lansbury was an idealist, benign though perhaps impractical. His popularity was the result of genuine and likeable qualities; by character and nature he disliked offending anybody. Few people can become effective leaders on such a basis, though they can mollify their critics.

Clem Attlee, amenable, fair-minded and deceptively mild in temper, probably represents the ideal Labour leader in the eyes of the majority of the factions that make up the Party. Fortunately for the movement, and still more fortunately for the nation whose Prime Minister he was in the most critical peace-time phase of its history, Attlee was shrewd and tolerant, though on occasion he could express himself with remarkable firmness. Like all his predecessors he experienced intrigue, dissension, and controversy, but never became fretful or disheartened. Nor did he ever lose his grip on the reins or seriously jeopardise unity by his decisions. Any displeasure he felt because of criticism of the wartime Coalition Government and through the attacks on himself and his colleagues failed to mar his judgment when in 1945 he appointed some of those critics as members of the Labour Cabinet. On his retirement he merited the approbation and affection of the Party.

Attlee was middle-class, with a cultured mind, and could be described as a middle-roader. Hugh Gaitskell, his successor, competent and intelligent, had much the same background, though naturally without the same experience. Where the two men differed was that Attlee was always approachable to diehard trade unionists, doctrinaire intellectuals and extreme left-wingers alike. Gaitskell created an impression of being less approachable except to those within his own coterie. Attlee, when occasionally he had to dictate, wore a velvet glove. Gaitskell, when arguments failed, or when assailed, was prone to exercise the authority of leadership, and display an excessive irritability which marred his judgment.

A formidable basis for Party unity between 1936 and 1950 was the close friendship between Attlee and Ernest Bevin. It was regrettable that neither the political views expressed with great sincerity by Frank Cousins nor the relationship between him and Gaitskell were conducive to the same kind of trade union support for the political leadership.

With the eclipse of the "ginger" groups typified by the I.L.P., the midwife and nurse of the Party in its formative years, the political consciousness of the trade unions has become the critical factor in

Labour's future. Failing a renaissance of a capable and responsible left group, free from careerism and embittered jealousies, the unions have the onus of fashioning Labour policy. With a trade union affiliation of almost six millions in the Labour Party, the union influence on the National Council of Labour on the National Executive and on the Parliamentary Labour Party is overwhelming.

Will the Labour Party survive basically in the form which has remained since 1906? Despite the specious criticism that its image is outmoded, that the working class which it was pledged to represent has largely disappeared, and that the bruises and wounds of internal strife have been so nearly fatal that a re-birth rather than a recovery offers the main hope, more reasonable judgment suggests that the Socialist movement in Great Britain will find its greatest opportunities in the reaffirmation of its basic principles.

That the Party has the capacity to restore unity and to recover from major setbacks is unquestionable. The impotence and indecision of the Party in the late fifties was an ephemeral phase, repeatedly experienced during this century, and of little consequence when placed in its historical context. A more effective Labour Opposition, and in the process of time an efficient Labour Government, are normal events in the evolution of the Labour movement.

An easing of the international situation and the resultant re-examination of defence matters would eradicate sources of internal controversy and revive the interest of the electorate in Labour's policies. Even if the tension among nations should continue, the current policies of the balance of terror will in time become sterile and futile; Labour's views on armaments might then be more widely recognised as in line with much expert, though less orthodox, military opinion, as well of ordinary people the world over.

Fundamentally the people's hopes of a design for living will demand attention instead of the mid-century's preoccupation with the means of survival for themselves through the means of mass death for the enemy. When this natural and inevitable change of mind occurs then Labour will take its accustomed place as the Party of youth, of imagination, and of change.

The lethargy which has enabled both young and old to accept the cynicism of never having it so good as an all-encompassing reason for satisfaction with the world as they find it, and hope to leave it, is passing. Men and women will tire of alternating booms and slumps, of economic brakes and accelerators, of the majority prospering while the minority suffer injustice and squalor.

They may then demand a Government ready to harness all the nation's resources, human, material and financial, for the common good, in co-ordination with other nations of similar outlook, for the welfare of mankind.

A greater problem for the Labour Party, and indeed for all Parties with respect for democratic government, will be to safeguard, modernise and adapt the system for the world of tomorrow.

There is force in the argument that the British system of Parliamentary democracy has continued in effective operation for so long that the ordinary citizen takes it for granted, believing that its functions and privileges are unassailable. It is true that periodic indications of the upsurge of a dictator either within these islands' shores or abroad can arouse the British people to an implacable defence of their heritage, but one might question whether they are quite so sensitive to the insidious and subtle erosions of our democratic way of life which now beset us.

Bureaucracy, scientific advance, supra-national bodies, public lethargy and cynicism, professionalism in political life, the Party machines—all are by nature hostile to the institution of a democratic Parliament, either consciously or unconsciously.

Political stability is one of Britain's greatest achievements. In periods of crisis the nation has always closed its ranks and spoken with one voice. Thereby Parliament has always contrived to rule. But the anxiety in recent times to achieve this stability in a world where the unexpected and the undesired are probable eventualities has produced trends where the Opposition—as vital to democracy as the Government—is deprived of its usefulness as a braking and equalising force. Meantime, while ministers in the Government exercise more authority and Parliament fails to exert its rightful discipline on the Executive, extra-Parliamentary forces gain greater control, steadily divesting themselves of the need of accountability to the tribune of the people.

Will the future struggle be between two major Parties, which come closer together in their ideologies and thereby produce something akin to a political stalemate, or between the Legislature and the Executive? The latter already often ignores the requests and advice of the Legislature. The characteristic attitude of bureaucracy, represented by the professional civil servant, vis-à-vis the amateur member of Parliament, is becoming more hostile.

Yet the amateur, with qualities of an open mind, independence, and incorruptibility, must be the final arbiter of the nation's political policies. Not least of the evils within the body of Parliament today is the careerist M.P., often a sycophant until he attains promotion, when he becomes dictatorial. The private member of Parliament is a vital force. In recent times he has been in eclipse. The hazards of political life and the comparatively low remuneration of M.P.s evoke a temptation that is almost overwhelming to seek sponsorship by a lobby group, to supplement income with outside work which frequently colours the political outlook, or to seek the rewards of a ministerial career bestowed on those who obey the Whip and are "reliable Party men".

Will foreign affairs, international trade, and the overall public welfare be controlled from some new supra-national Parliament on the continent of Europe, leaving Westminster with the trivia of internal affairs?

Can one claim that the Party with a traditional hatred for reaction will be more successful in safeguarding democracy?

The political future of Britain is obscure and it would be presumptive to dogmatise. It is possible only to pose questions. Has, for instance, the Party system changed so fundamentally that it no longer creates the sort of legislature which is the wish of the people? Since 1950 the electorate's views have changed at general elections by tiny percentages, giving a change of Government but not a major change of policy. It is comparatively simple for either of the two major Parties, aided by pollsters and advertising agencies, to ensure that they pursue a policy so that they retain control once they attain it. One may question whether a sequence of Governments of the same political colour is right for a nation where nearly half the population adheres to the rival opinion.

Should public disquiet result in some success for a third Party, can the dilemma be resolved? One may envisage a Coalition of Labour and Liberals, a retrograde step with painful lessons from the Lib.-Lab. period. Or in the formative years could both the Labour and Tory Parties be persuaded to embrace tokens of Liberal policy in order to woo the diffident elector, thereby raising the prestige and influence of the Liberals to a point far beyond their importance?

For the Labour movement the delicate balance of power seems fraught with dangerous temptations. Further setbacks at elections or through major internal dissensions might influence some members either to join the Liberal Party or to form a Lib.-Lab. group. One cannot ignore the fact that some trade union leaders might applaud such a move.

Decisions at recent Labour Party Conferences indicate that one out of three Party members disagreed with the Gaitskell leadership, or at least allowed their votes to be used to reflect an absence of agreement. It is impossible to analyse the proportion of this hostility which could be ascribed to the right or the left, but it is apposite to suggest that a far greater source of discontent lies to the left than is generally believed.

Nearly two thirds of the world is now Socialist or Communist. This anti-capitalist preponderance may be compared with the significant trends in the capitalist countries. The capitalist state interferes more and more in industry and commerce, and business in its turn is more ready to approach the State for financial and legal aid when trade becomes difficult. Some degree of public ownership of the means of production and distribution and some State supervision of welfare and social services appear to be more likely to be sponsored, as well as accepted, by non-Socialist political Parties.

Does this mean that the Labour Party in Britain has failed to benefit from the lessons it has taught its rivals? Is some criticism not justified for the contention that an almost indecent haste to depart from Socialist principles was exhibited, as for example in the controversy over Clause Four, cited by some as a reason for election defeat?

It is notable that the word Socialism is rarely mentioned in Parliament, unless used as a sneer by Tory and Liberal members. Yet there exists a hard core of the Labour Party, the stalwarts who have experienced its vicissitudes, who are Socialists in mind and heart. The political Party with ideals and vision has probably a better prospect of long-term progress than the Party which caters for electoral support on a popular, but superficial, policy.

Labour is pressed by domestic and international events to make its decision. It can move to the right, seeking to maintain the *status quo* of a mixed economy where Capitalism and Socialism have reached a compromise as uneasy and suspicious bedfellows. Would it then be a close replica of a future Tory Party, which since 1950 has learned to abandon its more reactionary policies and is making concessions to public opinion?

Or will Labour continue on its leftward path and endure temporarily the setbacks and failures which beset the road to success in 1945?

What Labour dare not be is a middle Party, moderate in its advocacy and out of date in its ideology. Neither moderation, in face of the tasks that lie ahead, nor mediocrity, in the presentation of its case, can achieve ultimate success.

The tragic death of Hugh Gaitskell has brought to an end an exciting and turbulent chapter in Labour history. By sheer perseverance he had gained an effective command of the Party, although the eulogies which naturally and deservedly followed his death failed to conceal the existence of considerable opposition to his leadership. The criticism to which he was subjected at Party Conferences had not been completely stifled; there remained a substantial minority of Labour M.P.s, and at least one third of the Constituency Parties, who were opposed to him.

Gaitskell's remarkable speech at the Brighton Conference in 1962 on the controversial subject of British entry into the Common Market gained him considerable advancement. His conversion from the policy described as "sitting on the fence" to actual hostility, his declaration that the economic advantages were evenly balanced, that the future of British agriculture was uncertain, and that the political implications would weaken Britain's control over foreign policy, expressed with lucidity of style, enhanced his prestige both in the Party and in the country.

Inevitably the impact of Gaitskell's speeches, his defeat of Harold Wilson in the contest for leadership, and the glaring deficiencies of the Prime Minister, Harold Macmillan, in economic affairs and the sphere of defence, had increased the electoral prospects of the Party, and his elevation to Prime Minister in a future Labour Government was assured.

Did Gaitskell's death in a pre-election year create a vacuum in Labour's political ranks? A similar question was asked when George Lansbury resigned and Attlee became the leader. Despite grave doubts Attlee proved a successful leader at a time when the fortunes of the Parliamentary Party were in decline. Labour has never regarded any man, whichever position he occupied in the Party, as indispensable.

The election of Harold Wilson to the leadership in February 1963 with 144 votes as compared with 103 for George Brown was decisive. But despite his immediate assurances that no change in policy was contemplated it must not be assumed that the course of events will continue to be affected by the policies associated with Gaitskell. Policy is often inspired and even biassed by circumstances, even more than by a leader. Wilson's outlook and character approximate more to Attlee than to Gaitskell, and for this reason he may inspire a unity of which the Party is much in need and could therefore prove a success.

Wilson's election was not a triumph of Left over Right. He had always been slightly left of centre, and in line with the general trend of Labour policy throughout its history, despite sporadic signs of reaction.

It is of interest to realise that Wilson's career was making an impression in the early years of the 1945 Labour Government. In the standard reference biography, *The British Labour Party*, published in 1948, T. N. Shane, a journalist who joined the TUC Publicity Department in 1926, wrote about Wilson:

"In less than ten years of public life Harold Wilson has moved at a speed which baffles prediction as to where he will be, if he maintains his present rate of progress, in another ten years' time. There are only so many places, after all, to which to go: it begins to look as if he will have had to occupy all of them before he can be classified as middle aged."

This was a remarkable forecast to have written fifteen years ago.

The auguries for the future chapters of the Labour Story, so far as they bear similarity to propitious phases in the past, are optimistic for Socialism, and indeed for Britain. But, as always, throughout the history of Labour, there will be the inevitable controversies and differences. They can be the necessary lubricant of a progressive and truly democratic movement.

INDEX

PRICE ONE PENNY.

SOCIALISM
and the
POLITICAL PARTIES.

By JEAN JAURÈS.

Translated by H. QUELCH.

THE TWENTIETH CENTURY PRESS, LIMITED
(Trade Union and 48 Hours),
37A, CLERKENWELL GREEN, LONDON, E.C.
1903.

The Unemployed Problem

Some Suggestions for Solving it.

J. Keir Hardie, M.P.

PRICE ONE PENNY.

Fabian Tract No. 5.

FACTS FOR SOCIALISTS

FROM THE

POLITICAL ECONOMISTS AND STATISTICIANS.

PUBLISHED AND SOLD BY

THE FABIAN SOCIETY.

NINTH EDITION (REVISED). NINETY-FIRST THOUSAND.

PRICE ONE PENNY.

LONDON:
THE FABIAN SOCIETY, 3 CLEMENT'S INN, STRAND, W.C.
JUNE, 1904.

"Clarion" Pamphlet
No. 8.

Land & Nationalisation

BY

ROBERT BLATCHFORD
(NUNQUAM)

PRICE ONE PENNY.

Published by the "Clarion" Newspaper Co., Ltd.,
72, Fleet Street, London.
1896.